IMAGES
of America

DOWNSHORE FROM MANAHAWKIN TO NEW GRETNA

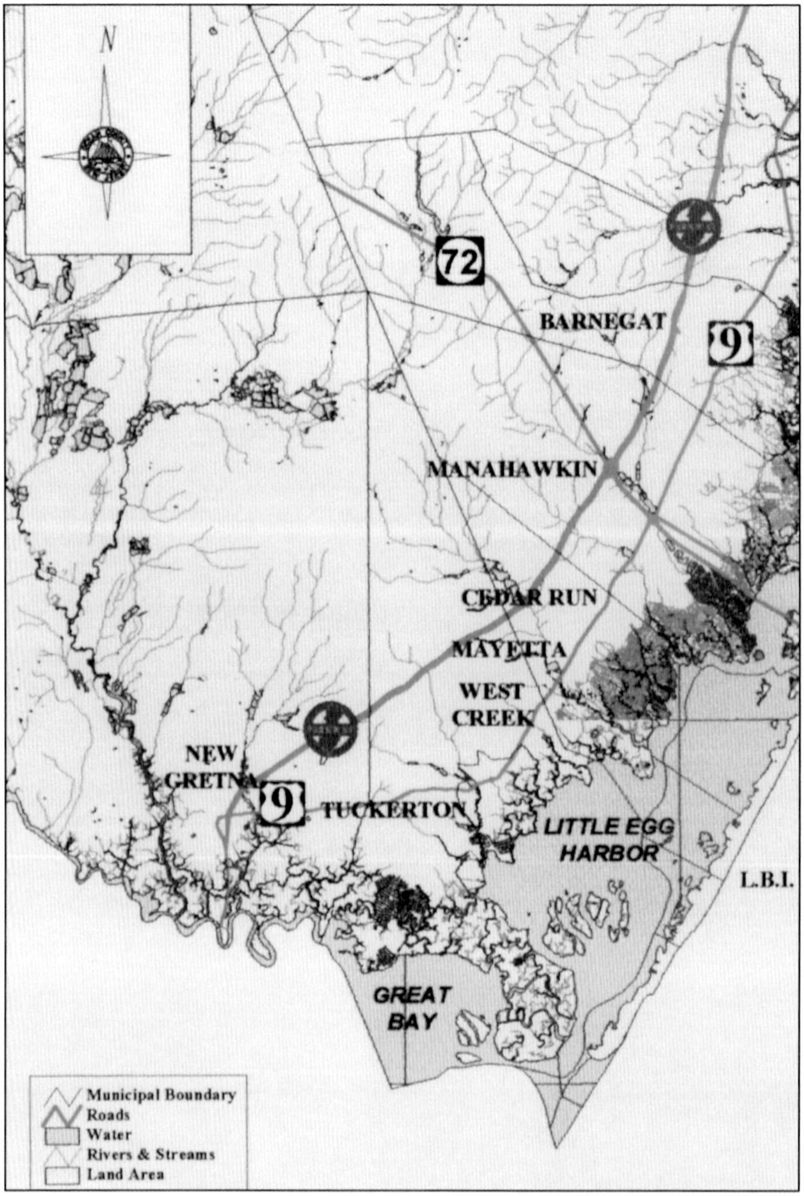

This recent map of the downshore area of New Jersey reveals that old names have scarcely changed. Thus, it forms a link with the old maps published in this book. The Tuckerton Railroad (1871–1940) stands out on old maps. It helped spur the growth of businesses in mainland communities as well as the building of resorts on the barrier island. Evidence of the railroad and its route can be found today, but modern maps tout the Garden State Parkway (1954). Geologically, the marshes along the bay shores increase in width going southwest to Cape May Canal. Old-timers wisely built on the fast lands (uplands) and not on tidal marshes or unstable barrier beaches. Access to bays and beaches was through villages which had strips of high ground along streams leading to the bays. Villages were established at the head of tide. Thus, early travel was by vessel. Route 9, the Main Shore Road, links the settlements only recently recognized as gems of our heritage. Here mankind has worked for generations on land and sea in harmony with the tides and seasons. (Courtesy Daniel Adams.)

IMAGES
of America

DOWNSHORE FROM MANAHAWKIN TO NEW GRETNA

The Publications Committee
of the Ocean County Historical Society
Carolyn M. Campbell (Chair), Anne L. Camp
Robert H. Camp, Mary Ellen Hudson
William A. King Jr., Jean C. Lacey
Elizabeth M. Morgan, Estelle M. Martin
Velma R. Oxenford, Martha T. Smith
Thomas M. Williams

ARCADIA
PUBLISHING

ISBN 978-0-7385-6445-6

Published by Arcadia Publishing
Charleston, South Carolina

Printed in the United States of America

Library of Congress Catalog Card Number: 2008941194

For all general information contact Arcadia Publishing at:
Telephone 843-853-2070
Fax 843-853-0044
E-mail sales@arcadiapublishing.com
For customer service and orders:
Toll-Free 1-888-313-2665

Visit us on the Internet at www.arcadiapublishing.com

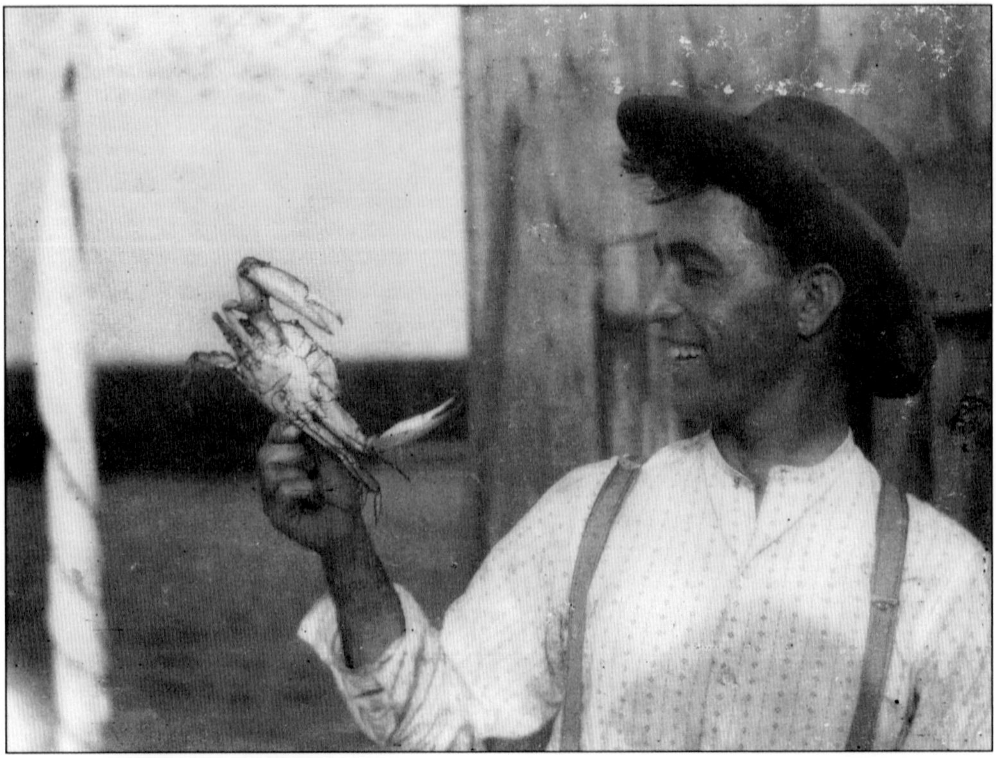

An unidentified man gleefully examines a large blue claw crab. The setting is West Creek in 1906. Among the creatures of the bay, crabs seemed to have fared the best in the centuries of life here. Even now on a summer's day there are hundreds of crabbers of all ages enjoying this form of recreation. They can be found along the streams and in the bays using a crab trap, crabbing from a boat, or simply dangling a fishhead on a piece of string from a dock. The blue claw is still the most common type in local waters. (Courtesy EHS.)

Contents

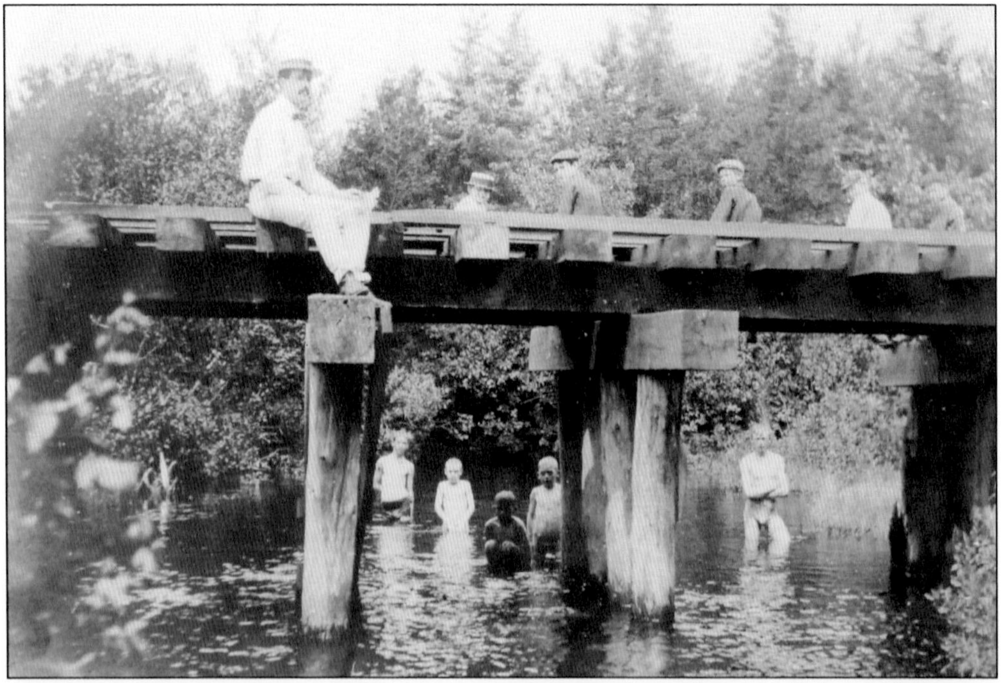
This favorite West Creek "swimmin' hole" was at the spot where Pharo's mill dam had operated for generations. The dam was built *c.* 1706 by Jarvis Pharo, the first settler of the village. Some remnants of the dam could be found as late as the 1930s. Archelaus Pharo, a direct lineal descendant of Jarvis, was instrumental in the building of the Tuckerton Railroad, which crossed this trestle for the first time on October 14, 1871. (Courtesy A.W. Kelly, Esq.)

Acknowledgments

This book was made possible through the combined efforts of the Bass River (BRHS), Eagleswood (EHS), Stafford (SHS), and Tuckerton (THS) Historical Societies; and the Barnegat Bay Decoy and Baymen's Museum (BBD & BM) in cooperation with the Ocean County (OCHS) Historical Society's Publications Committee. Key individuals who assisted were Alvah and Burrell Adams, Harry DeVerter, Steven Eichinger, James Estelle, John Gormley, June LeMunyon, Gladys Loveland, Michael Mangum, Elaine Mathis, June Methot, Terry O'Leary, Minnie Richards, Peter Stemmer, and Helen Wisner.

Credit has been given for each photo. If credited to one of the participating groups, names have been abbreviated. Beside those mentioned above, we thank a host of citizens from these communities who contributed photographs and information. Many of the photographs gracing the pages of our book are from the collection of Arthur W. Kelly, Esq., grandfather of June Methot. We would also like to acknowledge the assistance of the Ocean County Planning Board for our introductory map. Special thanks go to the Methodist Church of West Creek who hosted many of our meetings.

Introduction

We are told that the only constant is change. Our country's growth and progress is a record of that change. When a community, a custom, or a way of life is seemingly idyllic, we often wish it were possible to freeze it in time, to somehow prevent this inevitable change. Such an idyllic way of life exists, though it is quickly disappearing, along the marshy shores of Manahawkin and Little Egg Harbor Bays and the fresh water streams like Cedar Run, Mill, Westecunk, and Tuckerton Creeks, and the Bass and Mullica Rivers. This area extends from 20 miles north of Atlantic City to 110 miles south of New York City. It reaches on the west into the great pine barrens which cover a large portion of all of southern New Jersey.

The communities of Manahawkin, Cedar Run, Mayetta, Staffordville, West Creek, Parkertown, Tuckerton, Little Egg Harbor, and New Gretna march along Route 9 from north to south. Even tinier settlements such as Spraguetown, Mathistown, Cranmertown, Giffordtown, and Galetown used to exist but their names have been absorbed by the larger towns.

Settlers began arriving here in the very late 1600s and early 1700s. Some came to hunt whales from the barrier island and moved inland; some came for timber. Others started farms and worked the waters of the creeks and bays. They were an intelligent, energetic, creative, and resourceful people who successfully wrested a living from this new land. From the bay came fish, oysters, clams, salt hay, and waterfowl. From the pine barrens came pine and white cedar, charcoal, glass, bog iron, moss, and other products of the woods. Gunning brought visitors to the area.

In 1698, gentlemen from upper Burlington County were the proprietors of surveys of land in Little Egg Harbor. Henry Jacob Falkinburg, an interpreter for the European settlers with the Native Americans, bought land comprising Osborn and Wills' Island (Tuckerton). Next came Mordecai and Edward Andrews to settle on the west and east banks of Tuckerton Creek. A man from Shrewsbury Township, Joseph Parker Sr., settled in today's Parkertown in 1721. A Joseph and his wife, maybe the father of the Parkertown settler or maybe no relation at all, had been granted 240 acres in 1675 in Monmouth County.

Westecunk Creek, a favorite Native American haunt, attracted the Spragues, Gaskills, Seamans, Bartletts, Willitts, Cranmers, and the Pharos, to name a few. Joseph Willitts was deeded 900 acres in 1706, and Gervas Pharo moved from Springfield, New Jersey, to West Creek shortly after 1706.

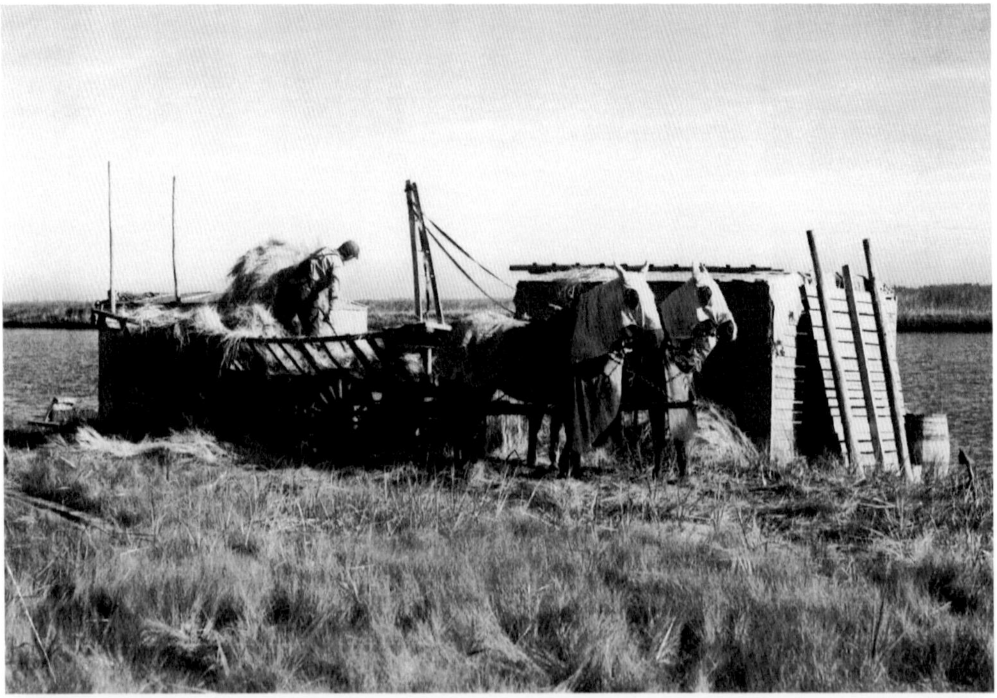

Salt hay is pitched from a wagon by Charles Weber Jr. of Lower Bank. The hay is cut, raked in windrows, put on wagons, and taken ashore and stacked. Farmers grazed their cattle on the salt hay meadows in the summer and used the hay for winter feed and bedding. In the 1840s, it was used for making wrapping paper, for mulching crops, and for packing glass, pottery, and bricks. (Courtesy William Augustine Collection, Rutgers University.)

Manahawkin, the "place of good corn," attracted its first white inhabitants about 1723. The banks of Manahawkin Creek—later Manahawkin Mill Creek, and now simply Mill Creek—were the site of the first settlers' homes. Nicholas Brown, who died about 1724, was one of the earliest persons to own land here. He was followed quickly by the Haywoods, Fitzrandolphs (later just Randolph), Cranes, Pangborns, Courtenays, Johnsons, Pearsons, Pauls, and Southards.

The construction of the Garden State Parkway in the 1950s, the opening of casinos in Atlantic City in the 1980s, and the migration of hundreds of people from the cities of metropolitan New Jersey beginning in the 1950s have caused a population explosion in Ocean County. That wave of growth has now reached the Manahawkin to New Gretna area. Families with surnames different from those which predominated for almost three hundred years have taken up residence here.

It has been this societal change that caused the members of the Ocean County Historical Society to consider preserving the heritage and lifestyle of this area through a pictorial in the Images of America series published by Arcadia. We hope that *Downshore: Manahawkin to New Gretna* will serve as a valuable source of information and as a vignette documenting the lives of these very resourceful people for the area's present and future inhabitants.

One

Downshore Life

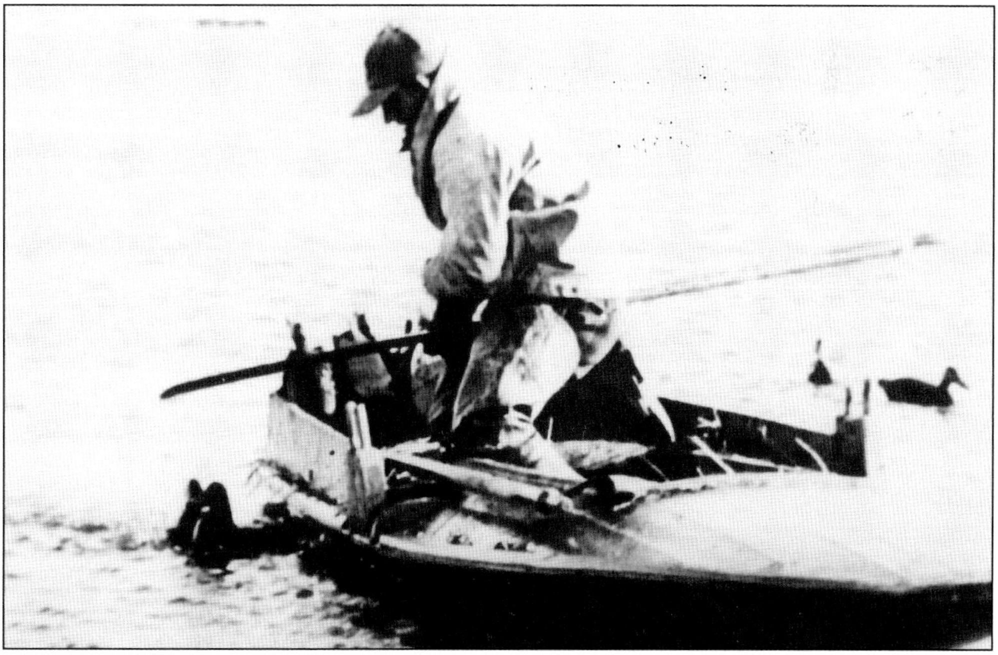

The Jersey shoreman, as each generation has passed, has sharpened his diversified skills and pursuits and has used his intellect to create a satisfying life for himself and his family. The area in which his ancestors chose to live provided an environment that encouraged woodland pursuits, manufacture of iron and glass; fishing, farming, and the cultivation of cranberries; gunning amidst an unbelievable number of wild fowl; and designing and building boats to match a perceived need and development of navigation skills. In this photo, Daniel O'Neill is setting out duck decoys. Philadelphia-born and a plumber by trade, he moved to Tuckerton from Audubon during the 1929 Depression. He quickly adapted to the shore lifestyle, becoming a clammer, duck hunting guide, and charter boat captain. He owned the 38-foot bateau *Marion* and sailed from Willow Landing dock on Green Street, along with the Smith brothers, Claude, Joseph, and Ralph—all natives of Tuckerton. (Courtesy June LeMunyon.)

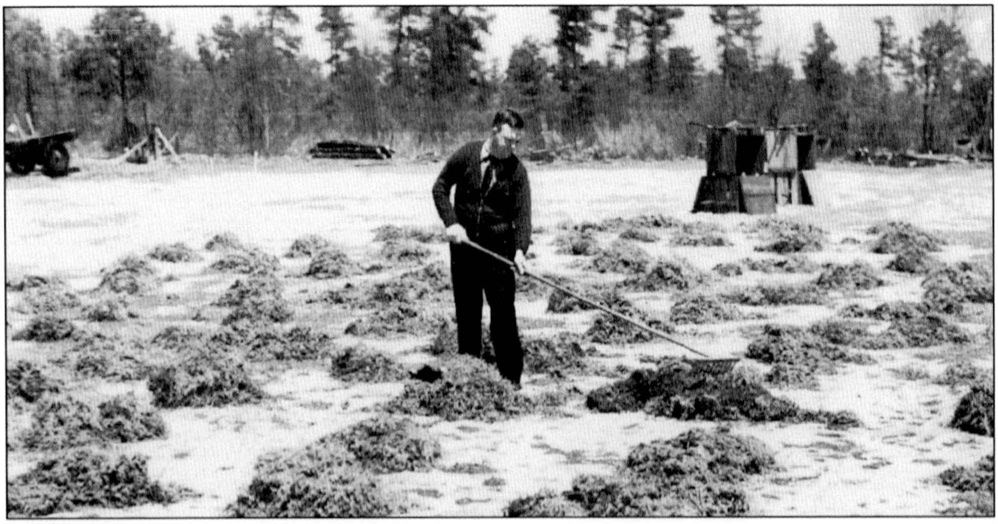

Sphagnum moss was gathered in the white cedar swamps of South Jersey with a long-toothed rake known as a moss dray and was dried in a cleared area called a moss landing. As the top of the moss dried, it was turned until it was mostly dry. It was then ready to be baled. After a few days, moss which formerly weighed 200 pounds had dried to a mere 15 pounds. Sometimes the moss was draped to dry over cedar hassocks, the gnarled and knobby roots that poke out of the swamp water at the tree's base. (Courtesy William Augustine Collection, Rutgers University.)

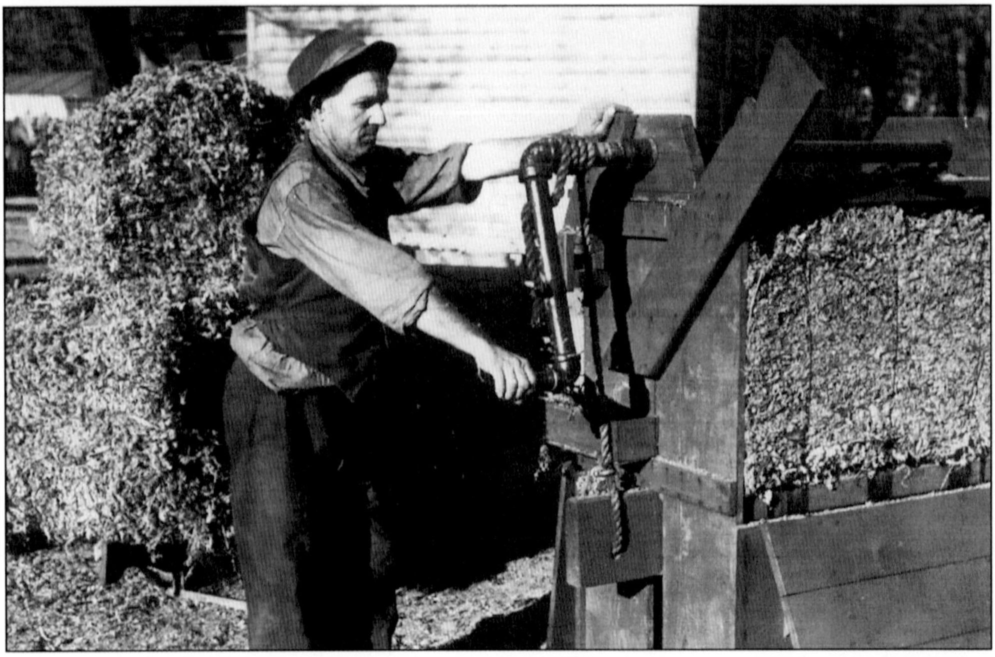

Dried sphagnum moss is being pressed by Sam Ford of Greenbank in a moss press. Most moss presses were homemade but of the same general design. The moss was pressed into 2-foot bales, held together with wire, and covered with burlap. The moss is antiseptic and was used for bandages during World War I. Later it was used as a packing material for flowers and plants. (Courtesy William Augustine Collection, Rutgers University.)

Arthur W. Kelly, photographer, relinquished his camera to pose for this duck-hunting shot with his favorite retriever, Mingo. Born in West Creek in 1869 and the son of Myles and Rebecca (Willits) Kelly, he attended and then taught at the West Creek School, studied law, and served as principal at West Creek for two years. After passing his bar exams, he married Anna Haywood. While living in Monmouth County, he recorded the scenes of his childhood in West Creek at every opportunity. (Courtesy A.W. Kelly, Esq.)

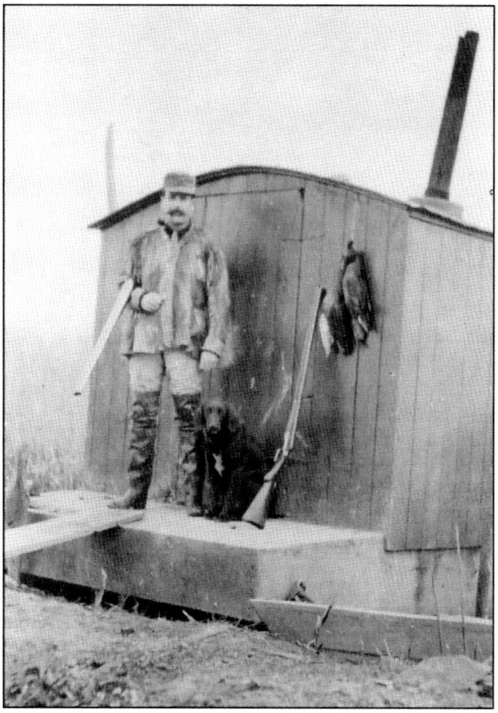

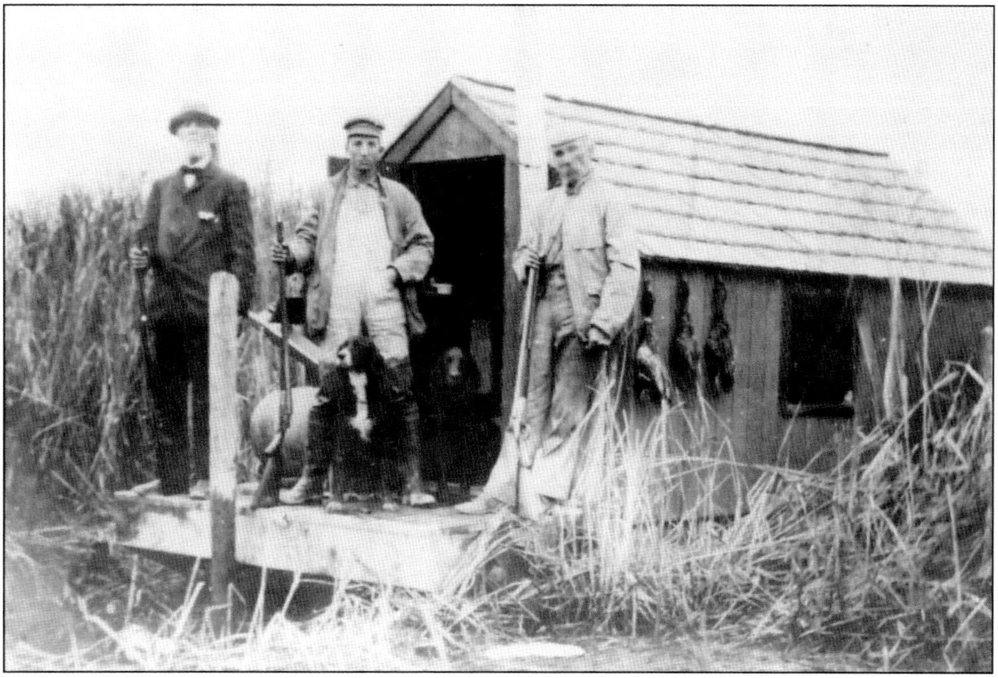

Duck hunting on the wide, windswept expanses of sedge lying between the village and the bay provided both sport and variety for the winter table. A gunning shack on a raft with a wood stove was a cozy retreat, giving these hunters and their retrievers a chance to warm up. (Courtesy A.W. Kelly, Esq.)

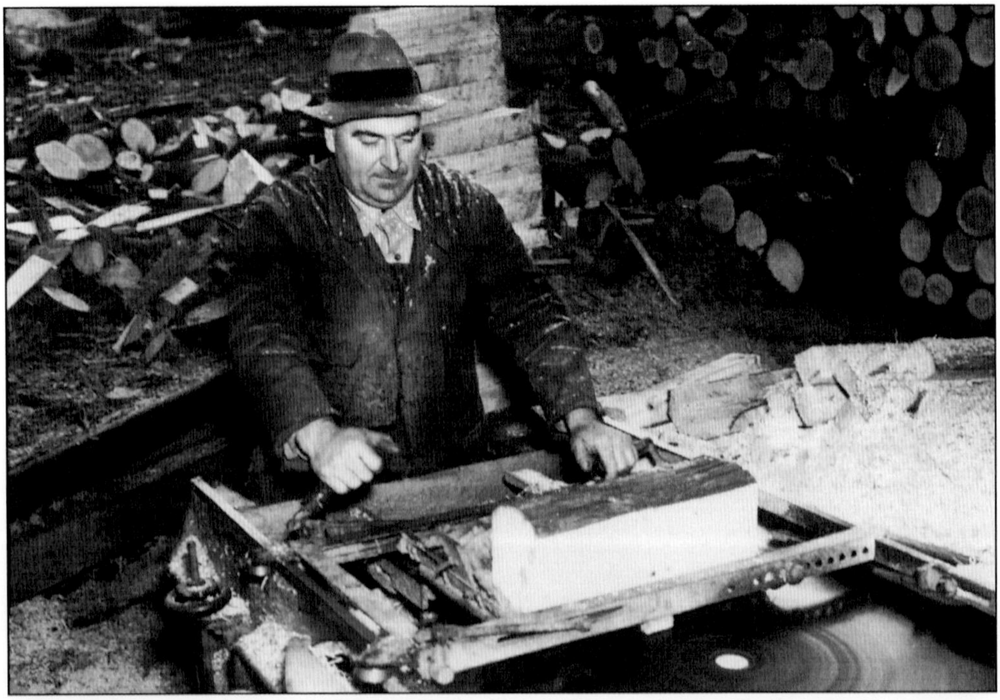

Cedar shakes, made here on a shingle saw by Joseph Ware in Lower Bank, were an important part of the large timber industry in the area. As the cedar block was cut, first one end was lowered and then the other between cuts to give the angle cut of the shingle. The most durable cedar for shakes was dug up or "mined" from the water of the cedar swamps. (Courtesy William Augustine Collection, Rutgers University.)

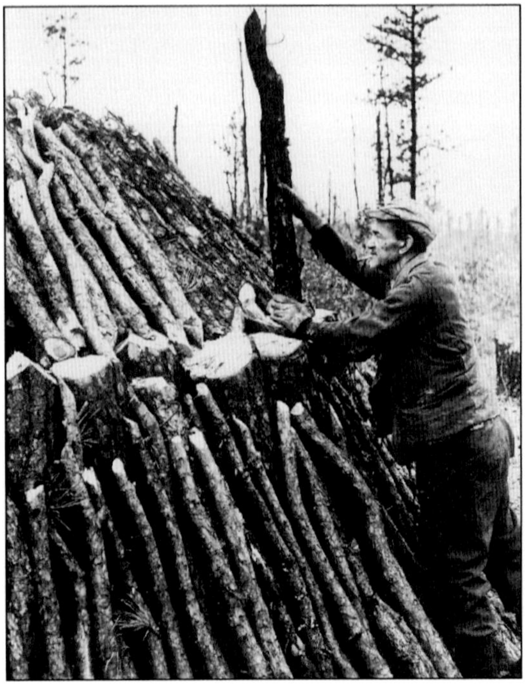

George Crummel of Jenkins Neck is piling pine to make a charcoal kiln. He constructs a chimney in the center by stacking short pieces and covers the outside with "floats" of turf to make the kiln airtight. The kiln will be set on fire and watched carefully day and night to make sure it will not burn too fast, thus turning the charcoal to ashes. An eight-cord kiln takes about ten days to burn. (Courtesy William Augustine Collection, Rutgers University.)

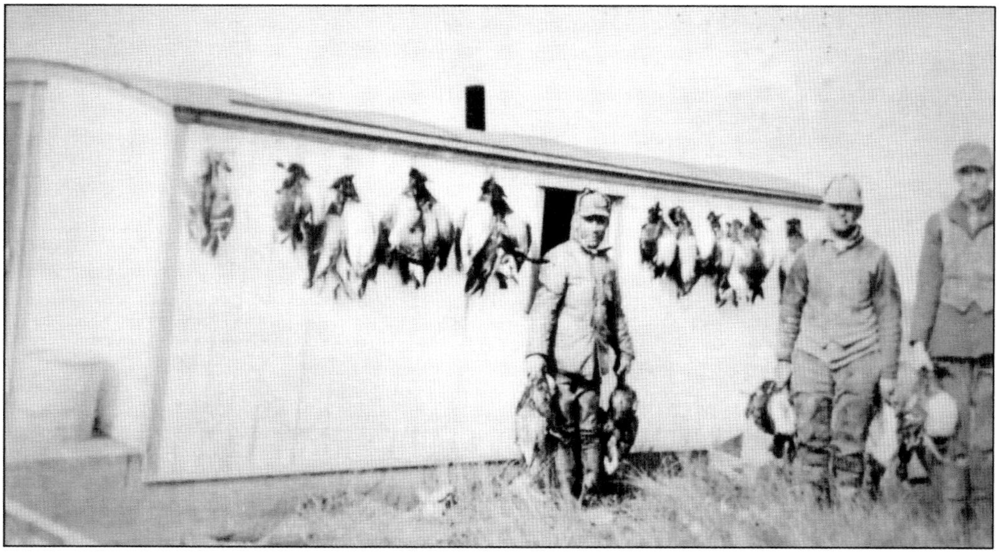

Jay Remington (left), guide Harvey Parker (center), and an unknown hunter (right) display their bag limit of ducks and brant at Harvey's houseboat, which was located on Shelter Island between Parkertown and Long Beach Island. Remington was a road engineer from Burlington County, who frequently hunted with Harvey. (Courtesy BBD & BM.)

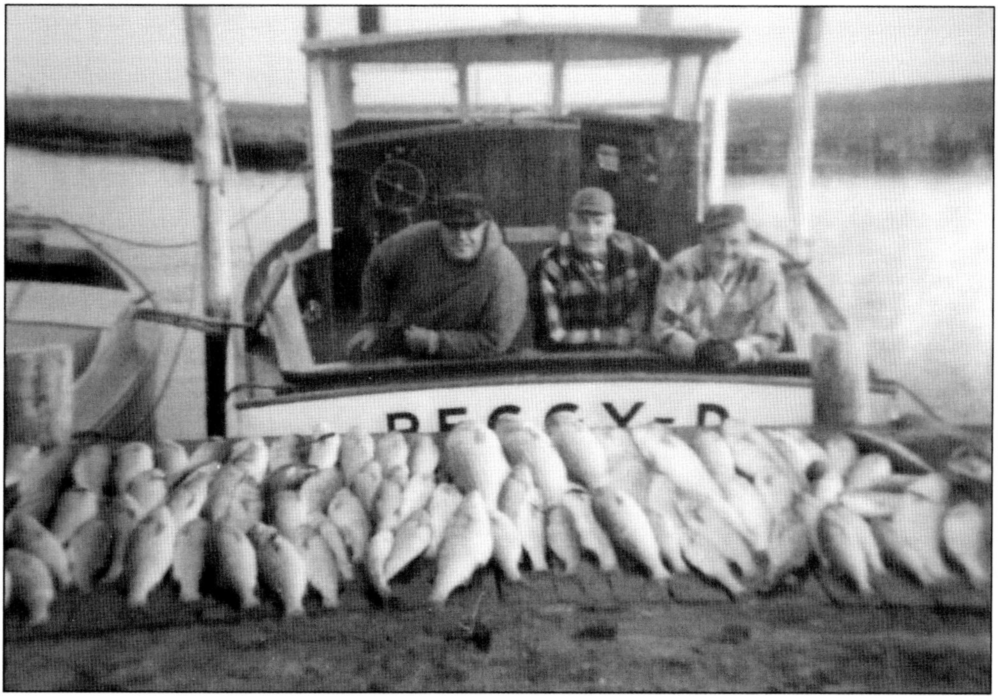

Captain Mason Price, Captain Chet Holman and Dick McKandless (from left to right), all of Parkertown, are seen at the Parkertown dock on Thanksgiving Day, 1958, aboard Captain Holman's boat the *Peggy D* with their catch of striped bass. These fish were caught outside Little Egg Harbor Inlet. They could have caught more if they hadn't become exhausted. They claimed they had never seen stripers any thicker. (Courtesy BBD&BM.)

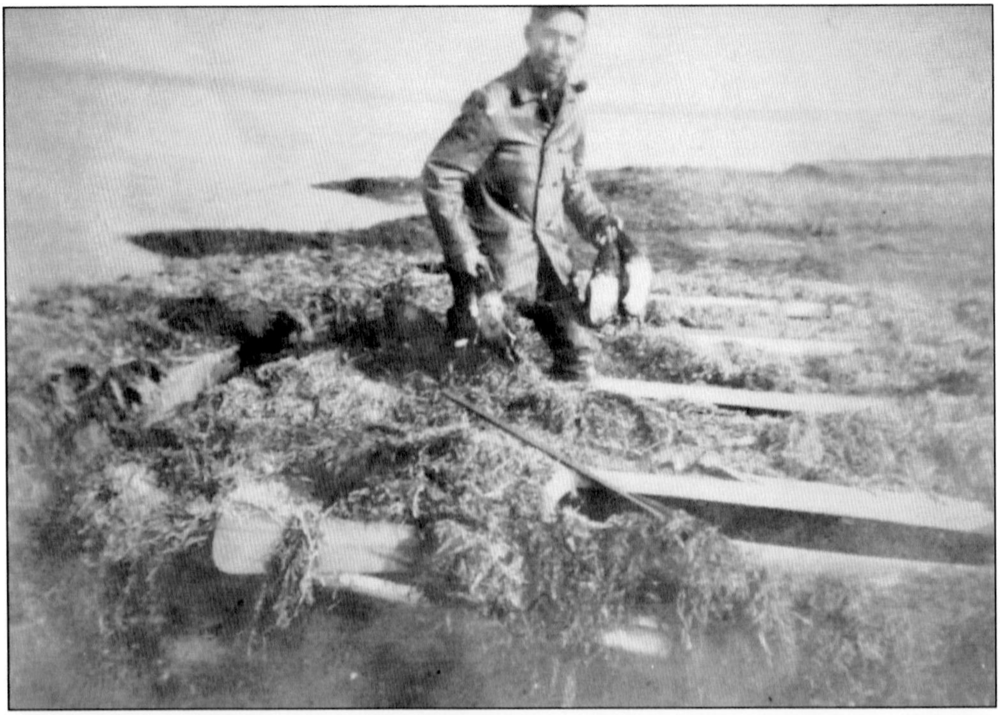

Camouflaged sneakboxes were used by duck hunters on Barnegat Bay. These boats were ideal for the shallow bay since they drew only 6 inches of water. This 12-foot long boat could easily be covered with marsh grass and converted into a blind. (Courtesy BBD & BM.)

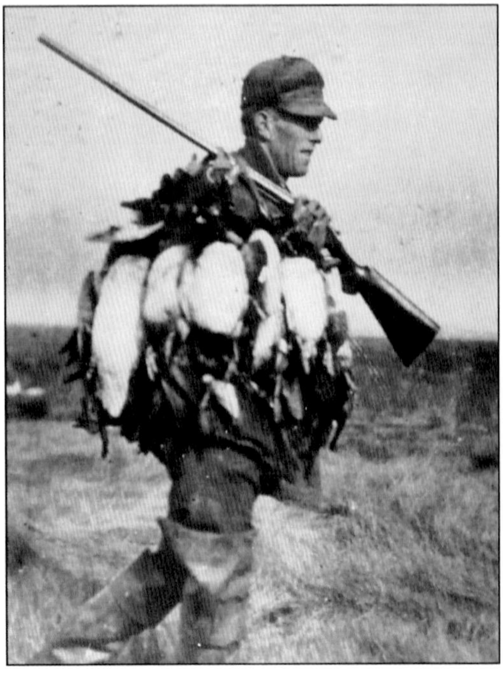

Captain John Cramer (1883–1956) of Parkertown is shown carrying his bag limit of ducks and brant. Captain Cramer was a partner of Harvey Parker in a houseboat on Shelter Island. He was a hunting guide for groups such as the Peahala Club and the Philadelphia Athletics. He ran a charter boat out of Parkertown Dock for years and carved a few decoys for his own use. (Courtesy BBD & BM.)

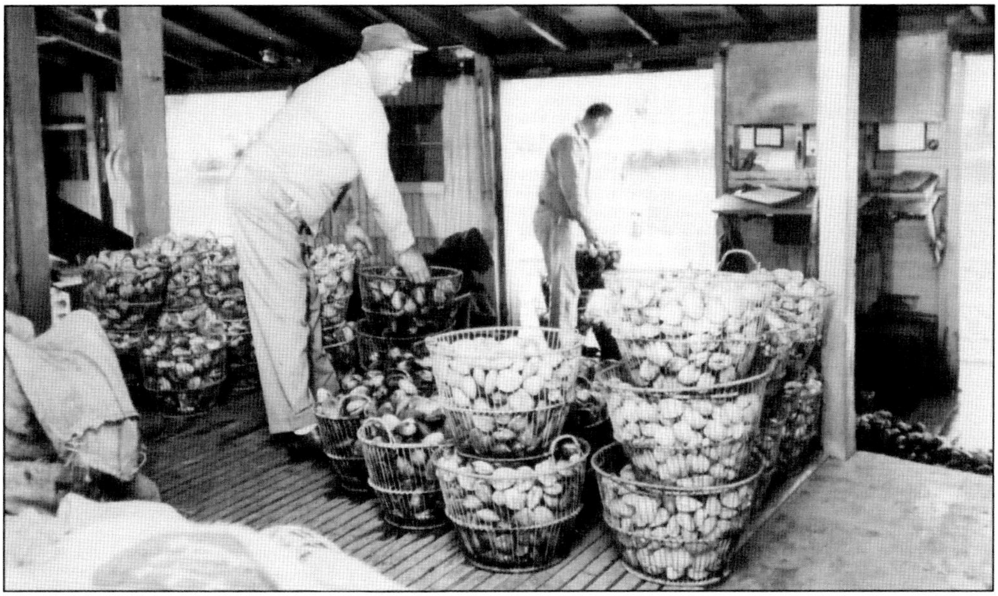

These men are working in Parsons' Clam House on Tuckerton Creek. In the 1940s Parsons' Seafood had clam houses in West Creek, Pleasantville, Smithville, Parkertown, and Tuckerton. Eighty-five full-time baymen worked for them. In its best year Parsons shipped more than nine million clams and they were only one of ten or twelve clam houses on Tuckerton Creek. During World War II, Parsons shipped five truckloads of clams daily to Campbell's Soup. (Courtesy BBD & BM.)

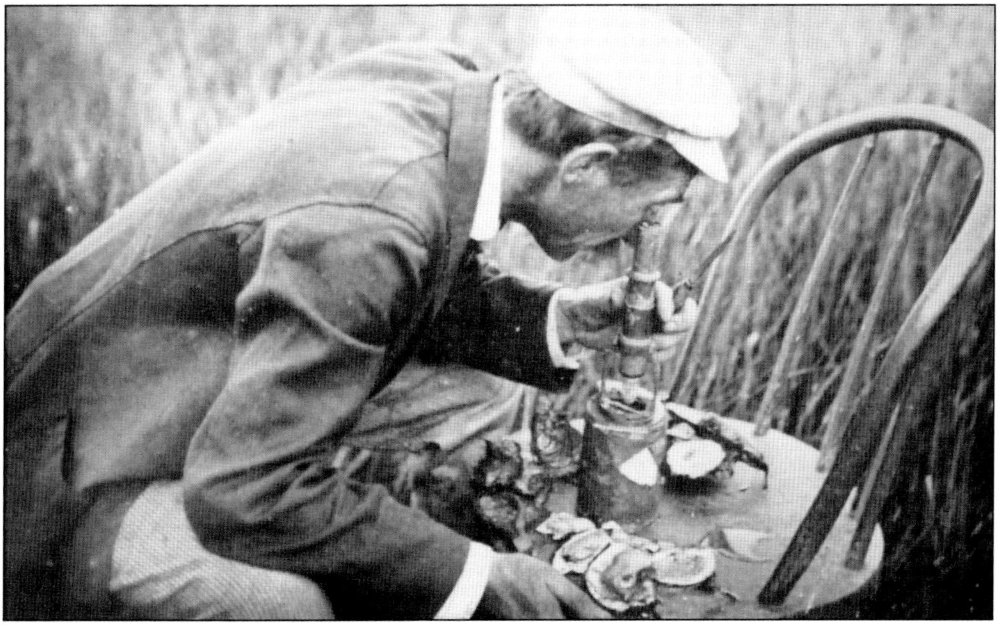

Julius Nelson was Rutgers University's first professor of biology. He was also the biologist for the New Jersey Oyster Commission. His report of 1898 estimated that there were 200,000 productive acres of oyster-growing lots along the New Jersey shoreline. In October 1905, over a hundred boats were seen tonging oysters at the mouth of the Mullica River. (Courtesy BBD & BM.)

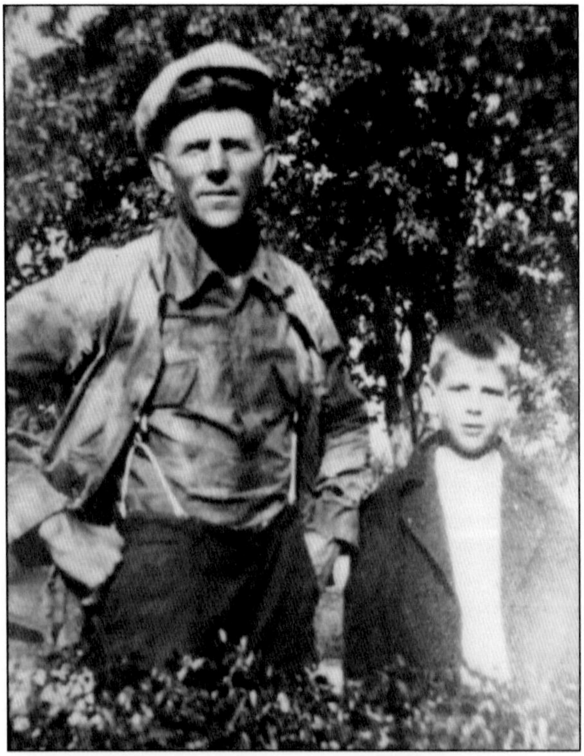

Nathan Rowley Horner (1881–1942) was a well-known carver of duck and goose decoys. His decoys are ranked among the finest made in New Jersey. He was a bayman, most of his life, but also worked for the *Tuckerton Beacon* and a printing firm in Philadelphia. He lived in Tuckerton until 1916 when he moved to Lavallette to work as a boatbuilder. Horner was a talented musician, playing the trombone and piano in local movie houses. He is shown in the photo with his son, Watson. (Courtesy Kenneth Tolbert.)

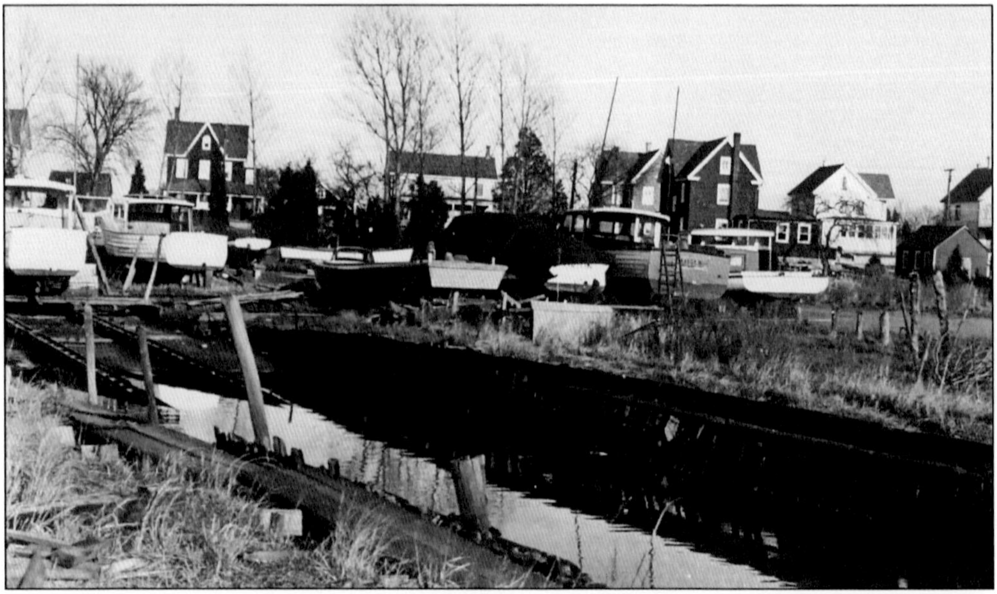

Sidney Pearce bought this boatyard about 1947. It was established in the late 1890s by Mr. Crozer for his and his friends' private use. Extra heavy ways were put in to accommodate large sailing vessels and racing sloops. William P. Smith took over its operation as a commercial facility. When it was sold to Sidney Pearce, it was described as the oldest established marine railway along this section of the coast. Mr. Pearce was a Tuckerton native, a graduate of New York Merchant Marine Academy, and a sea captain for eighteen years. (Courtesy BBD & BM.)

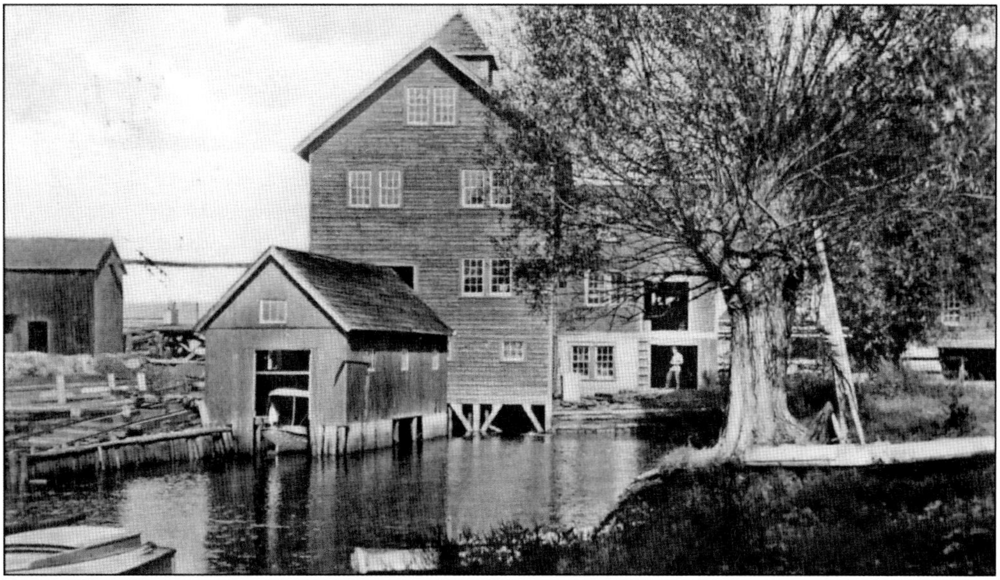

Edward Andrews built the first gristmill in 1704 on Pohatcong Creek. In 1812 Andrews made a will in which he bequeathed the mill to his wife during her life and then to his son Samuel. From Samuel it passed through many hands: Samuel Shourds Sr., David Shourds, David's son Samuel, Shinn Oliphant Sr., Eayre Oliphant Sr., Simeon Haines, Timothy Pharo, and A.R. Pharo. A.R. Pharo had the old mill torn down and a large mill (pictured here) put on the site. (Courtesy Michael Mangum.)

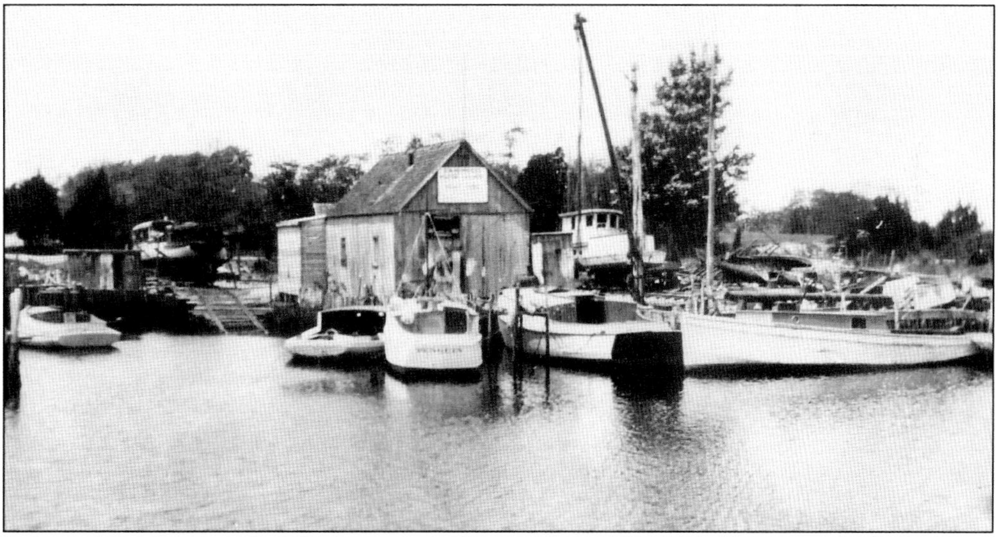

Heinrichs' Boat Works and Marine Railway was located at the head of Tuckerton Creek next to Crowley's Basin. The facility was owned by Captain Edward "Socks" Heinrichs around 1920. The railway made it possible to launch boats and to haul them out for maintenance, repair, or winter storage. The biggest boat built was 50 feet long. Heinrichs also held a Master Mariner's license for many years. Heinrichs' four sons Gus Sr., Frances, Joseph and Eddie Jr. all worked for him at various times. Heinrichs operated the boat works until the late 1940s. He lived until age eighty-eight. (Courtesy BBD & BM.)

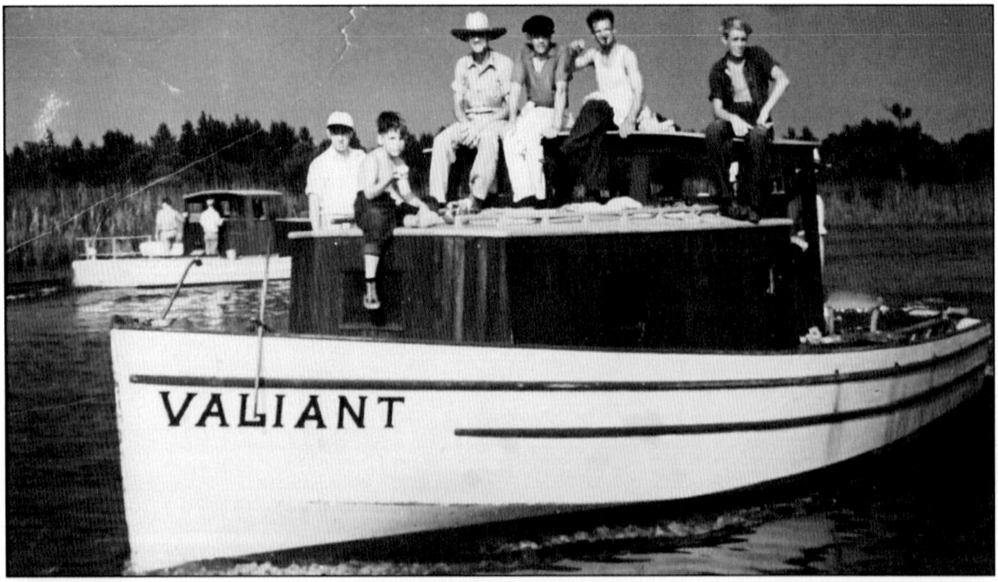

Captain Chester Allen was the owner of Allen's Dock & Marina in New Gretna. His party boat, the *Valiant*, was named for his wife, Edna Valiant. A man named Robert Allen married Edith Andrews in 1716, daughter of Edward, one of Tuckerton's first residents. The Allens settled near Bass River in 1721 and were the first white neighbors Great John Mathis had. Since Chester Allen was a "New Gretna Allen," it is likely he was descended from that first Robert. (Courtesy BBD & BM.)

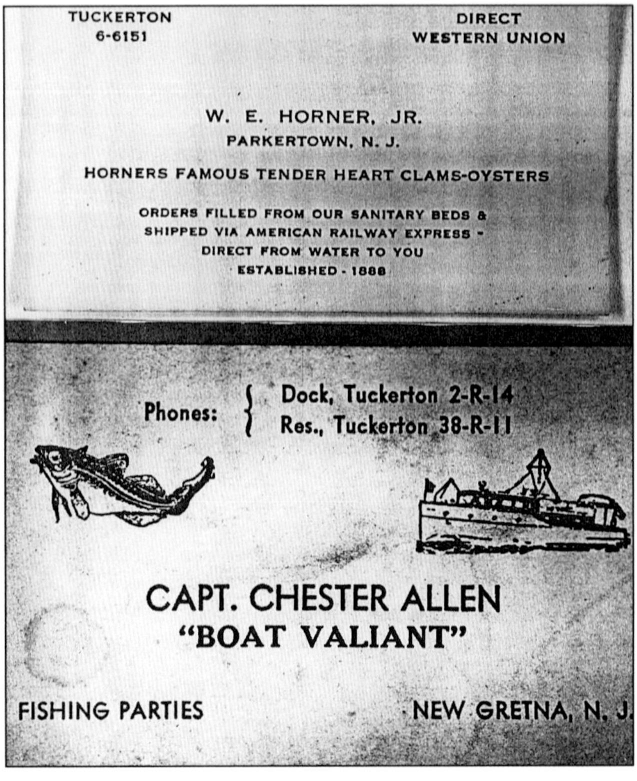

These two business cards are samples of the many which must have been distributed in the early 1900s. Chester Allen was taking fishing parties from New Gretna, but listed two phones, one at the dock and one at his residence in Tuckerton. W.E. Horner Jr. of Parkertown advertised his specialty: tender heart clams and oysters direct from the water to you via the American Railway Express. (Courtesy BBD & BM.)

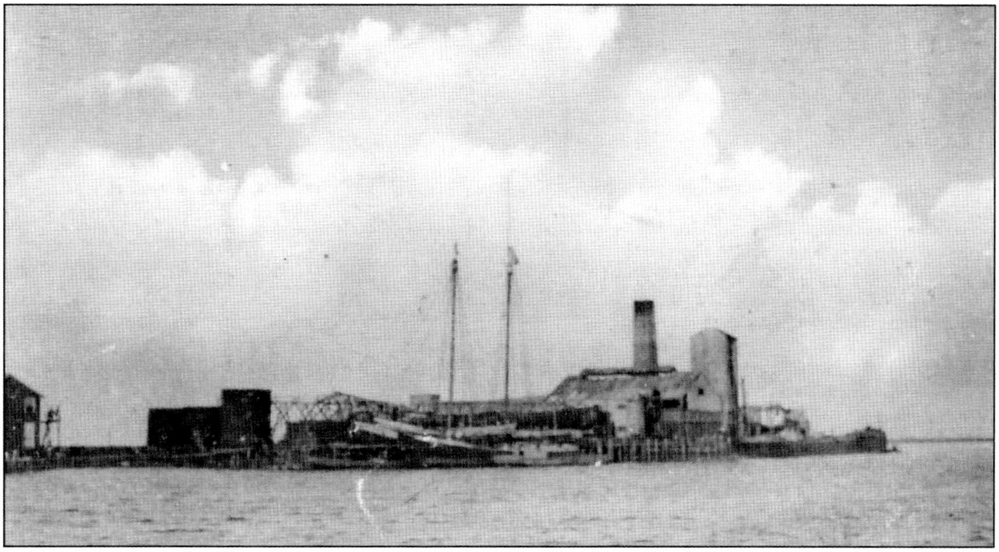

In 1912 Great Bay was one of the leading centers of the fish oil and fertilizer business in the United States. Two factories were in operation, the McKeever Brothers factory on Crab Island and the Atlantic Fisheries Company (shown here) on Story's Island. The menhaden swarmed by the millions along the Jersey shore. The annual catch averaged about six hundred million fish. From these about 65,000 tons of scrap and 35,000 barrels of oil were produced. The scrap was used for fertilizer and the oil was used to manufacture soap, paint and varnish, oilskin garments, and plastics. (Courtesy Michael Mangum.)

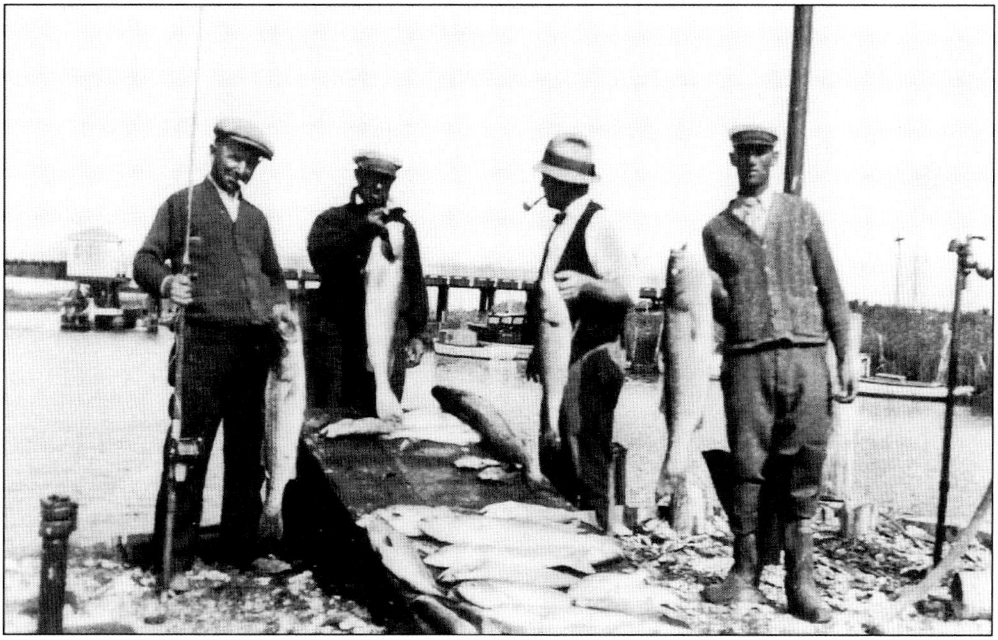

Sports fishing has been an important industry along the south Jersey coast throughout the years. Here, *c.* 1938, "Piper" Allen, Chet Allen, Levi Downs, and Les Allen (from left to right) display their catch of stripers at Allen's Dock along the Bass River. The Bass River bridge can be seen in the background. (Courtesy Earl and Sally Allen.)

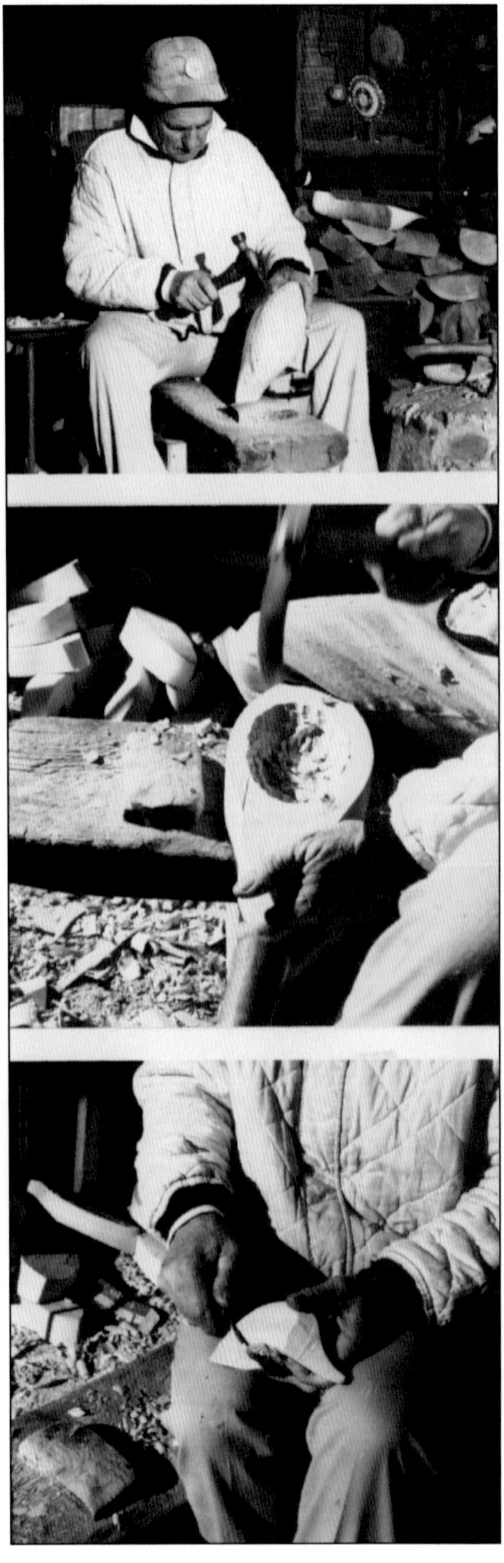

Hurley Conklin was born in Manahawkin in 1913. He started making decoys when he was fifteen years old and estimated that he had made over twenty thousand decoys in his lifetime. After serving in the army during World War II, he worked as a guide for the Marshelder Gunning Club. Conklin was also noted for carving miniature Barnegat Bay sneakboxes. Most carvers had distinctive features which make it possible to identify individual artists. The ballast could be a lead pad or molten lead poured into an opening in the bottom of the decoy. The tails differed in height and the amount of rounding on the bottom often varied. Eye grooves might be wide-eyed or tight. Some decoys had ice catchers behind the necks. Each year at the annual Old Time Barnegat Bay Decoy and Gunning Show, those folks who lived their lives in the Barnegat Bay tradition are honored with a Hurley Conklin Award. With each passing year, there are fewer and fewer people who we can say make a living from the bay and the pinelands. (Courtesy James Estelle.)

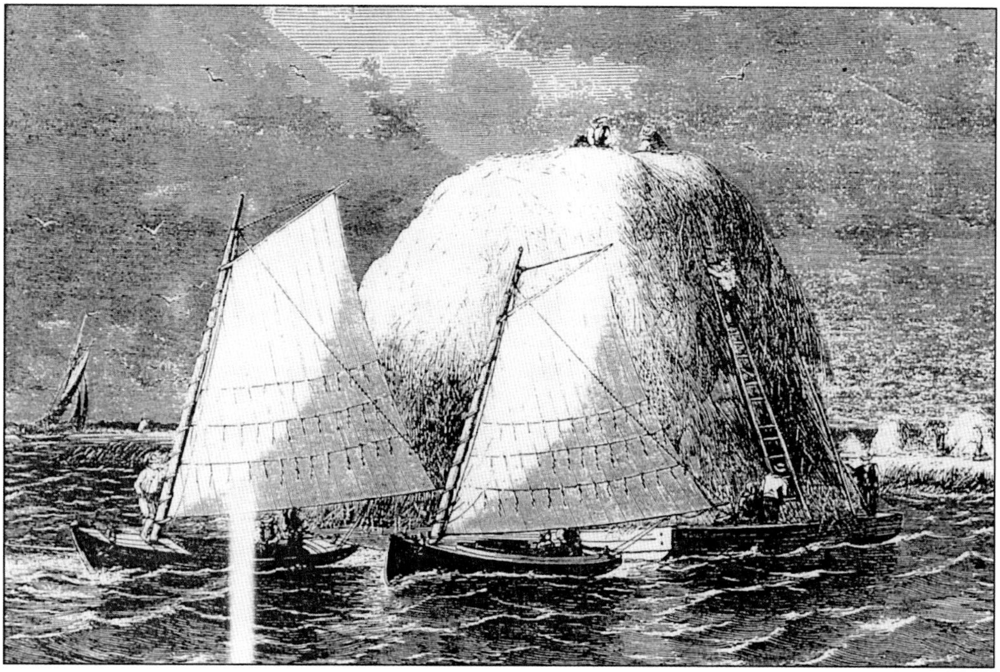

Gathering salt hay from the meadows along the coast was a major industry in the early nineteenth century. Salt hay was used for feeding cattle, packing glass or pottery, fertilizer, mulch, and insulation. It was cut with scythes, raked into windrows, and stacked on scows. The hay was then towed across the bay and shipped by rail to New York or Philadelphia. As much as 100 tons per week were shipped. (Courtesy BBD & BM.)

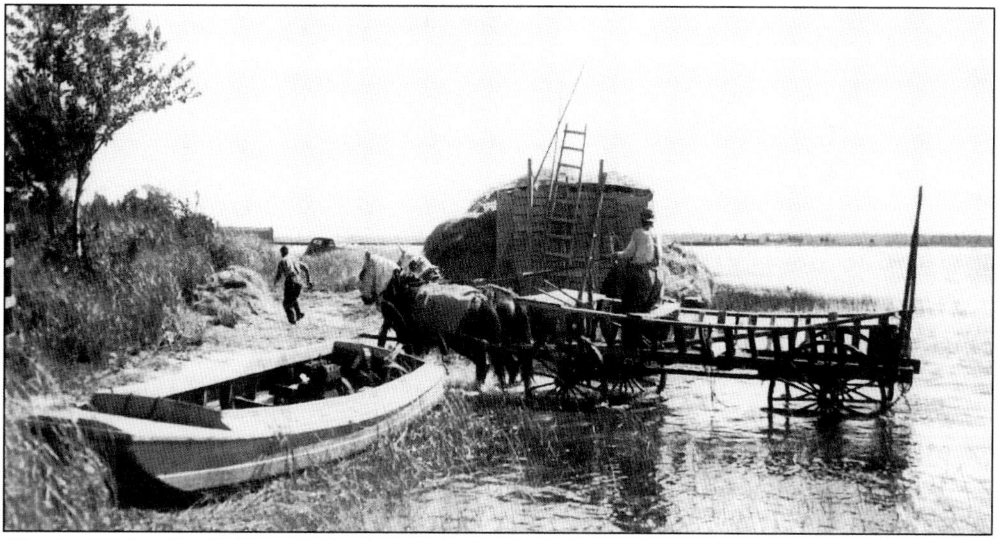

Charles Weber Sr. (left) and Charles Weber Jr. (right) of Lower Bank are seen harvesting salt hay from meadows in the Lower Bank-Bass River area. Harvesting, usually done between June and January, was hard work made more difficult by the heat, mosquitoes, and green head flies. In this photograph, the horses' heads and bodies are covered to protect them from the insects. They also wear "mud boots" to keep from sinking into the soft meadow's surface. (Courtesy William Augustine Collection, Rutgers University.)

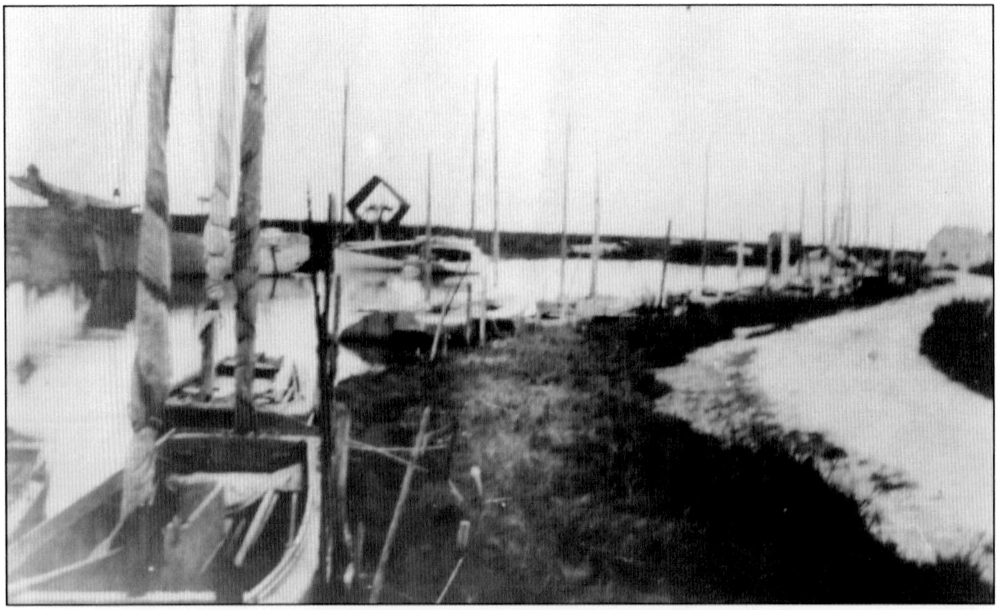

Against the far bank a typical coastal sloop is moored, perhaps one of the many built at Tuckerton. More garveys and various other types of boats line the near bank of Westecunk Creek as far as the eye can see. This creek had many bends, which made sailing rather difficult. (Courtesy A.W. Kelly, Esq.)

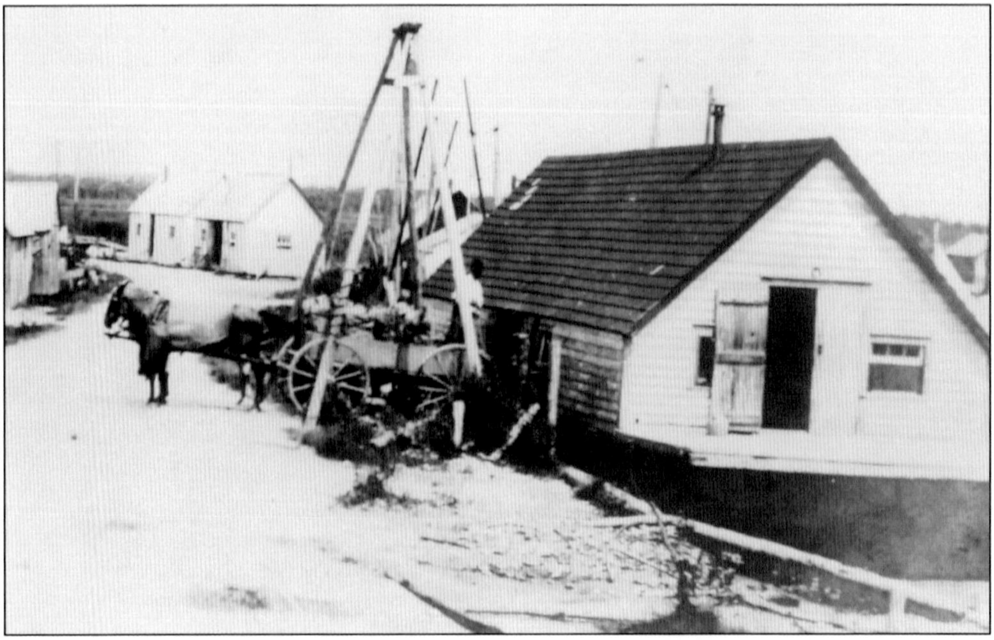

Sacks of oysters are being hand-loaded for shipment from one of the numerous businesses which lined Dock Road c. 1900. When the oysters or clams were to be shipped by rail, they were usually loaded in heavier barrels, which explains the presence of the overhead hoist. Before rail service, large shipments to New York or Philadelphia went via coastal vessels. (Courtesy A.W. Kelly, Esq.)

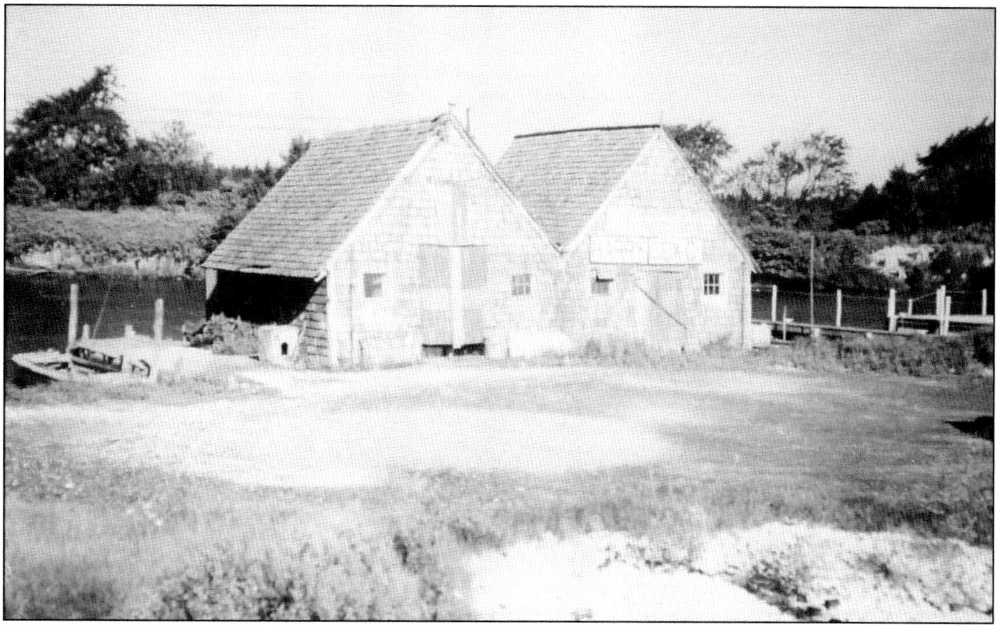

When the oysterman made his way homeward with the day's harvest, he often headed for a dealer or buyer. Sheds were built along the creek and situated so that the bayman could dock his boat, transact business, and unload right from the boat. The oysters were frequently placed in floats until needed to fill an order, at which time they were packed in barrels and shipped to market. These sheds, whether for oysters or clams, belonged to Harry Cox. (Courtesy BBD & BM.)

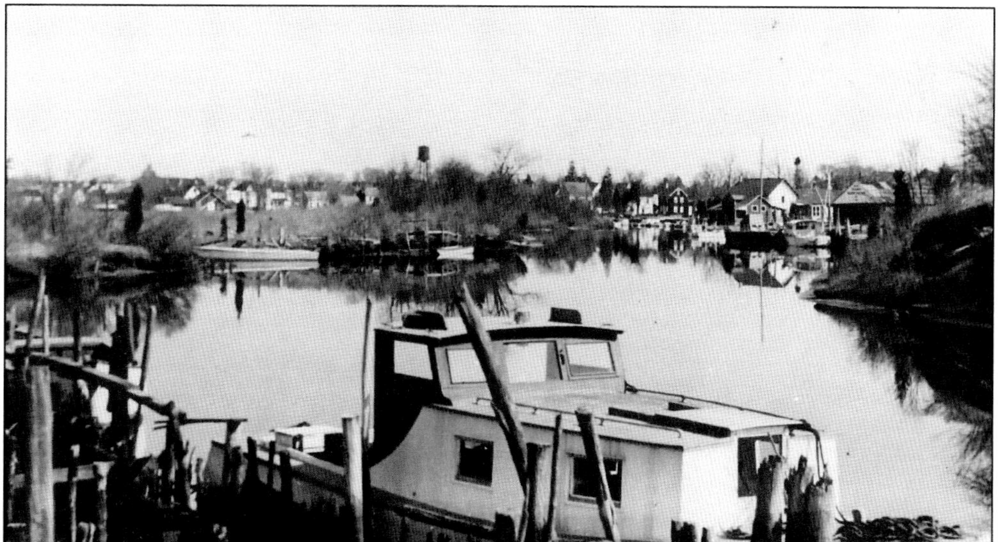

This peaceful scene is along Tuckerton Creek looking toward town. The firm ground along the northeastern bank of the stream made it possible for the community to spread out along the waterway. (Courtesy BBD & BM.)

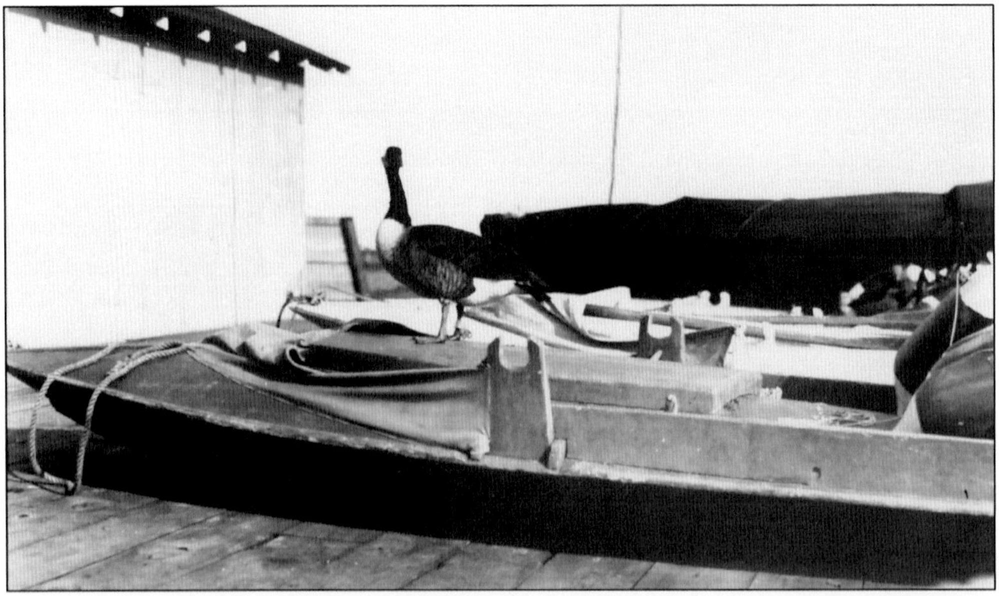

The tame goose on this sneakbox in Manahawkin could be taken out into Barnegat Bay with the hunters to serve as a live decoy along with the wooden ones. (Courtesy James Estelle.)

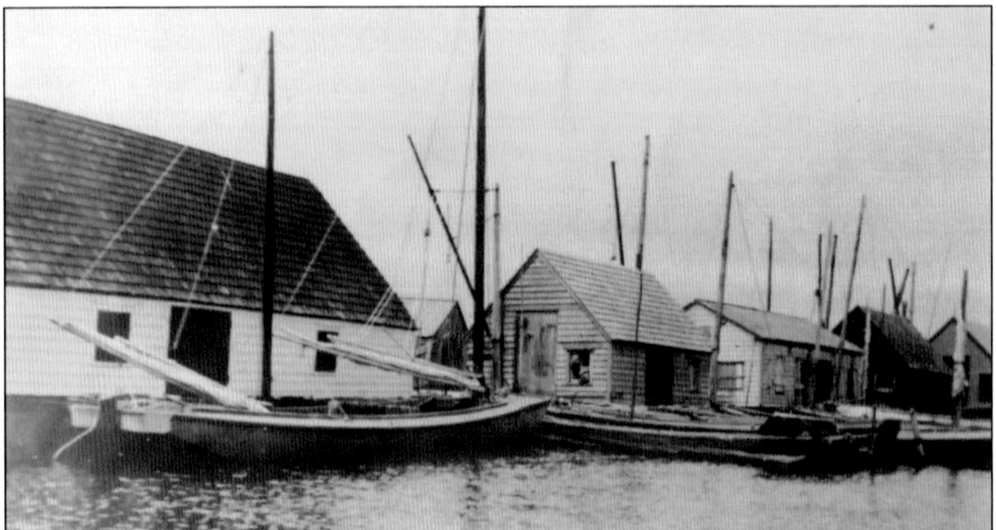

Sailing garveys, whose flat bottoms were stable platforms for working in the bay chop, were tied up rail to rail on a Sunday. Any other day it would have been hard to find one, for shell fishery was the economic backbone of the town. After World War I most garveys were converted to gasoline engines, but the basic design remained little altered. (Courtesy A.W. Kelly, Esq.)

In the background is a net drying reel. Half out of the water is an oyster raft which, when floated by the two large cedar logs at its sides, permitted the water to flow freely through the slatted bottom, thus keeping oysters and clams fresh while awaiting shipment. Discarded shells provided surfacing for dirt roads. (Courtesy A.W. Kelly, Esq.)

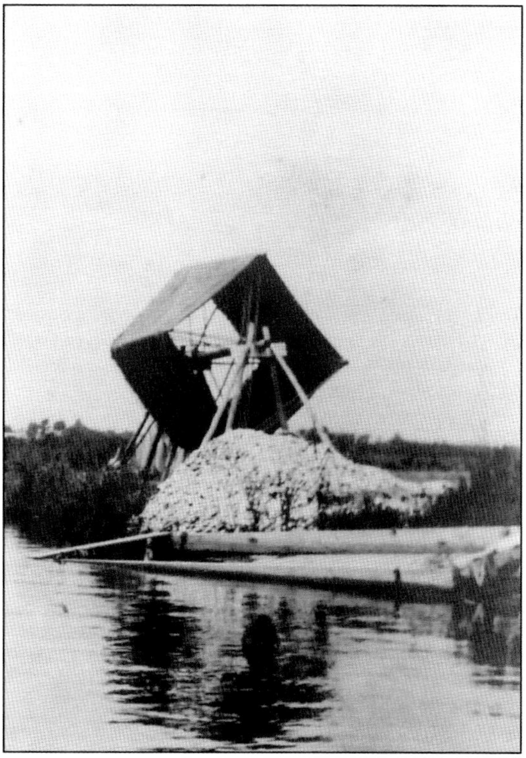

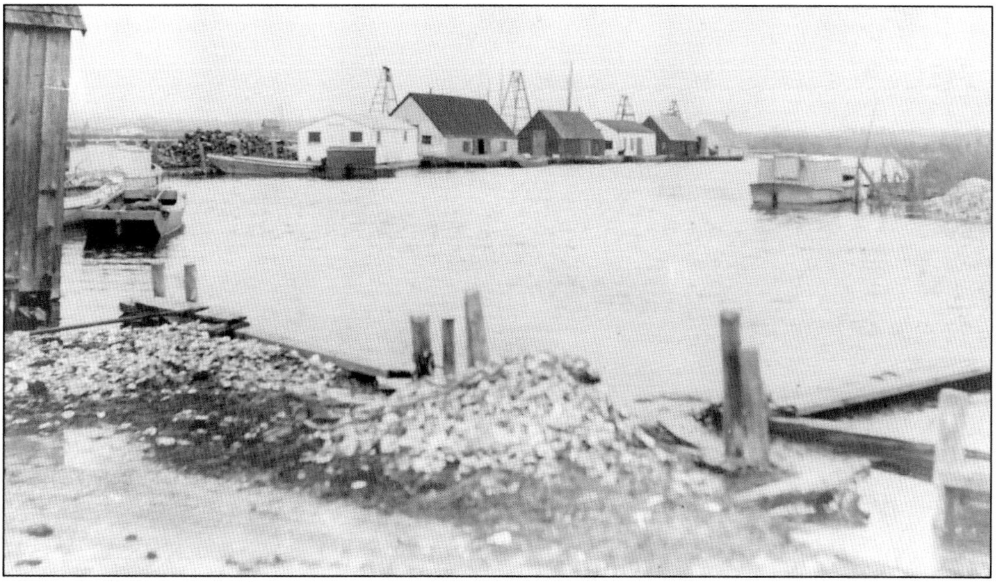

West Creek was not only the town's "business district," but it also attracted photographers and artists who liked the old sheds, quaint boats, piles of oyster shells, and winding creeks. Most of the docks and sheds were on the south bank. The urgency of getting clams and oysters to city markets quickly created a busy scene, as the baymen brought the results of their day's work to the docks. After being prepared for market in the sheds, the shellfish were loaded on wagons and later trucks, and taken to the railroad station. (Courtesy EHS.)

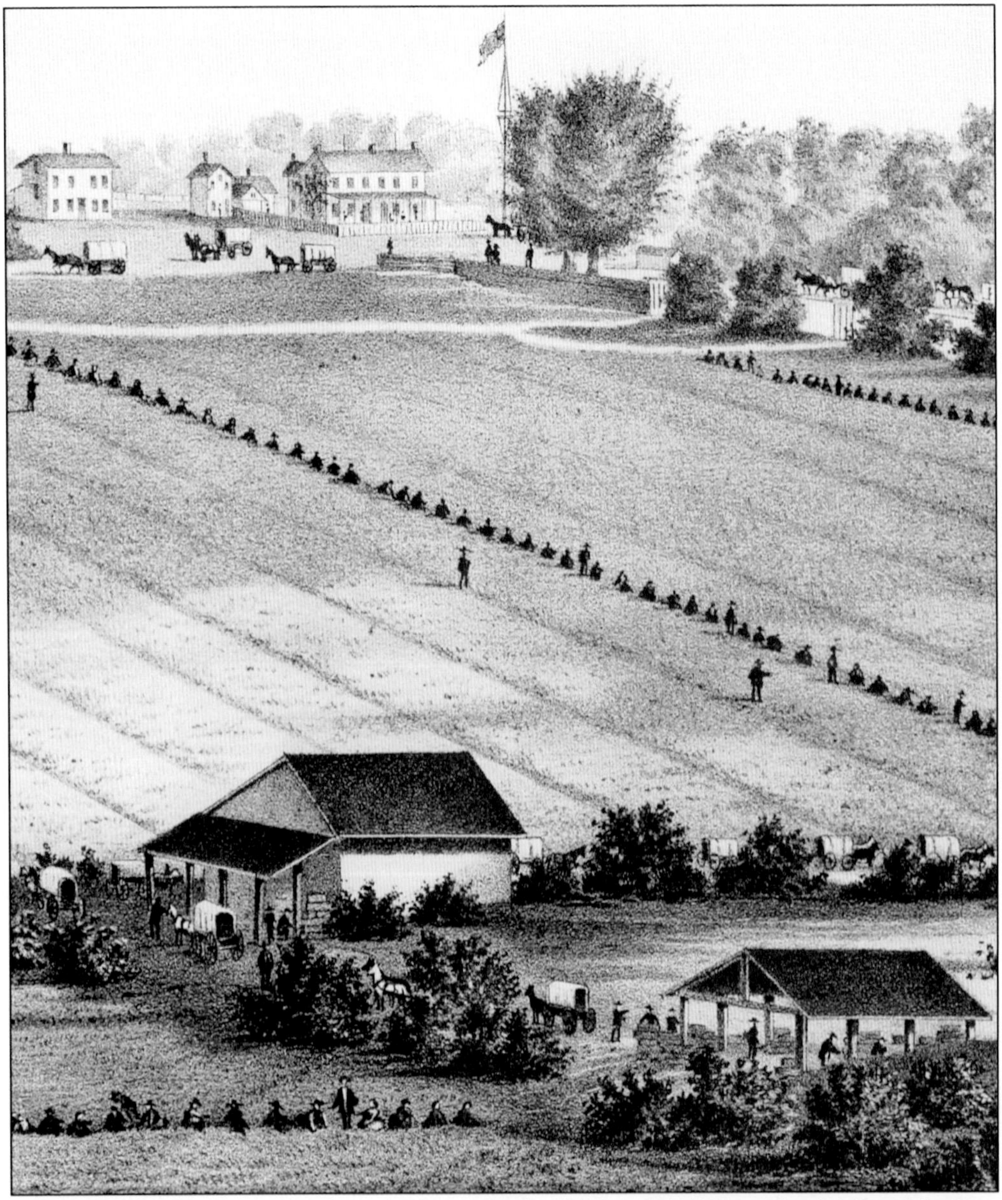

In this illustration from part of an engraving in the *Historical and Biographical Atlas of the New Jersey Coast* by Woolman and Rose (1878), cranberries are being harvested on the 150-acre bog owned by Daniel Gowdy, who came to New Jersey in 1855 from Massachusetts. He and two brothers planted fifty bogs under contract and also sold about one hundred and fifty more which they made. Daniel Gowdy was highly successful in the cranberry boom era. The plantation shown was once the site of Stafford Forge, which was built by John Lippincott from Howell Township in 1797 on the north branch of Westecunk Creek. The double forge was conveyed to John Youle, New York iron merchant; Joseph Walker of Washington Township (Burlington County); and Henry Kimble of Stafford Township in 1808. Later Youle bought up Walker's and Kimble's interests. The forge was abandoned *c.* 1838. A later owner was Jesse Richards of Batsto. In 1965 New Jersey bought up the land, which is now called the Stafford Forge Wildlife Management Area. (Courtesy OCHS.)

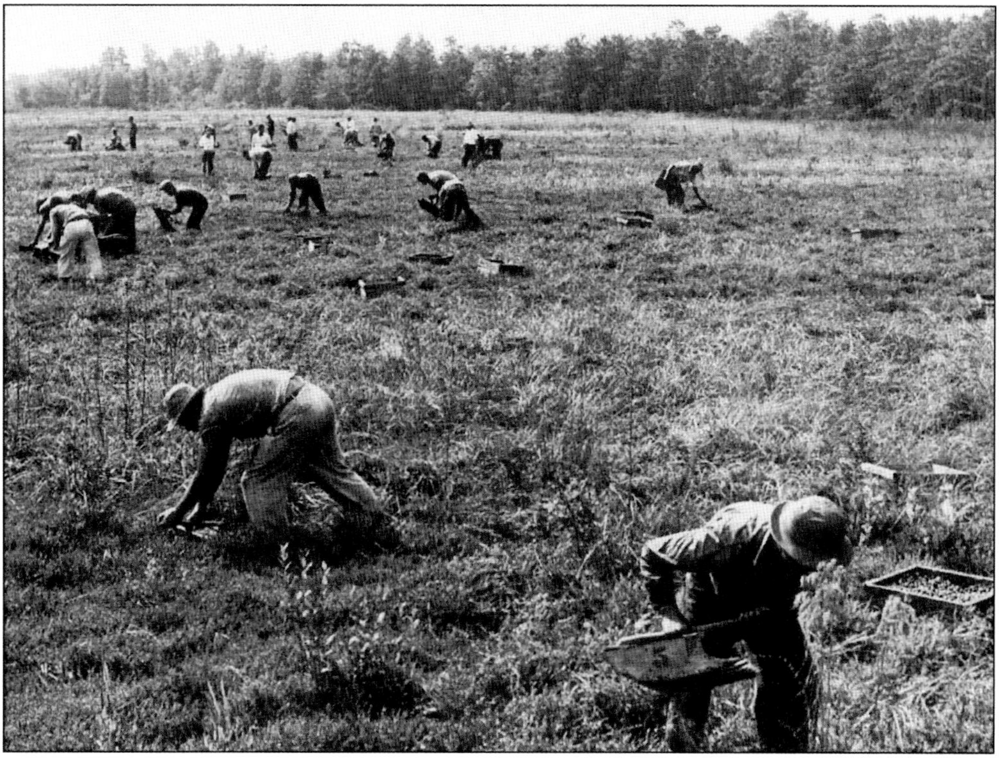

Many cedar swamps were converted to cranberry bogs after the timber was depleted in the mid-1800s. Two large plantations were Sim Place in Bass River and Stafford Forge in Eagleswood Township, both along the pine barrens's streams. First, picking was done by hand, then by scoop in the early twentieth century, and after the 1960s the "wet method" involving machines was introduced. Hand-picking and scooping were backbreaking jobs. Berries were placed in a 1-peck box and later transferred to a 1-bushel packing box. (Courtesy William Augustine Collection, Rutgers University.)

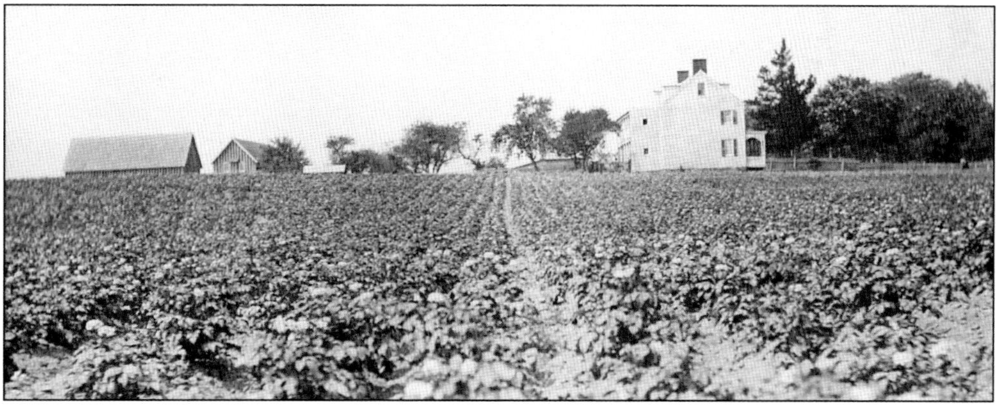

Sometime after 1904 this potato farm and buildings belonged to J. Franklin Dye, New Jersey's secretary of agriculture. It was along the Main Shore Road south of West Creek's center. The original grant to the Willits family for this property lay across the East/West Jersey line which divided Burlington and Monmouth Counties. John Willits built this large farmhouse on the Burlington side of the line. Arthur T. Willits inherited the farm, but when he died in 1904 it was sold. (Courtesy EHS.)

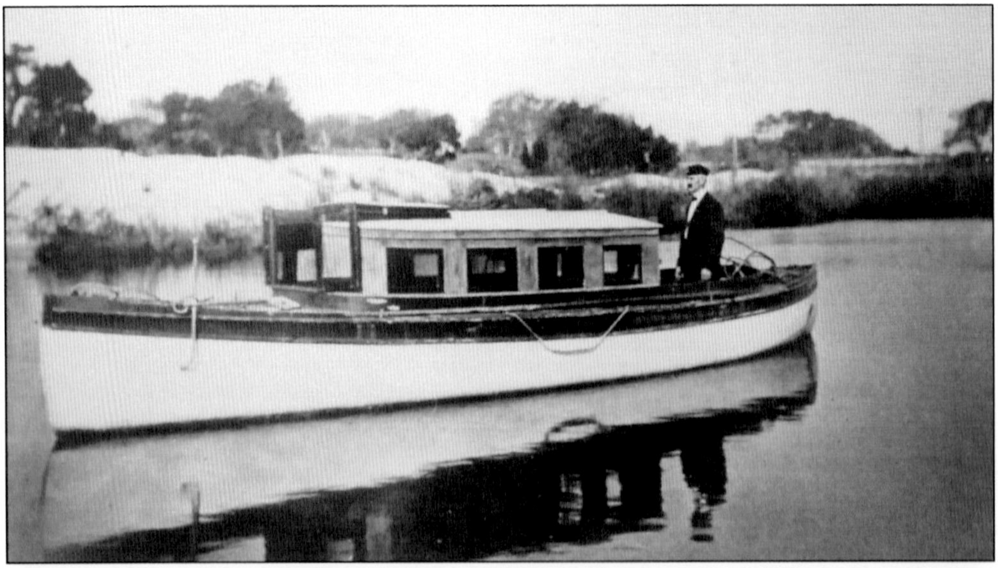

Mr. E.A. Horner, superintendent of the N.J. Oyster Commission, traveled up the Tuckerton Creek in 1905. Mr. Horner patrolled the oyster grounds daily, inspected licenses, and insured that the oystermen were on their own leased lots. This was the same man who rented the tracks from the Tuckerton Railroad for the Clamtown Sailcar. (Courtesy BBD & BM.)

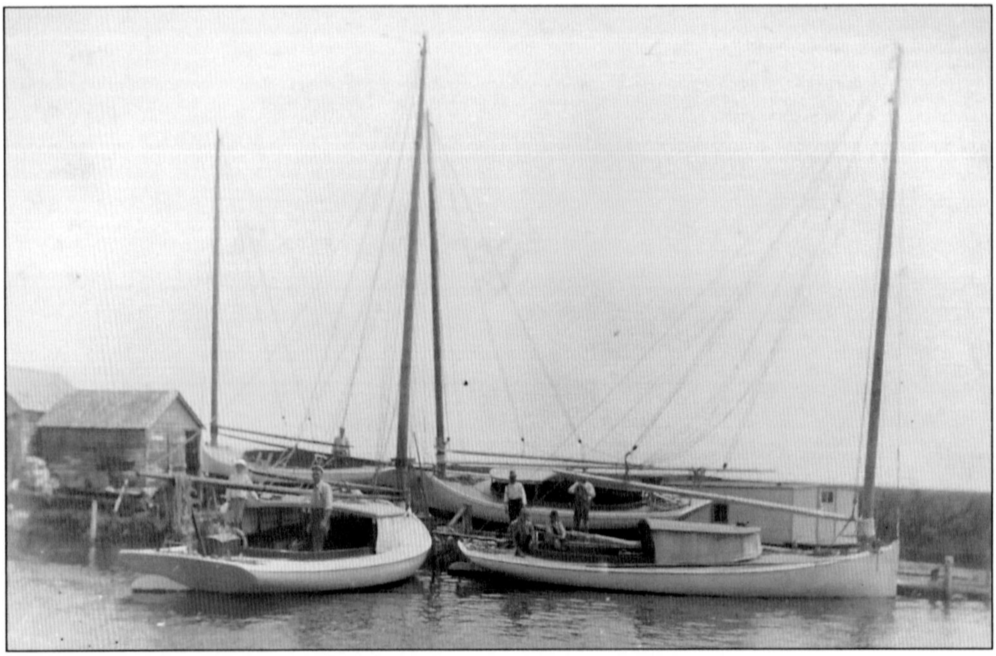

These catboats are docked on Westecunk Creek. The catboat was usually about 30 feet long. It had a tall mast, large mainsail, broad beam, and shallow draft. It was an important means of transportation to the baymen. Like the sneakbox and the garvey, catboats were designed and built to help the bayman make his living and get from place to place. They have all developed into racing craft, though the garvey, still working, can be seen in every creek flowing into Little Egg Harbor Bay. (Courtesy A.W. Kelly, Esq.)

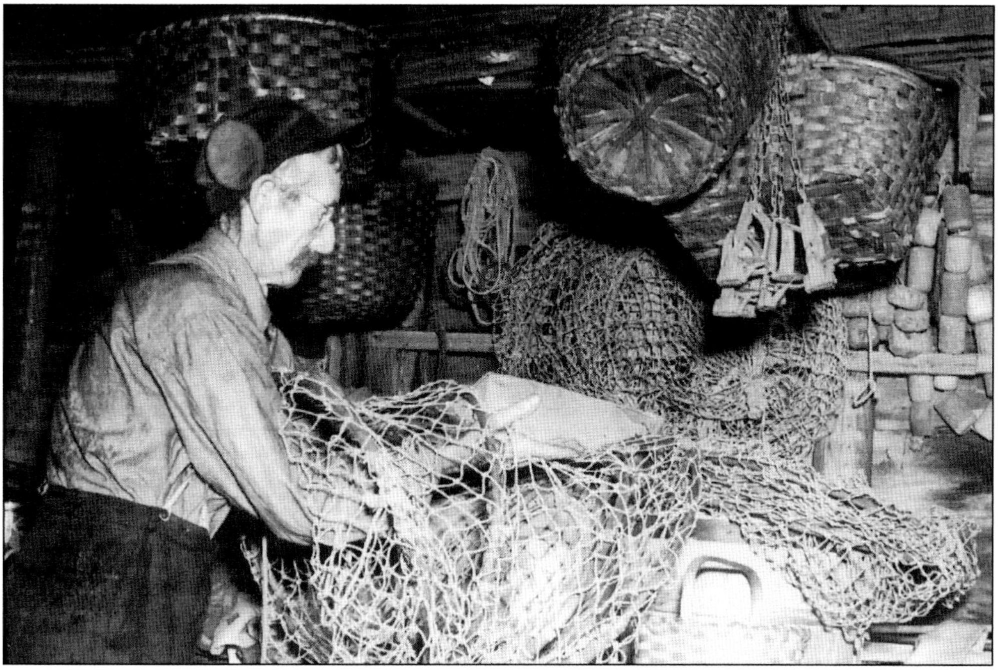

Fyke nets, long round nets which are held open with hoops and with a funnel built into one end, are repaired by Lance Cobb of Herman City. The nets are used to catch snapper blues, eels, and turtles in the area's many rivers and streams. (Courtesy William Augustine Collection, Rutgers University.)

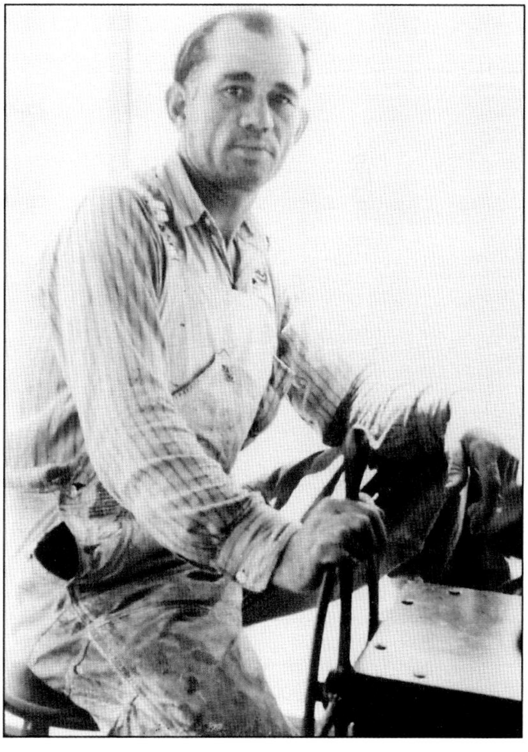

Captain Joseph Dayton of Parkertown was the owner of a sawmill off Dock Road, but like many downshore residents, he had more than one vocation. In addition to operating the mill, he had several charter boats which were used to take parties fishing. Mr. Dayton was born in New Gretna but spent most of his life in Parkertown, where his daughters still reside. (Courtesy BBD & BM.)

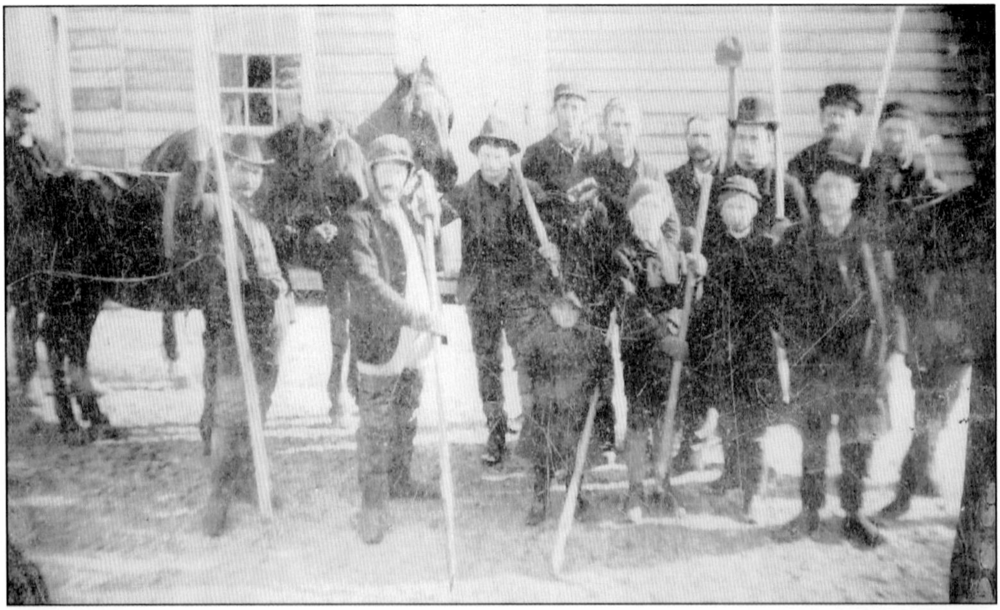

The cutting of ice from ponds was necessary for food preservation in the pre-refrigeration era. The ice was first marked in large squares. Often a sled with very sharp runners was used. Then the cakes were broken off with long-handled bars with sharp spade-like ends. The ice was then stored in icehouses, which were insulated with salt hay or sawdust. (Courtesy THS.)

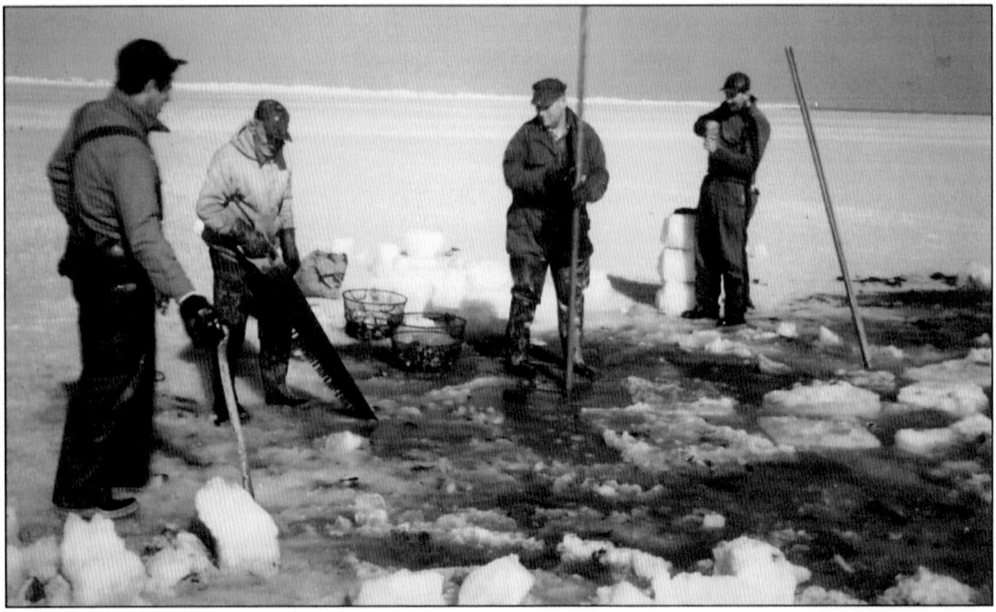

Dick Cavileer and his friends are tonging clams through the ice off Tuckerton Beach in Little Egg Harbor Bay. When the ice became too thick for boats, the clammers would walk to their clam lots, cut holes in the ice, catch their clams, and carry them on sleds to the nearest road. The earliest method of clamming was treading with bare feet. Rakes were developed for use in deeper water, often from a boat. Tongs act like scissors. They dig into the bottom and close on the clams. One usually tongs from a garvey. (Courtesy BBD & BM.)

Prices charged for decoys, feathers, and crabs are listed here by Harry V. Shourds. Decoys ranged in price from "1 pair ducks—50¢" to "1 pair brant—$1.25." Two lots of feathers cost $6 and $7. Crabs went for $10 per dozen. Dr. Reeves purchased these items in the 1889–1895 period. Shourds' son Harry M. (Mitchell) of Ocean City still makes decoys in the tradition of his father. (Courtesy BBD & BM.)

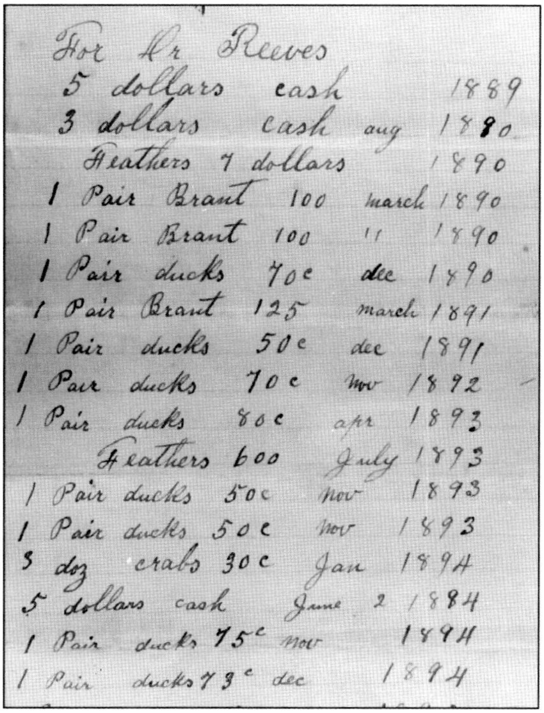

For Dr Reeves
5 dollars cash 1889
3 dollars cash aug 1890
Feathers 7 dollars 1890
1 Pair Brant 100 march 1890
1 Pair Brant 100 " 1890
1 Pair ducks 70c dec 1890
1 Pair Brant 125 march 1891
1 Pair ducks 50c dec 1891
1 Pair ducks 70c nov 1892
1 Pair ducks 80c apr 1893
Feathers 600 July 1893
1 Pair ducks 50c nov 1893
1 Pair ducks 50c nov 1893
3 doz crabs 30c Jan 1894
5 dollars cash June 2 1884
1 Pair ducks 75c nov 1894
1 Pair ducks 73c dec 1894

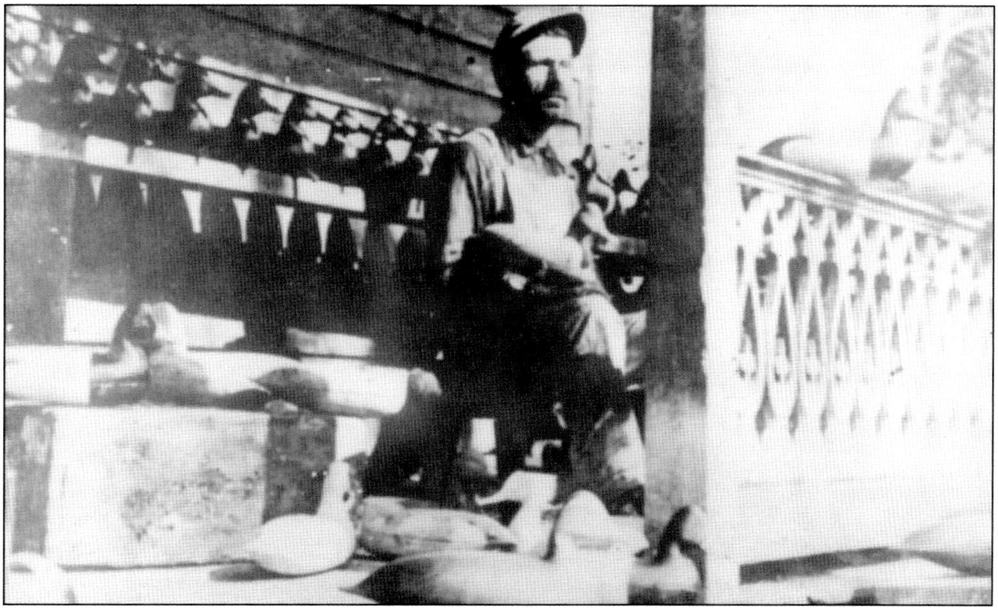

Harry V. Shourds (1861–1920), a painter by trade, was the master decoy carver. Buyers up and down the East Coast bought many of his more than fifty thousand decoys, which are highly prized by collectors today. He packed the decoys in barrels and took them by wheelbarrow to the train. The Shourds are an old family in Tuckerton. A branch of the creek bears the name Shourds. Harry V., the sixth of ten children born to Samuel and Josephine Shourds, also built his home just a few feet from Tuckerton Creek, and he raised five children there. (Courtesy BBD & BM.)

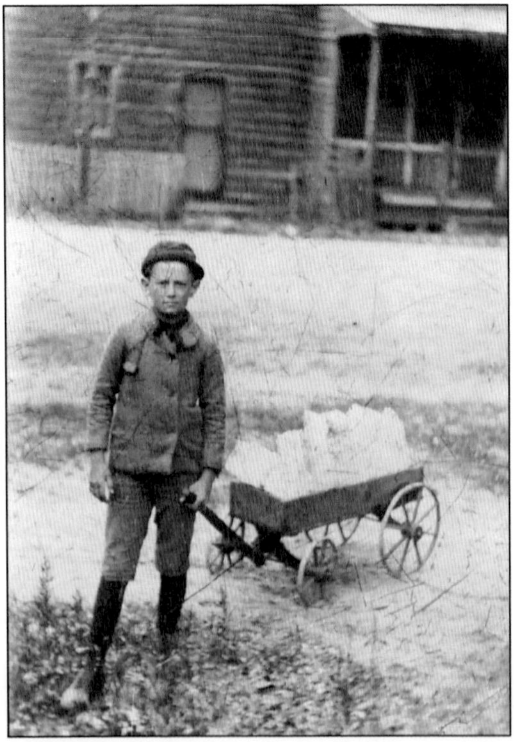

William E. Blackman Jr. began a successful ice business from his express wagon at the age of thirteen. He became a Trenton lawyer and was nominated for Congress unsuccessfully on the Republican ticket in 1912. He was the grandson of Leah Blackman, who wrote the *History of Little Egg Harbor Township*. (Courtesy THS.)

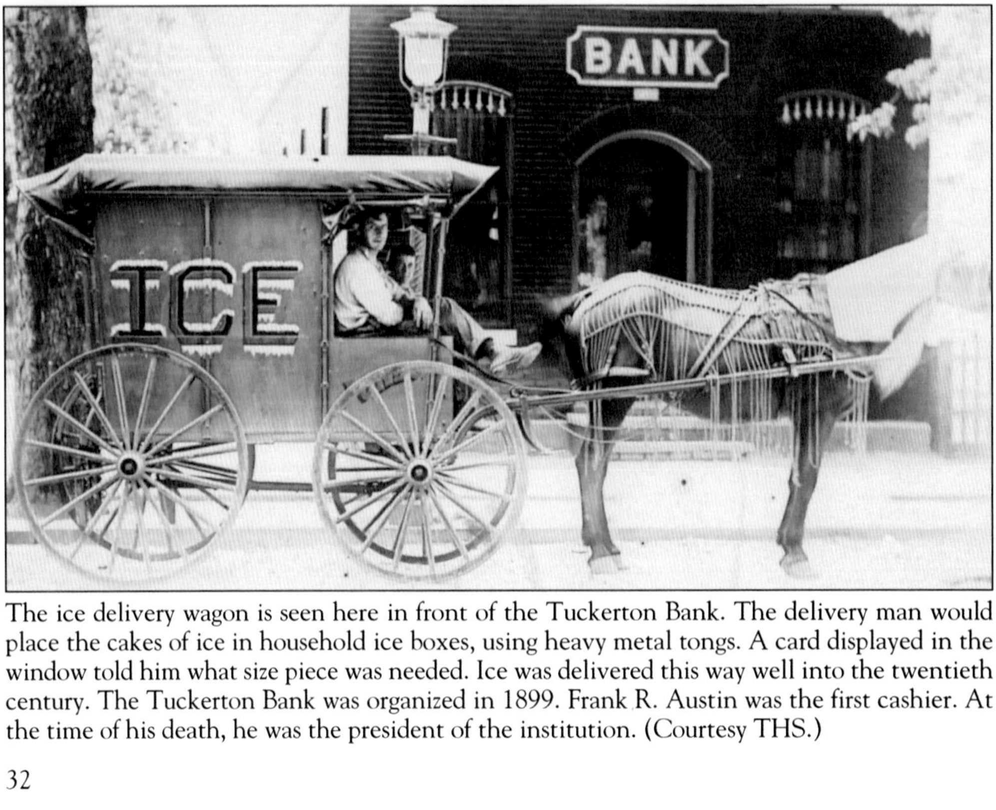

The ice delivery wagon is seen here in front of the Tuckerton Bank. The delivery man would place the cakes of ice in household ice boxes, using heavy metal tongs. A card displayed in the window told him what size piece was needed. Ice was delivered this way well into the twentieth century. The Tuckerton Bank was organized in 1899. Frank R. Austin was the first cashier. At the time of his death, he was the president of the institution. (Courtesy THS.)

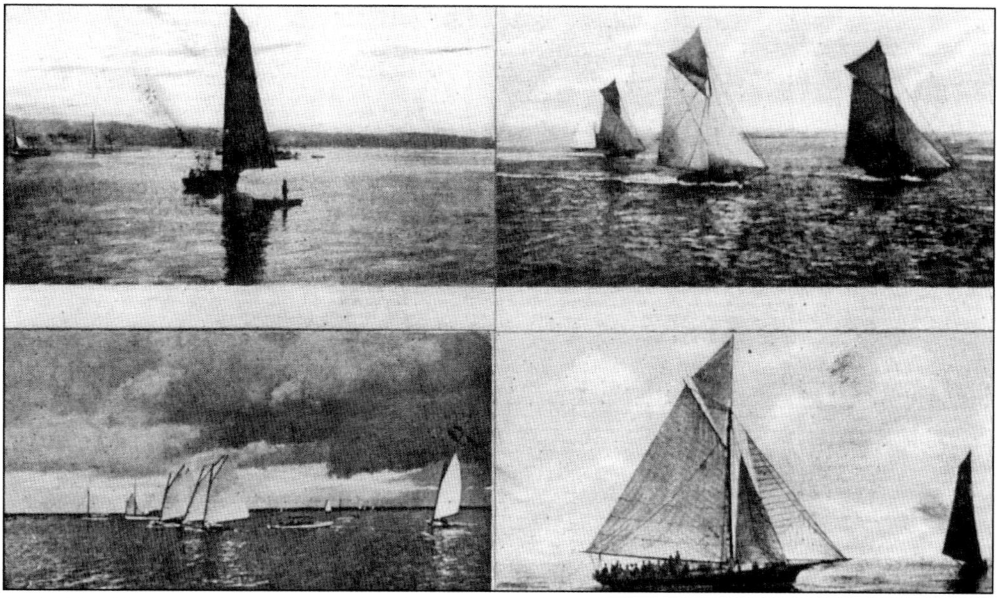

Little Egg Harbor Inlet to the south of Long Beach Island, though a constantly changing inlet, provided access to and from the ocean for sailing vessels. Its position almost directly to the east across the bay from Tuckerton contributed to Tuckerton Creek's being the port of call for many sea captains. Most sailboats that sailed the bay required little water beneath them or had a centerboard which could be raised or lowered. The above were yachting types seen on the bay at Cedar Run. (Courtesy James Estelle.)

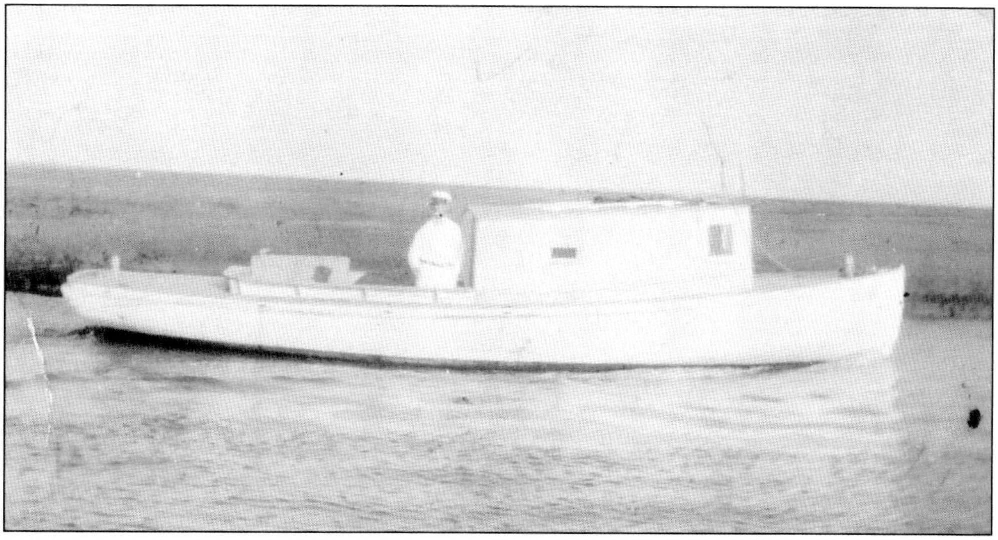

Ralph G. Cummings was a party boat captain in the warmer weather and a member of the lifesaving crew stationed on Tucker's Island in the stormier months from September to May. His home was in Parkertown, where he docked the *Olive* in 1919. Captain Cummings and his whole family moved to the island in September. The children attended the Sea Haven School taught by Miss Florence Morss. (Courtesy BBD & BM.)

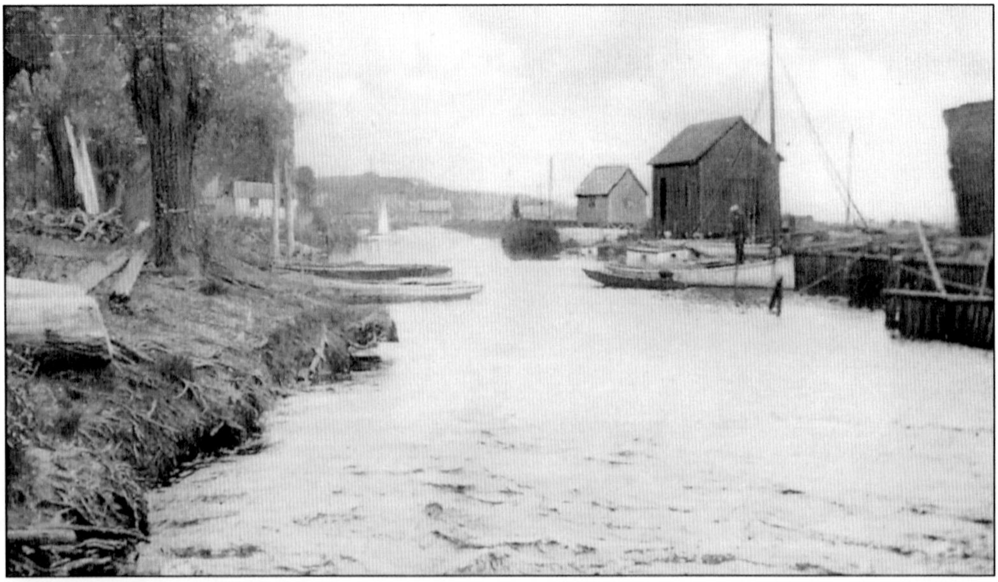

This scene taken along Tuckerton Creek may be of the stretch between the old mill and Willow Landing. The familiar sheds that were found along any busy creek in the mid-to-late 1800s, a catboat, two sneakboxes, a small sailboat, and a very natural looking bank on the left give us a tiny look at how Tuckerton used to be. (Courtesy Michael Mangum.)

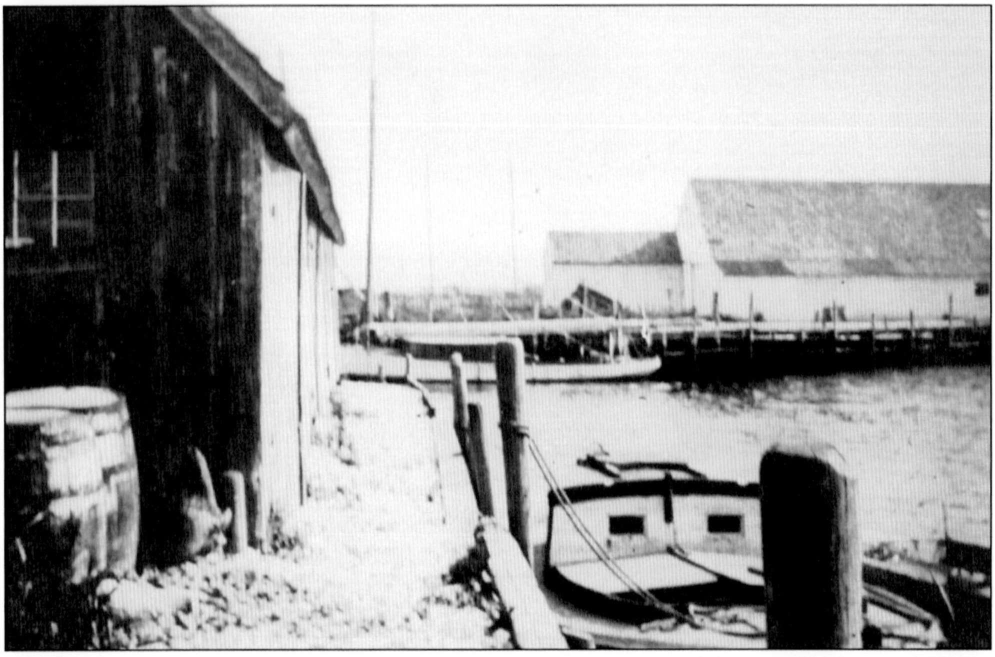

These sheds at Scow Landing in Tuckerton were the destination of thousands of tons of Ocean County oysters and clams. A less-plentiful catch of oysters between September and May 1934 still exceeded 250,000 bushels. A good clammer's catch could average several thousand clams a day. During the 1935 season they earned about 50¢ per hundred. An ambitious clammer could earn $2,500 for the eight-month season. (Courtesy BBD & BM.)

Noted decoy carver, Brad Salmons (left) and his brother John (Doc) display their turn-of-the-century (1900) bathing suits. These costumes were generally made of heavy flannel. Ladies wore even more clothing while swimming in the ocean. Their garments would generally include long sleeves, skirts, pants, stockings, and a hat. The apparel was so heavy that it is doubtful that they did any real swimming. (Courtesy Donald Salmons.)

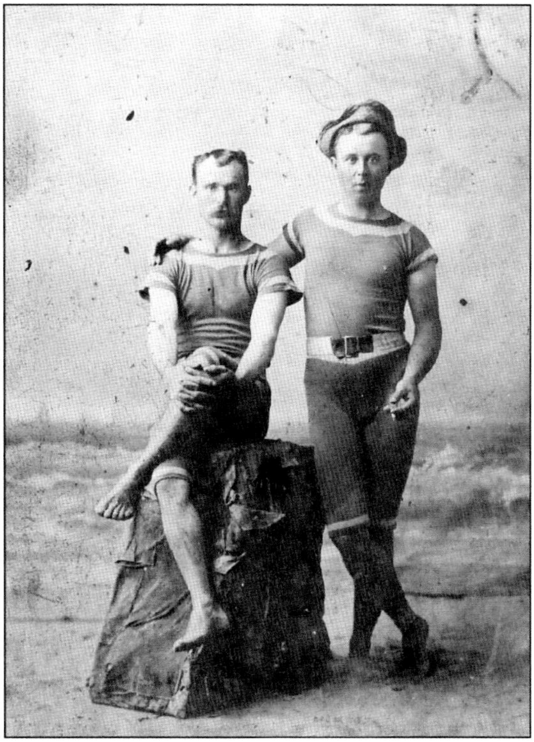

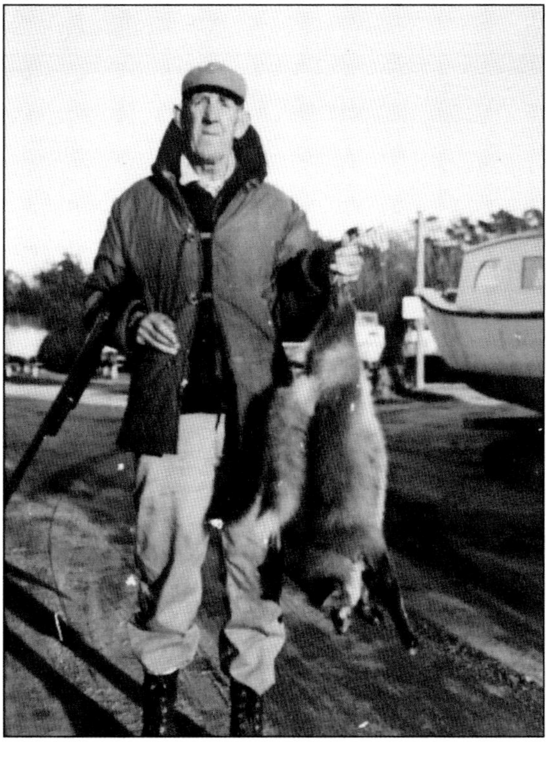

Captain Harland Price apparently took to the land long enough to kill two foxes. There are docks in the background so perhaps the foxes were shot in the marshes or around the docks themselves. Hunting was surely a part of life for those hoping to stock their tables with the foods available on land and water. Deer have always been plentiful, as have small game animals. (Courtesy BBD & BM.)

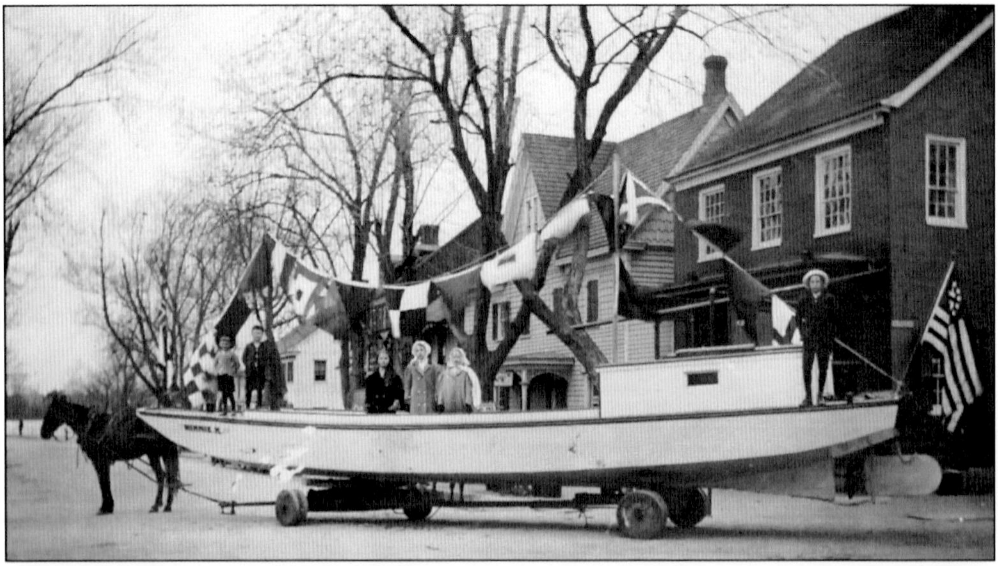

The garvey *Minnie H.*, which was built by Captain Edward "Socks" Heinrichs of Tuckerton, is being towed from his garage on Green Street to his boat works. Aboard are his children Gus (stern), and Pat and Joe (bow), along with Mae McConomy, Della Smith, and Elsie Kelly (center, from left to right). (Courtesy Marjorie Heinrichs Holloway.)

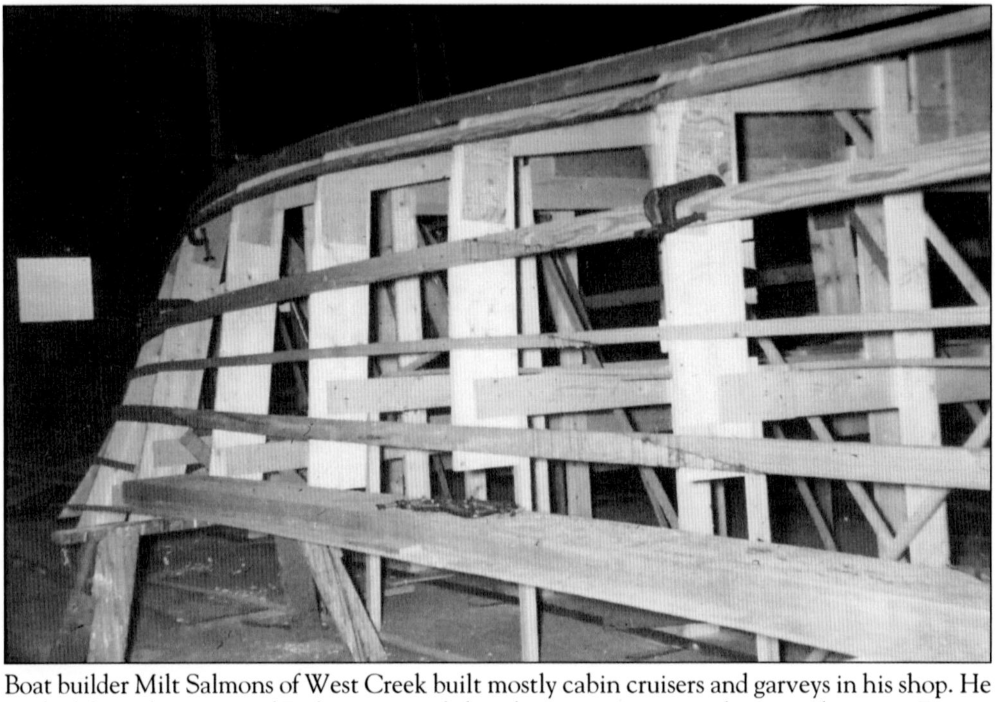

Boat builder Milt Salmons of West Creek built mostly cabin cruisers and garveys in his shop. He worked for Adam Price of Parkertown and then began constructing boats on his own. During World War II, Mr. Price's boatyard produced over six hundred landing craft that were used in the South Pacific. (Courtesy BBD & BM.)

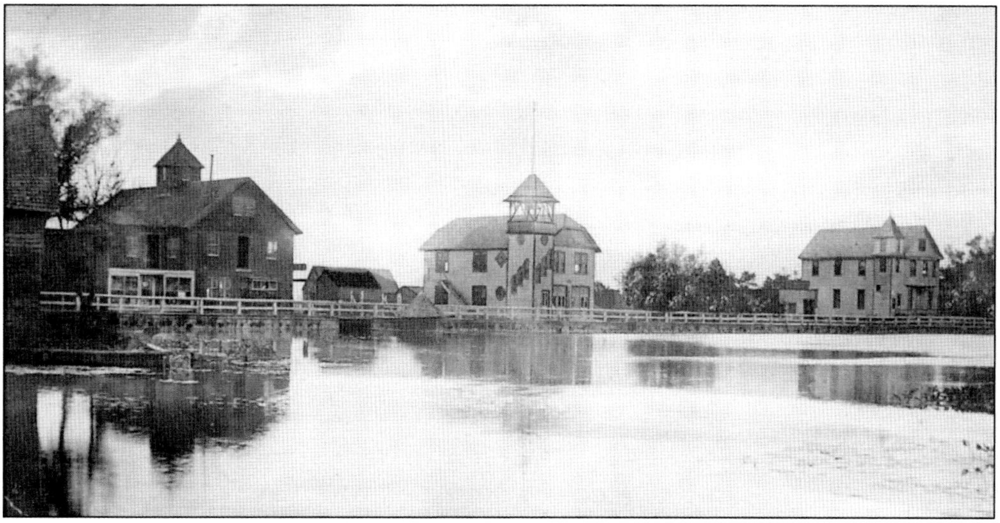

Attractive buildings were created in Tuckerton as evidenced by the mill, firehouse, and YMCA (from left to right). Each had its peaked cupola or bell tower which made a distinctive skyline if one were coming up the creek or looking across the lake. The millpond to their north-northwest provided a mirror for reflections. The earliest mill was built in 1704. This one dates from the mid-1800s, the firehouse from the 1890s, and the YMCA from 1905. (Courtesy THS.)

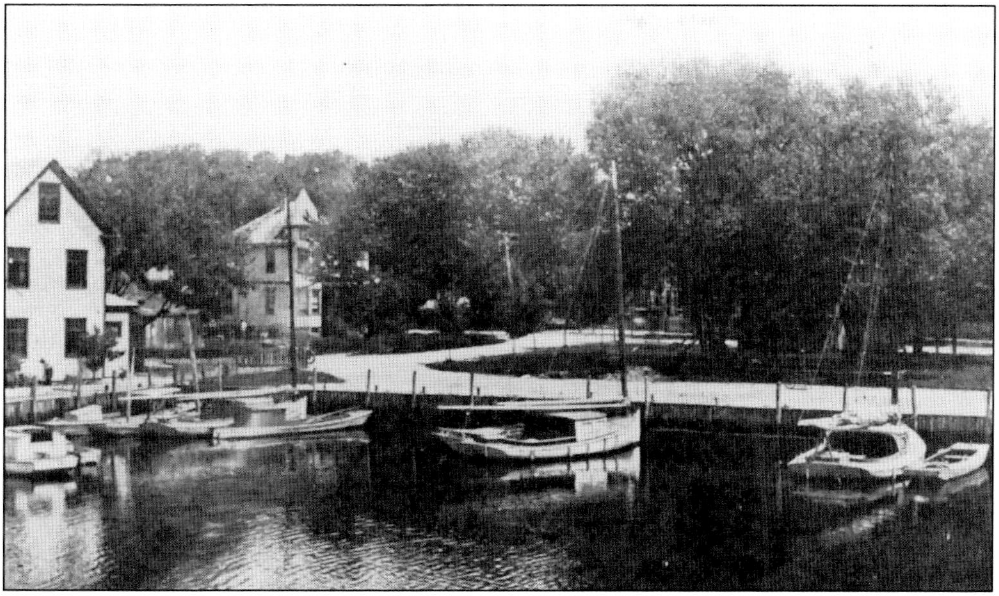

Much of the activity of Tuckerton's waterfront was centered at Willow Landing for more than one hundred and fifty years. Privateers sailed from here in the American Revolution, trading ships from many ports docked here, passengers disembarked here, gunners were transported by their guides to their favorite clubs from here, and new schooners were constructed in nearby shipyards. Willow Landing was located along Water Street, one block from Main Street, the mill, lake, YMCA, hotels, and businesses. (Courtesy BBD & BM.)

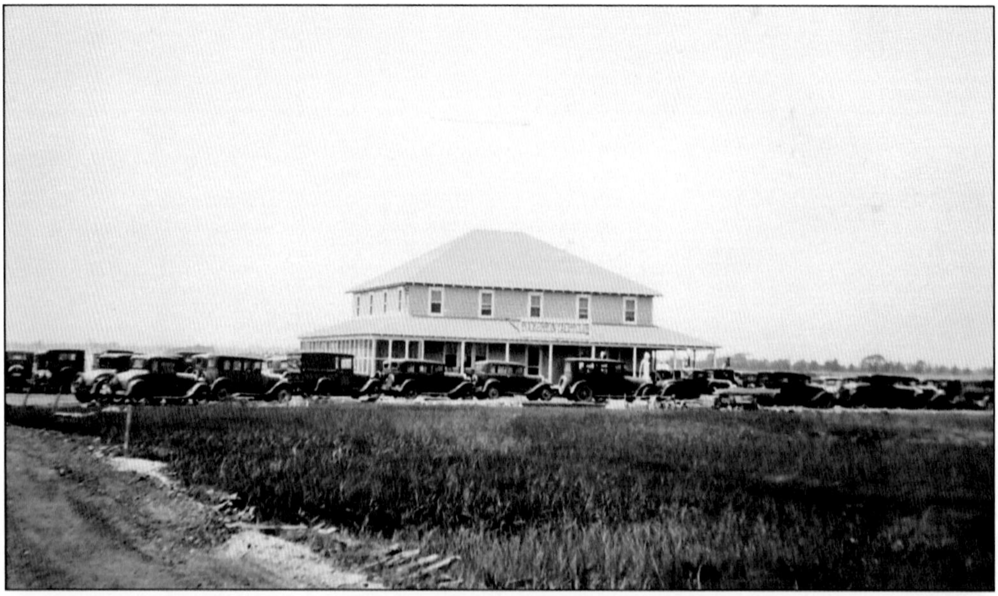

The Tuckerton Yacht Club was built in 1929 at the end of Carroll Avenue in Tuckerton Beach. The yacht club changed owners a few times. The cost for a charter boat for a party of six was $12 on weekdays and $15 on Sundays and holidays. The Tuckerton Yacht Club came to an end in a fire on January 18, 1973. (Courtesy BBD & BM.)

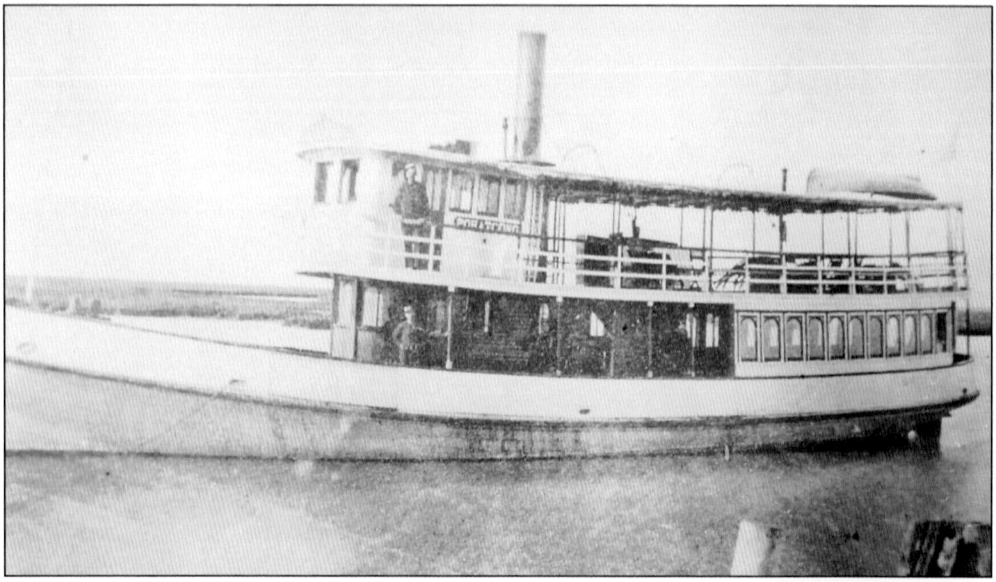

In the summer of 1874 the Tuckerton Railroad was extended from its Tuckerton terminus one mile to bayside at Edge Cove. The new four-story Parry House opened at Beach Haven that year, so the tourist trade was on its way. In the ensuing years, small steamers, the *Barclay* of the Haines Rancocas Steamboat Company and the *Pohatcong*, conveyed passengers across the bay 4.5 miles to Beach Haven. The *Pohatcong* (pictured here) had two levels, one open and one enclosed. Passengers were entertained by the G.T. Parry Cornet Band. (Courtesy THS.)

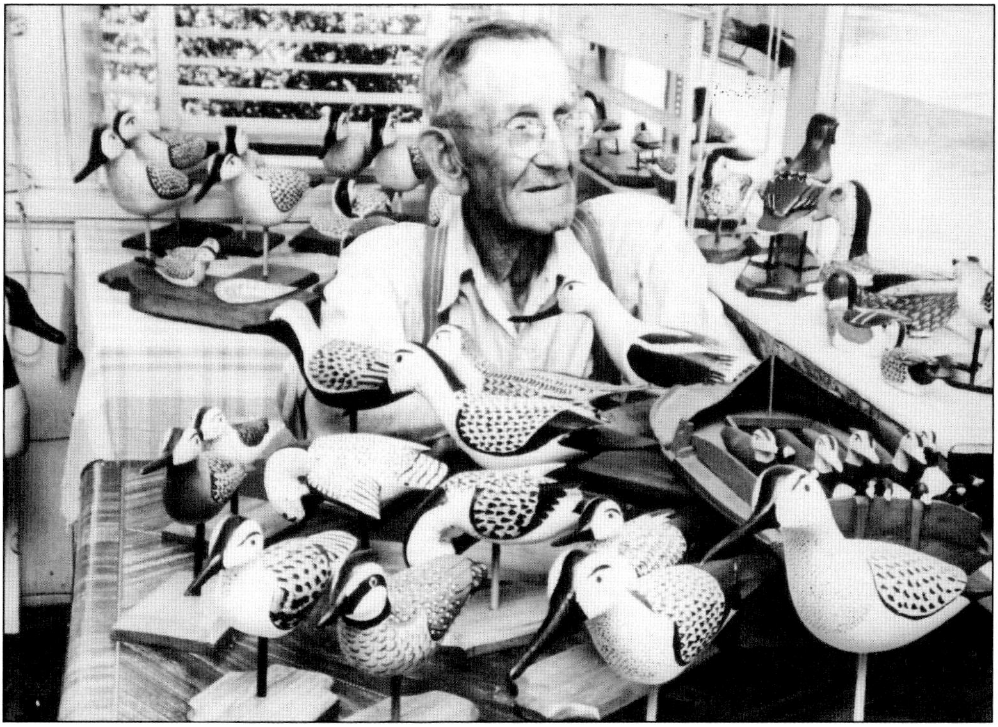

Jay C. Parker is surrounded by the shorebird decoys he carved. Parker was one of the last old-time carvers, and he received little money for his efforts. In 1964 his work was exhibited at the New York World's Fair. He wrote a multitude of shorelife observations in logbooks, which today constitute a priceless addition to the Barnegat Bay Decoy and Baymen's Museum. (Courtesy BBD & BM.)

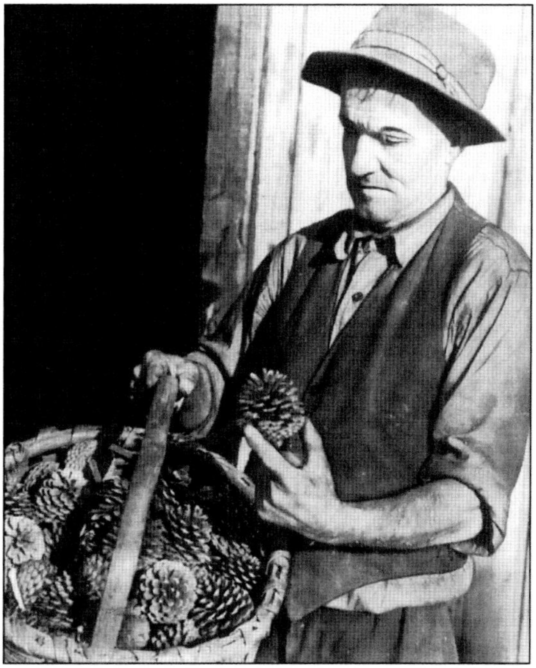

Sam Ford from Herman City displays some of the pine cones he has collected in the New Jersey area known as the "pine barrens," which borders the coastal areas along much of the Jersey shore. The cones are best collected after the first frost when they are mature and have less pitch in the stem, thereby snapping off the tree more easily. Cones from pitch pine trees open only with heat, so they must be roasted in a "pine cone popper" to make them desirable for marketing to craftspeople and florists. (Courtesy William Augustine Collection, Rutgers University.)

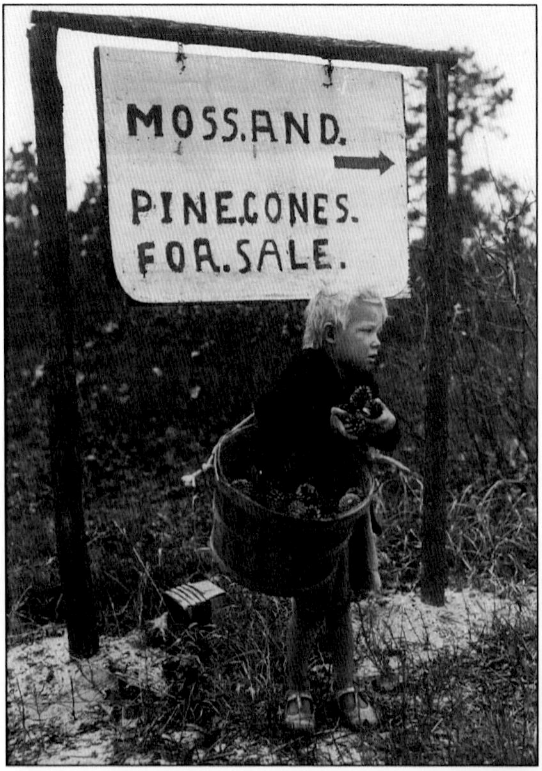

Many of the baymen and their families turned to the woodland in the fall and winter months to supplement their incomes. Lumbering, cutting cedar, cutting cordwood, drying plant materials, gathering acorns and pine cones, making acorn sprays, picking cranberries and swamp huckleberries, and guiding deer hunters were activities in which different family members could engage. This little girl has the fruit of her efforts for sale. (Courtesy William Augustine Collection, Rutgers University.)

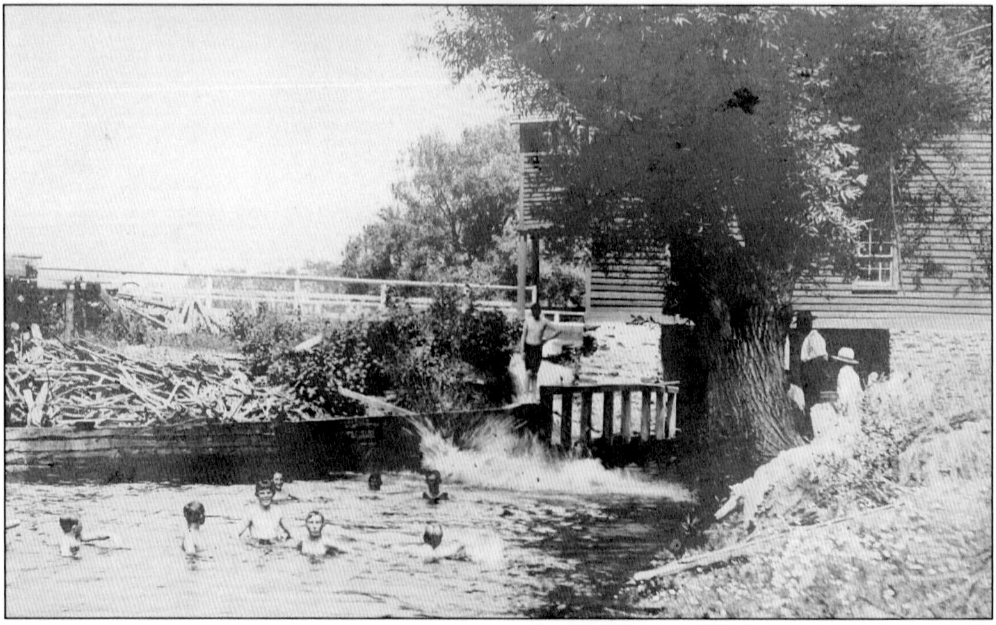

There were always those lazy summer days when a swim in the "crik" was most refreshing. Tuckerton Creek has always attracted swimmers, and for a number of years there was a small bathing beach on the lakeshore in what is now Tip Seaman Park. These youngsters, all boys, are enjoying the water that comes through the dam and under the old mill with a little extra force. (Courtesy Michael Mangum.)

Two

Communities

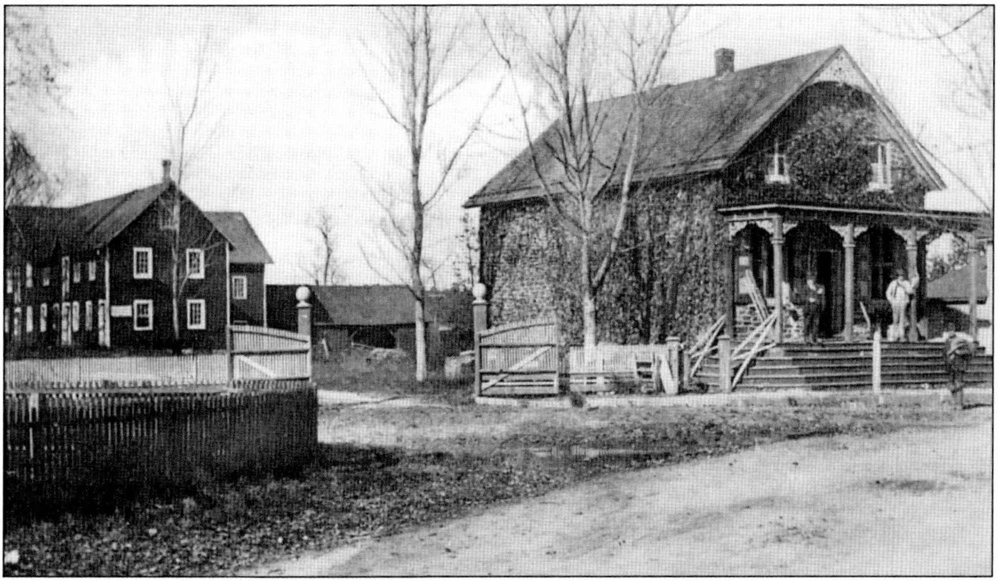

The communities of today from Manahawkin to New Gretna are largely inhabited by descendants of the earliest settlers. Marriages within this 100-square-mile area for many generations have produced a complex relationship among the families. Names like Hazelton and Haywood, Salmons and Seaman, Cranmer and Cox, Kelly and Kelley, Mathis and Falkinburg, Pharo, Price, and Parker predominate in the cemeteries and among today's residents. Now as the twenty-first century nears, the area's residents are faced with drastic changes in all aspects of life. The peaceful, pretty, out-of-the way communities will be a thing of the past. This stone store, built in the mid-1700s, probably by one of the Fitzrandolph brothers, has witnessed it all—it is truly a landmark. The store was reinforced *c.* 1838 with a stone exterior by Benjamin Oliphant, who also operated the adjacent grist and sawmill and carved the date on the structure. Early in this century, it was used as a residence. Today, after being vandalized and burned, it has been repaired and preserved as a local museum. It is encircled by a contemporary highway interchange, a sight which would have utterly stupefied its earlier proprietors. (Courtesy James Estelle.)

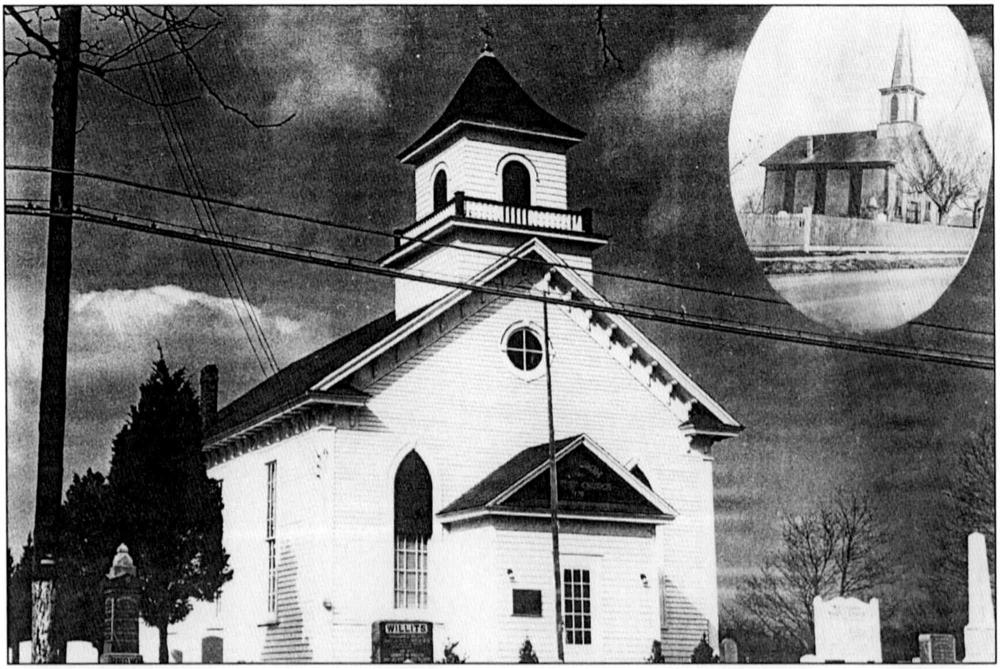

In 1758, when there were about twenty families living in Manahawkin, land was acquired and a building was erected for the First Baptist Church Society. The church organized with "nine souls," one of whom was James Haywood. This church is credited with offering instruction to children before a public school was started. Today the church is still in the field of education with its Lighthouse Christian Academy for age three through grade six. The inset shows the original building and spire. (Courtesy Burrell Adams and James Estelle.)

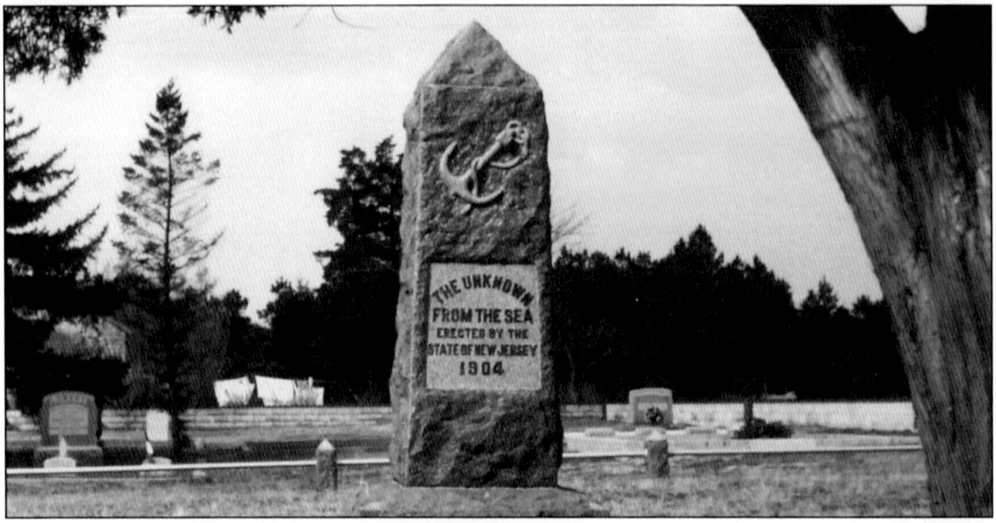

This monument reads, "THE UNKNOWN FROM THE SEA." It is centered in the huge fenced-off burial plot behind the Manahawkin Baptist Church. It marks the final resting place of all who were found following the wreck of the *Powhatan*, which foundered on the shoals off Long Beach Island in a late spring blizzard on April 18, 1854. More than three hundred passengers, mostly German, and twenty-nine crew members were aboard; none survived. (Courtesy Burrell Adams.)

Edna Hazelton (1910–1991), a lineal descendant of Jarvis and Ann (Haywood) Hazelton who settled in Manahawkin in 1743, taught school at Beach Haven and in Stafford Township for most of her life. Edna was a well-respected and civic-minded citizen who served many local organizations long and well, and a member of the Methodist church. She was photographed seated atop a salt hay press at the end of Meadow Lane, now Beach Avenue. Perhaps she and her friends were out for a Sunday afternoon stroll. (Courtesy BBD & BM.)

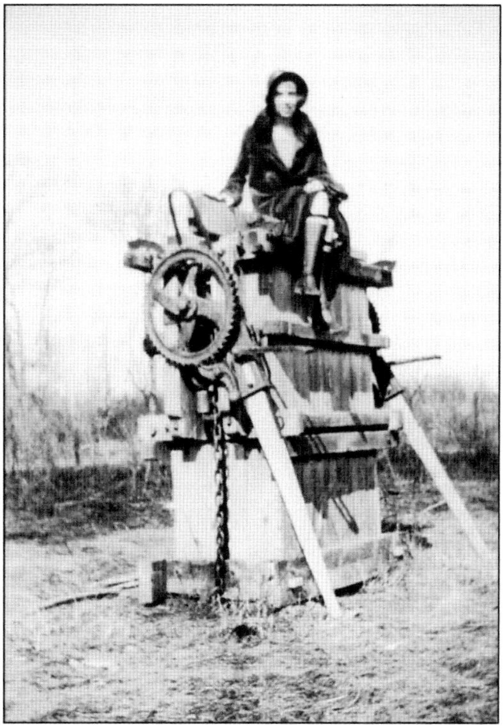

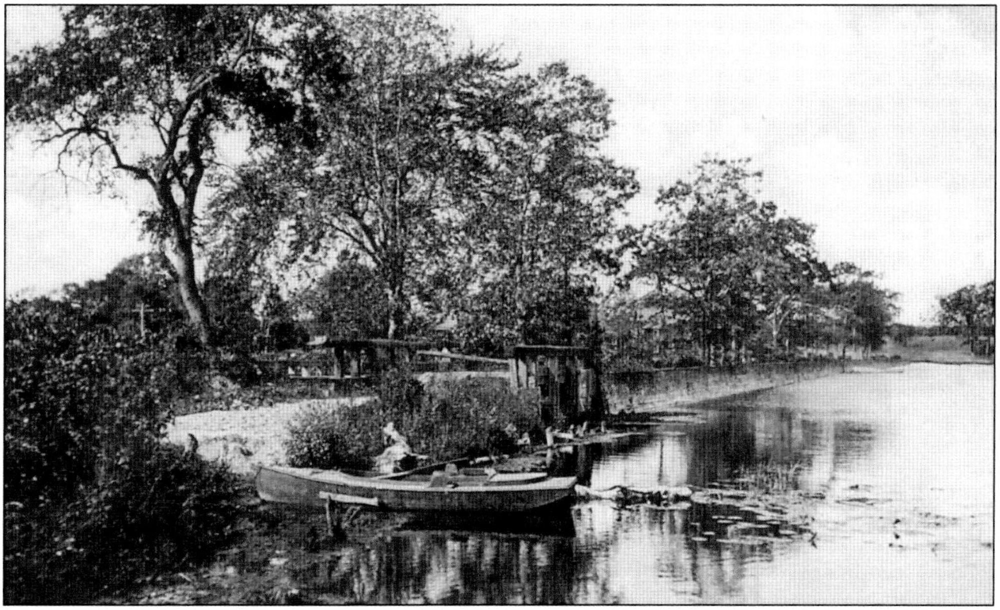

Manahawkin Pond was created by the construction of the dam for the sawmill associated with the old stone store. The cedar forest which was inundated was some of the first cedar cut in the area and provided fine materials for the construction of both houses and boats. Since Jersey cedar is virtually impervious to water, the numerous stumps remained well into the present century, as seen here. (Courtesy James Estelle.)

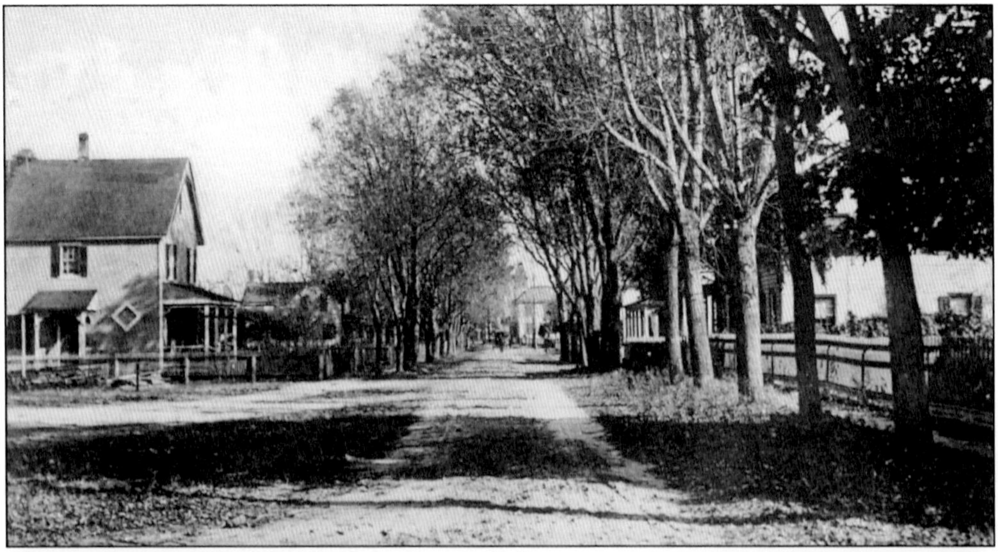

This view eastward on Beach Avenue around the turn of the century shows the Grammar School, just beyond the Methodist church's cemetery hidden behind houses and trees. Those who wished to continue their education in the early part of this century were transported daily to Tuckerton by what was called a "truck bus" to attend the Tuckerton High School. (Courtesy James Estelle.)

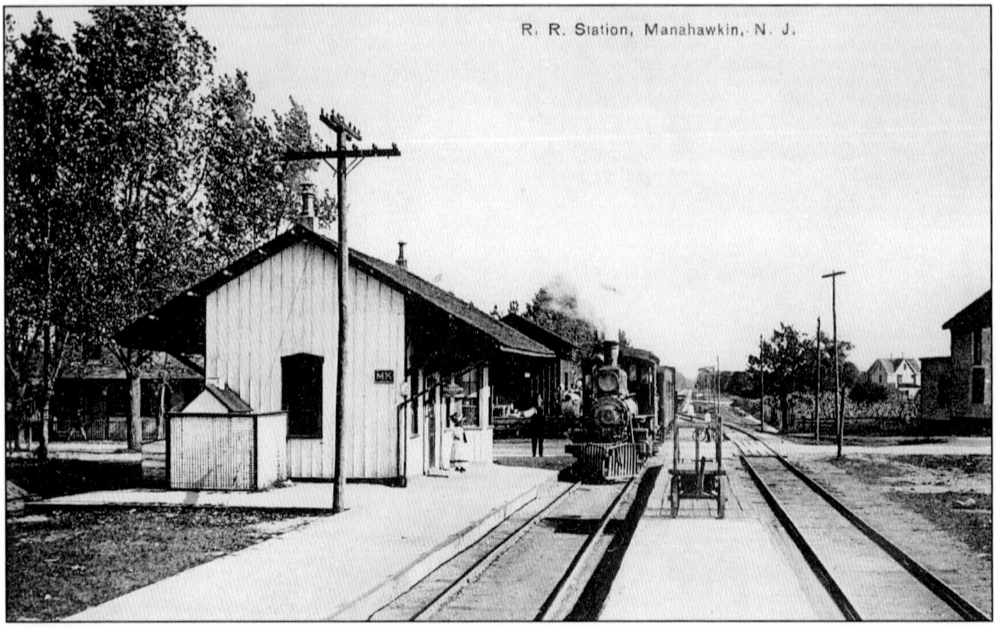

Manahawkin's railroad station was at the Stafford Avenue crossing east of Route 9. The first train arrived here from Whitings Junction on October 14, 1871. This postcard view was c. 1911. Manahawkin also was the departure point for trains going to Long Beach Island, a route leased to the Manahawkin and Long Beach Transportation Company in 1893. The cars, called Yellow Jackets, were painted yellow with green trim. Derailments, washouts, ice damage to the bridge, and one train destroyed by fire caused the Manahawkin and Long Beach Transportation Company to end service. (Courtesy James Estelle.)

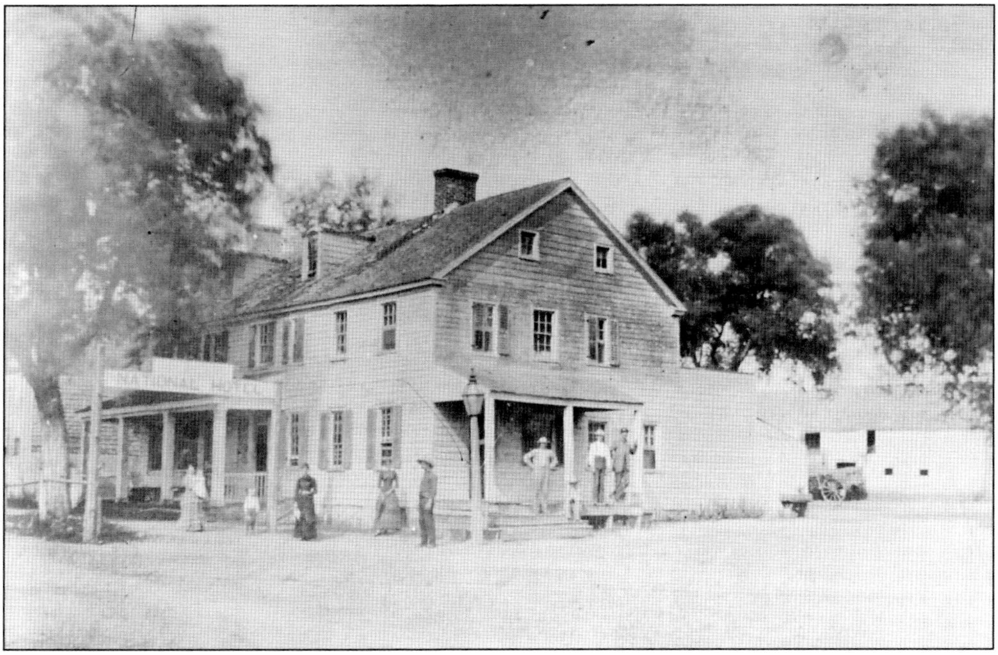

The historic National Hotel, built *c.* 1750 by Reuben Fitzrandolph, became the scene of uncounted gatherings during its landmark existence on North Broadway. Seen here, after gas streetlights were installed early in the present century, its appearance was later considerably altered by enclosing the porch. (Courtesy OCHS.)

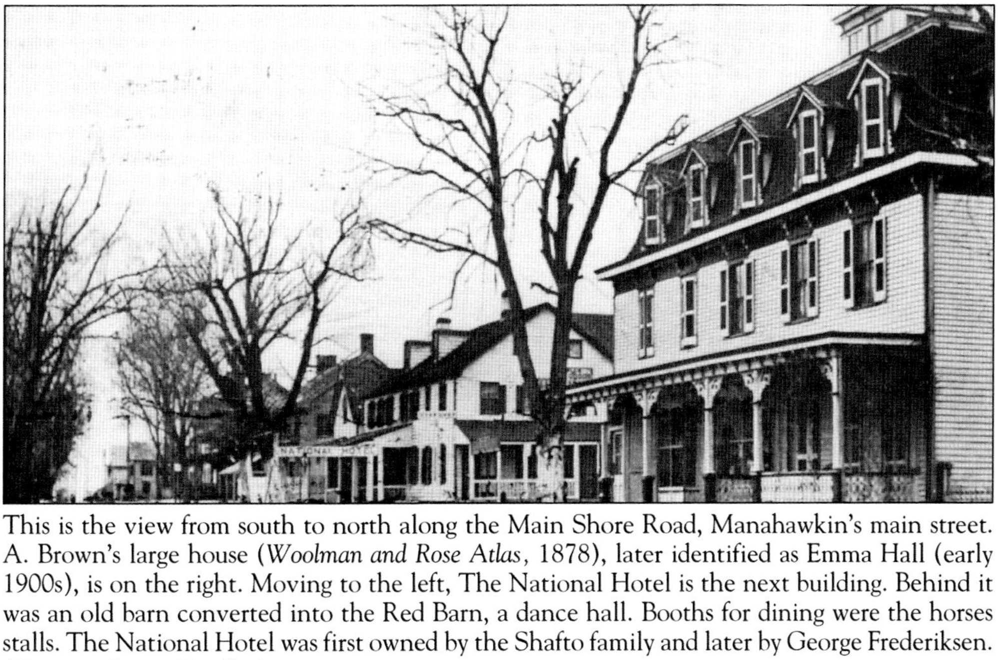

This is the view from south to north along the Main Shore Road, Manahawkin's main street. A. Brown's large house (*Woolman and Rose Atlas*, 1878), later identified as Emma Hall (early 1900s), is on the right. Moving to the left, The National Hotel is the next building. Behind it was an old barn converted into the Red Barn, a dance hall. Booths for dining were the horses stalls. The National Hotel was first owned by the Shafto family and later by George Frederiksen. (Courtesy James Estelle.)

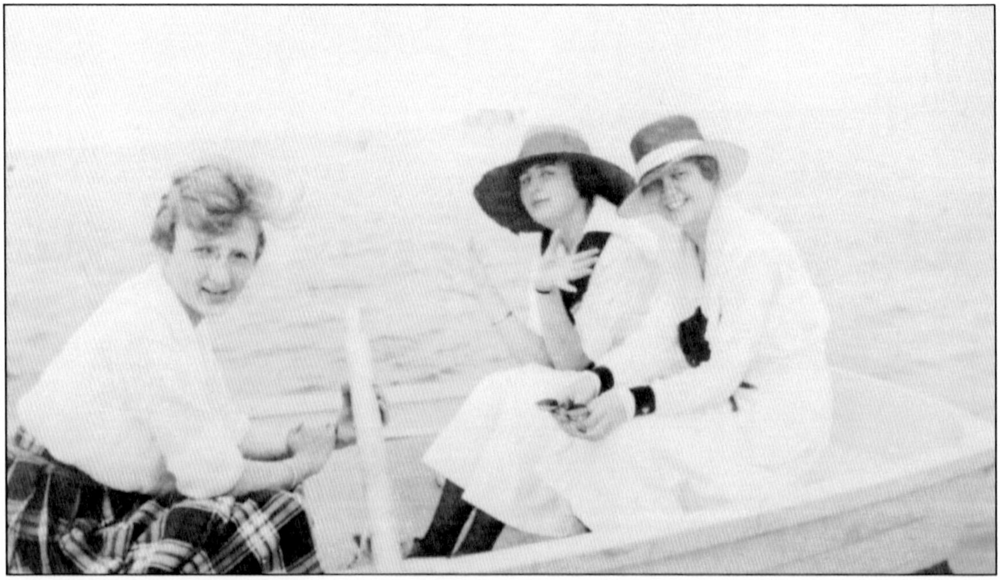

Olive Cranmer at the oars is rowing Margaret Ridgeway and Dorothy Chadwick on a sunny afternoon. The girls are dressed in middy blouses and long black stockings, which were in style in 1919. Brimmed hats keep their faces shaded from the sun. (Courtesy Blaine I. Pope.)

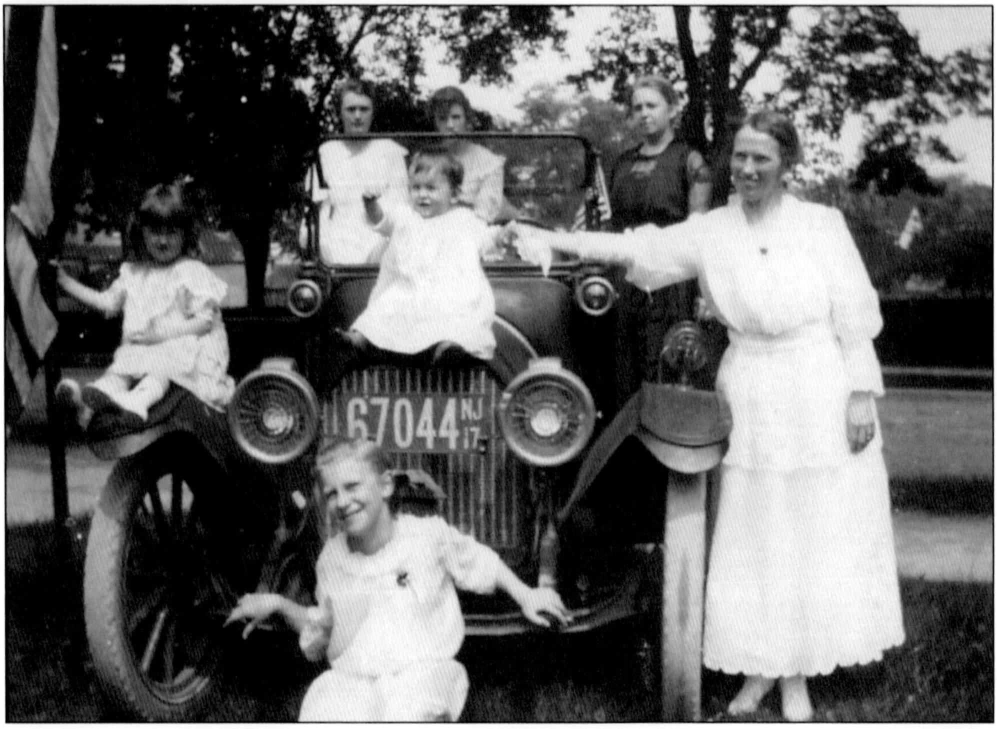

The license plate on this Maxwell car is dated 1917. This well-dressed family is undoubtedly ready to enjoy a Sunday afternoon drive. They are Dorothy Jones (on fender), Verna Jones (standing in rear), unidentified boy (in front of car) Charles Jones (on hood), Olive Cranmer (behind boy), Susie Cranmer (dark dress), and Blanche Cranmer (white dress). (Courtesy Elaine I. Pope.)

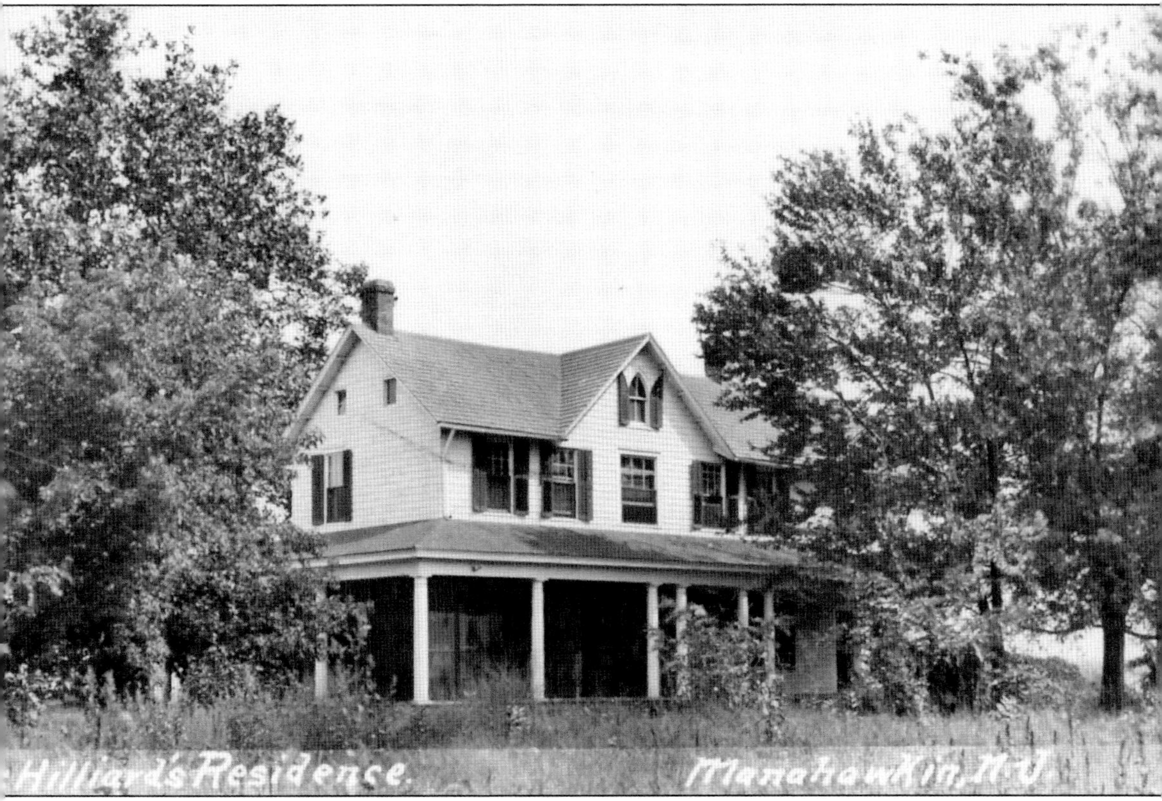

This house, recalled today as "Dr. Hilliard's place," is doubtlessly the most historically important residence in the town. It was built and occupied about 1750 by Reuben Fitzrandolph and his wife Mary Herriot, whom he had married February 8, 1737, at Woodbridge, New Jersey. He served in the Revolution as captain of the 5th Company of Monmouth Militia based in Manahawkin. (After the war, this family dropped the British prefix "Fitz.")

The next known occupant of this house was Dr. William A. Newell, a New Jersey state assemblyman and governor from 1857 to 1860. He is best remembered as the father of the U.S. Lifesaving Service. He came to Manahawkin as a young physician to visit an uncle and happened to be on Long Beach Island in 1839 when the Austrian brig *Terasto* was wrecked. All fourteen men aboard were drowned before the eyes of would-be rescuers, who were unable to reach them. The horror of what he had seen resulted in his determination to do something to help prevent such catastrophes.

The next owner of the home was Dr. Joshua Hilliard, who, throughout his life, cared for the real and imagined ills of area residents and made house calls, regardless of the time of day or night. The core of the original house is said to exist today, although a bit lost in the numerous additions, some of which were made by the present owners, Shinn Funeral Home. (Courtesy James Estelle.)

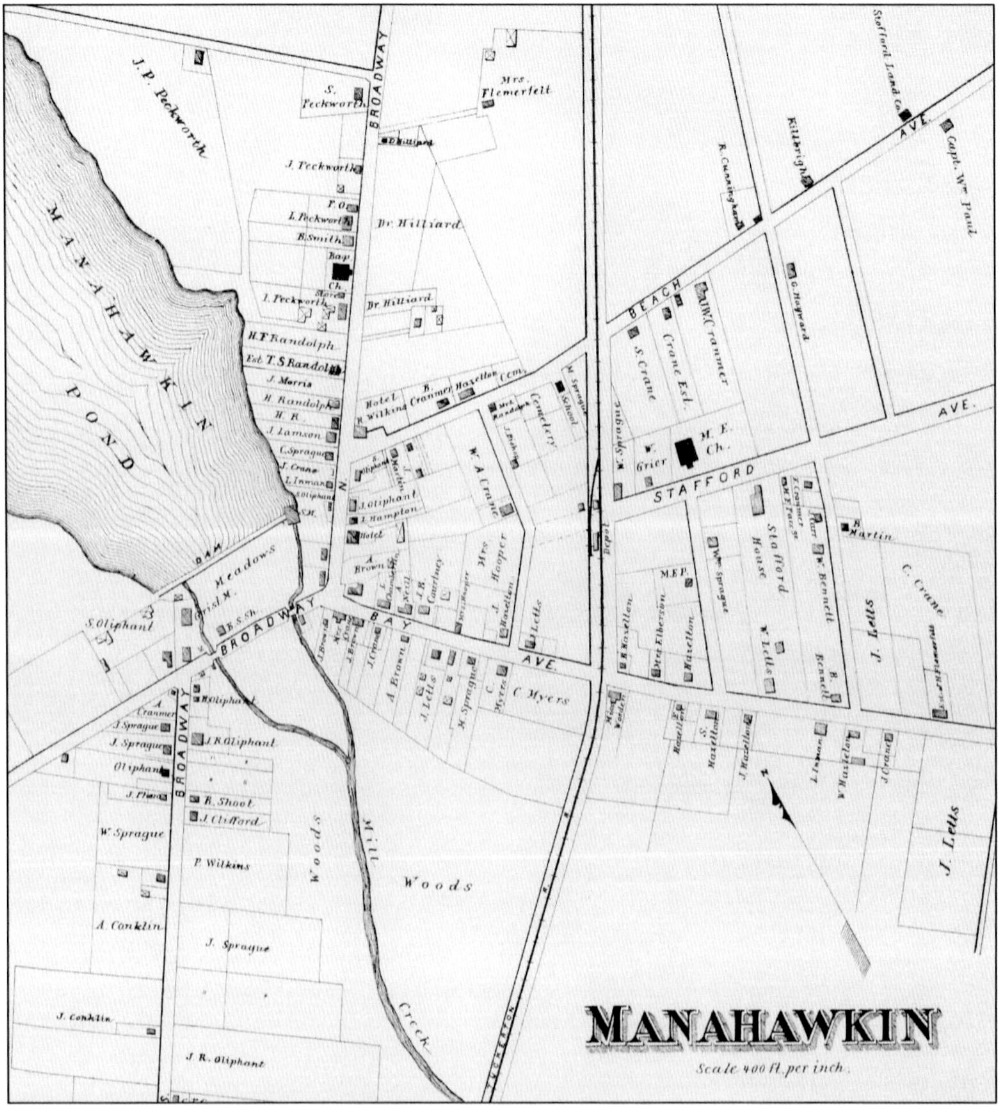

Native Americans called their "place of good corn" Manahawkin and the white settlers accepted the name. North of the village (between Route 9 and the Marsh) was Great 'Hawkin Swamp, the largest Ocean County coastal swamp. It was a forest of huge trees, predominantly cedar, which provided men with a living for over two hundred years. It was one of the last haunts of bears. Route 9 today follows the course of North Broadway and Broadway, which were also called Main Shore Road. Bay Avenue goes east to the bay from their juncture.

The dam built across Mill Creek provided waterpower for a sawmill by one outlet and a gristmill at the other. The old stone store was located near the gristmill. The area near Manahawkin Pond became the center of business, while farms extended to the east and south. The tracks of the Tuckerton Railroad (1871–1940), which lay east of Broadway, continued south to the Tuckerton terminus. In 1886, a spur going to the east and across the bay crossed Bay Avenue twice. Both the railroad trestle and the bridge for automobiles caused a real estate boom on Long Beach Island. The good corn land vanished as Manahawkin became the gateway to the island. Fortunately, much of the surrounding land is in the public domain and protected from development. This map is from the *Woolman and Rose Atlas* of 1878. (Courtesy OCHS.)

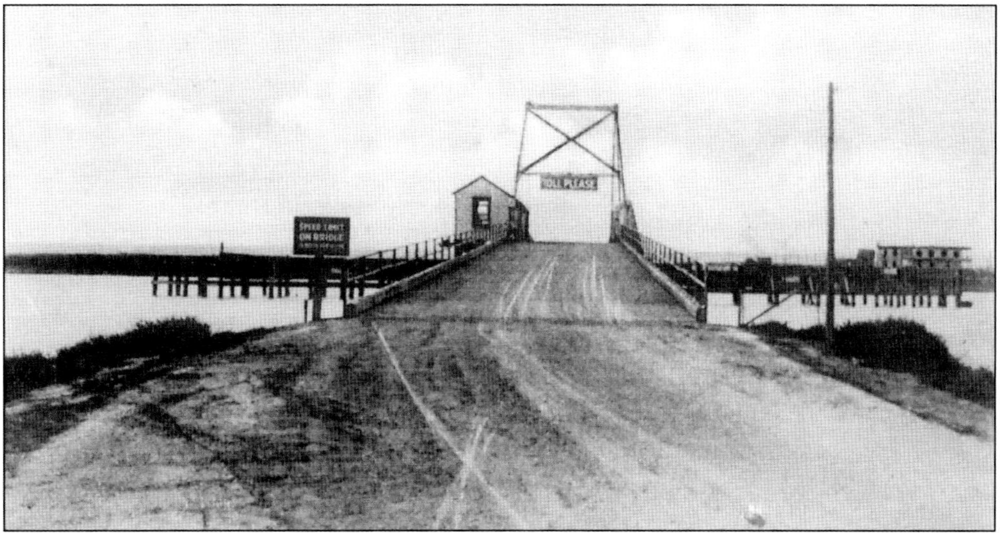

The first automobile bridge from Manahawkin to Long Beach Island opened in 1914, six summers after the last train run. The new bridge ran parallel to the old railroad trestle, separated by perhaps 100 yards. It introduced a whole new era in private transportation. The highest annual earnings by the Tuckerton Railroad, ironically, occurred in 1925 when it hauled in all the stone, cement, sand, and supplies used for the construction of Route 9 (the route of the old Main Shore Road), which eventually resulted in the Tuckerton Railroad's demise. (Courtesy James Estelle.)

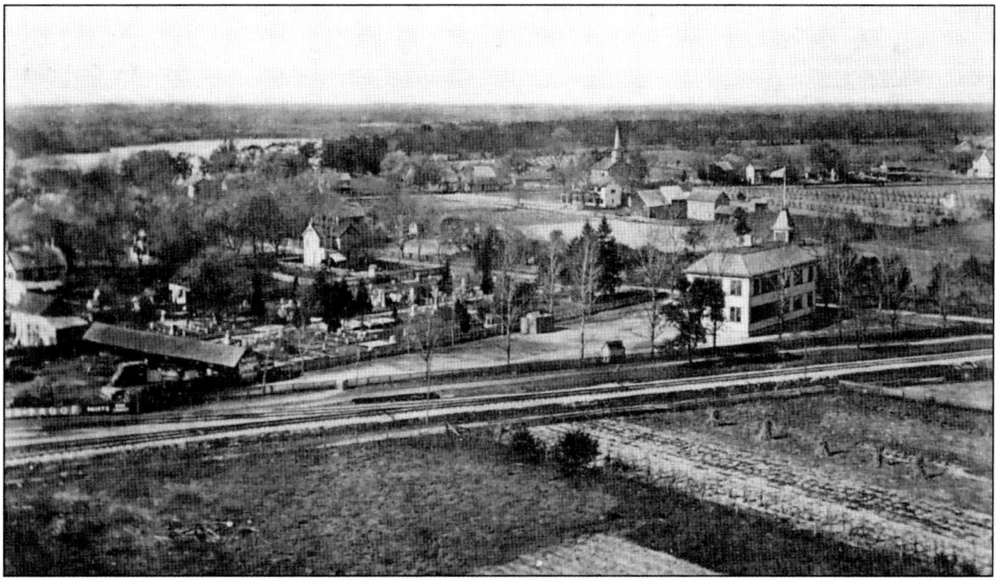

This is an overview of Manahawkin early in the present century, photographed from the steeple of the Methodist church. In the foreground are the Manahawkin Grammar School and the Methodist Cemetery. Beyond the farmhouse and farm buildings seen over the school, the Main Shore Road can be traced by the houses built along it and the Baptist church, still with its tall steeple. At top left, beyond the unseen downtown business district, lies Lake Manahawkin. (Courtesy James Estelle.)

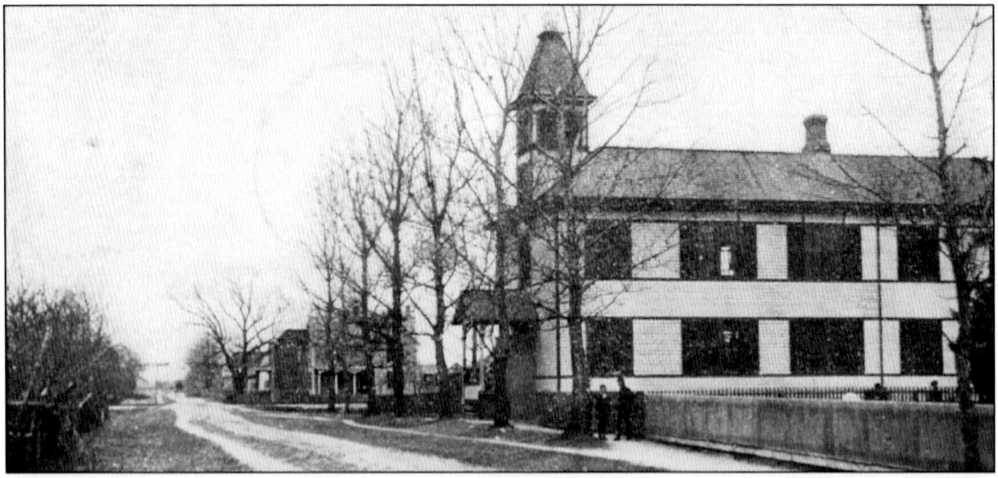

This large two-story school building dated from 1887. It began as a two-room school, but as enrollment increased, both floors were partitioned, thus making four rooms. In time, a third room was created on the first floor. The school continued in operation until 1951. The first public school financed with tax money was erected on Beach Avenue next to the cemetery after the American Revolution. This 1887 building was constructed on the same site. (Courtesy James Estelle.)

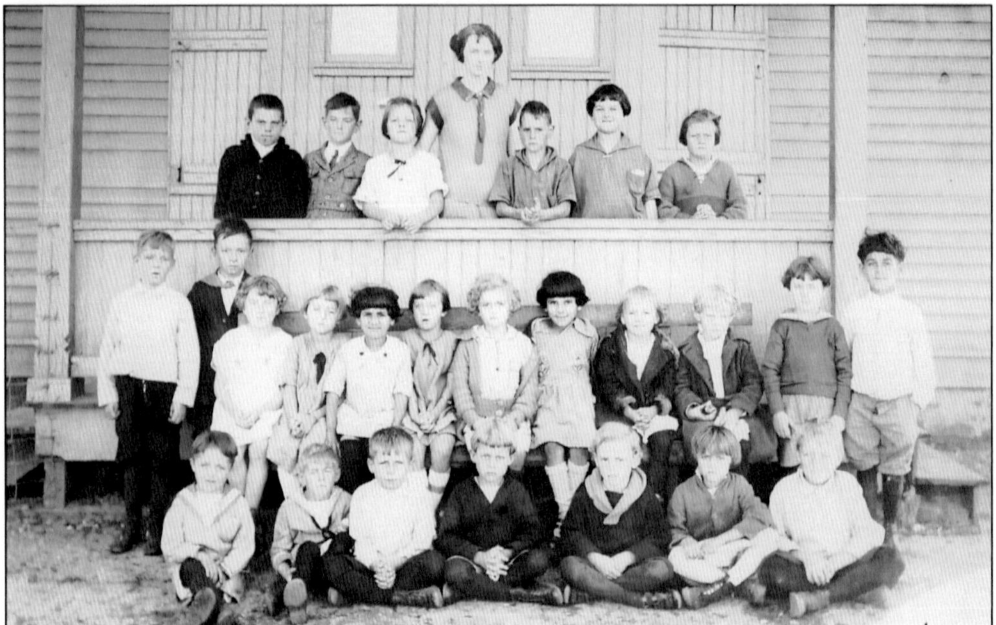

Mrs. M. Irene Hazelton (Cramer) was the teacher of these first and second graders in 1923/24 in Manahawkin. From left to right, students (and teacher) are as follows: (bottom row) Norman Pharo, Franklin Martin, Vincent Becker, Elmer Aker, Franklin Salmons, Bertha Jarossy, and William Cranmer; (middle row) Alfred Pharo, George Schingloff, Carolyn Corlis, Ruth Sprague, Blanche Boreedy, Althea Frederickson, Ethel Carr, Mary Boreedy, Pauline Giberson, Clara Salmons, John Camp, and Philip Boreedy; (top row) Daniel Michel, Alden Cranmer, Evelyn McAnney, Mrs. Cramer, Paul Salmons, Ada Jeffries, and Phyllis Jablonski. Students were also from Staffordville, Cedar Run, Mayetta, and Warren Grove. (Courtesy James Estelle.)

Railroads were largely responsible for the residential and economic development of Ocean County. Manahawkin became a busy center especially in the 1909–1923 period shown here. Long Beach Island was growing from Sea Haven to Barnegat City, and all the traffic was funneled through Manahawkin. Two stops were made on the trip to the island: Hilliard's and Martin's. Hillard's Station was the address of Thomas H. Cranmer's Bay Side Inn and Bay Side Inn Market while the Bonnet Gunning Association gave its address as Martin's. (Courtesy John Brinckmann, The Tuckerton Railroad.)

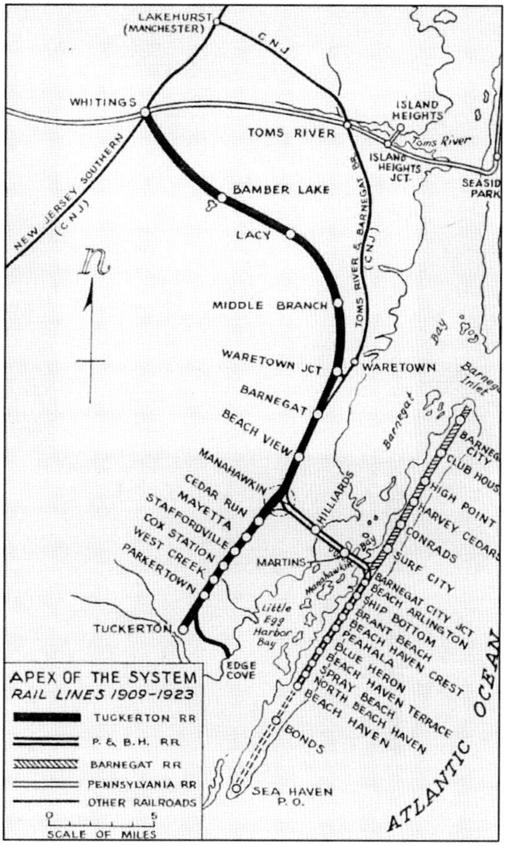

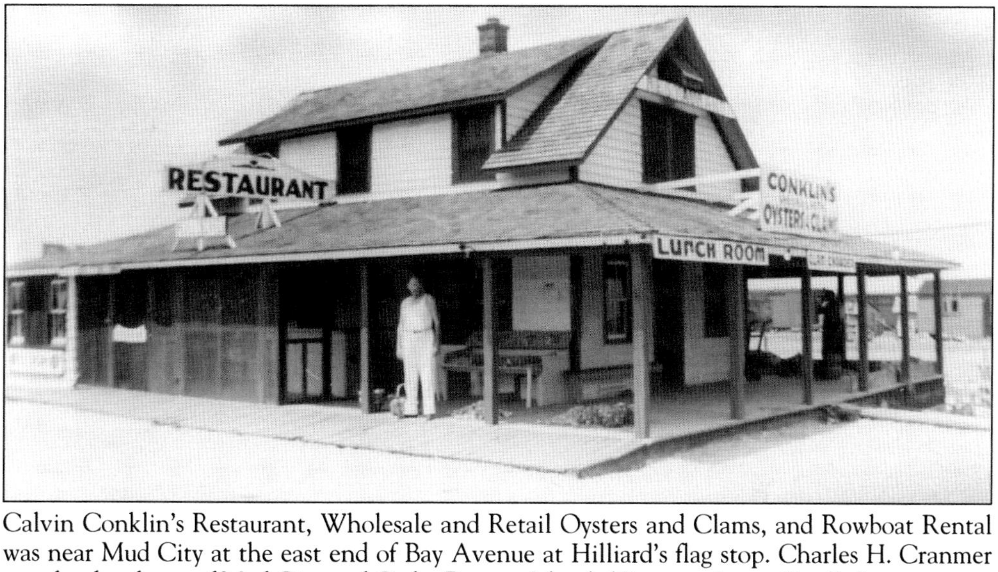

Calvin Conklin's Restaurant, Wholesale and Retail Oysters and Clams, and Rowboat Rental was near Mud City at the east end of Bay Avenue at Hilliard's flag stop. Charles H. Cranmer was the developer of Mud City and Cedar Bonnet Island. (Courtesy James Estelle.)

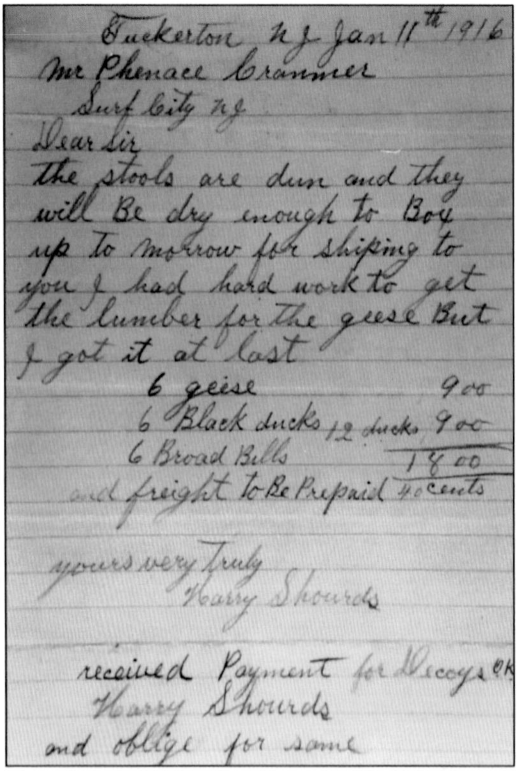

Tuckerton N J Jan 11th 1916
Mr Phenace Cranmer
Surf City N J
Dear Sir
the stools are dun and they will Be dry enough to Box up to morrow for shiping to you I had hard work to get the lumber for the geese But I got it at last

6 geese	9 00
6 Black ducks 12 ducks	9 00
6 Broad Bills	18 00
and freight to Be Prepaid	40 cents

yours very Truly
Harry Shourds

received Payment for Decoys OK
Harry Shourds
and oblige for same

Decoy collectors should drool over this bill addressed to Phineas Cranmer of Mayetta for eighteen handmade stools for $18—plus 40¢ postage to ship them from Tuckerton to Surf City! (Courtesy James Estelle.)

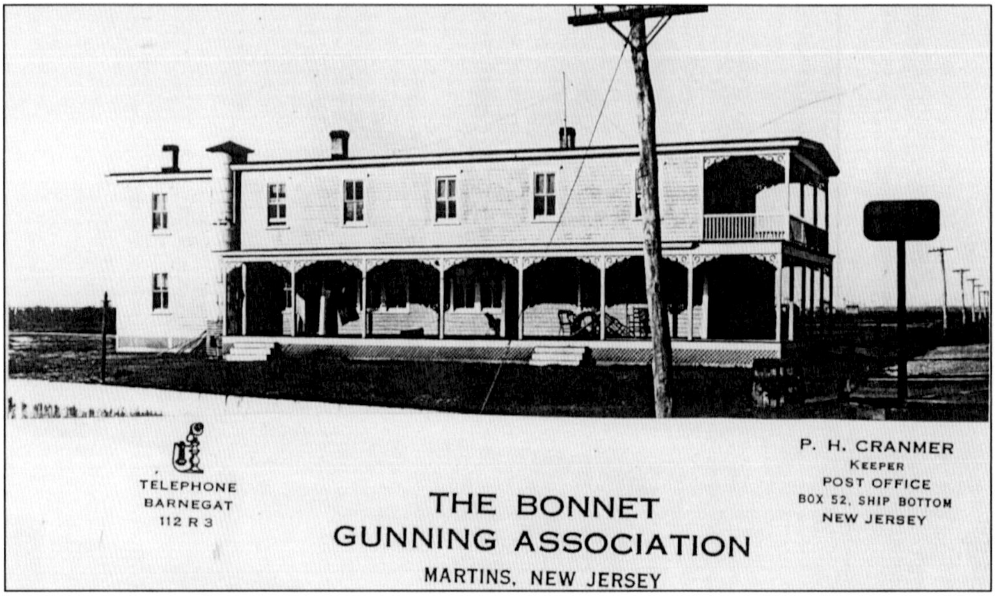

The Duck Inn on Bonnet Island in mid-bay catered to boaters, fishermen, and duck hunters. It was known, at the time when the railroad bridge crossed there, as Martin's Box for its builder, Humphrey Martin, and later as the Bonnet Club. Phineas Cranmer was the club's guide and his wife Rebecca was the cook. The club has been there since *c.* 1886 and was once a flag stop on the way to Long Beach Island. (Courtesy James Estelle.)

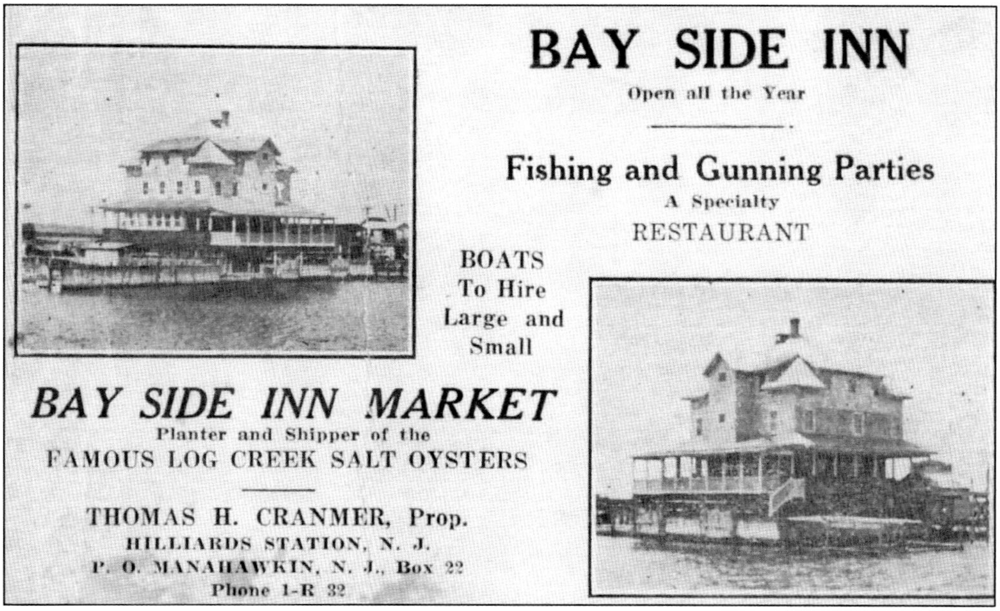

Thomas Cranmer's Bay Side Inn, built in 1917 and located at the edge of the bay, was no small operation. It was at a prime site and still stands today as Margo's boatyard. Despite the addition of a few outside stairways and other exterior changes, it is easily recognized as the old Bay Side Inn. (Courtesy James Estelle.)

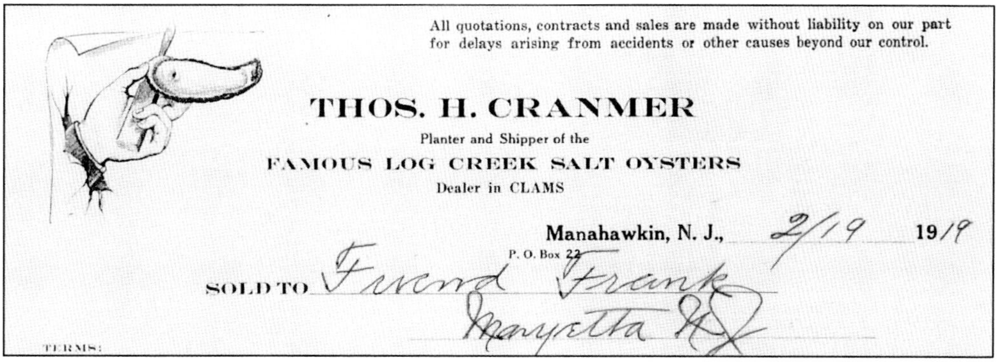

Thomas H. Cranmer's 1919 billhead for his "Famous Log Creek Salt Oysters" features a clever sketch of a hand offering an oyster on the half shell freshly "cracked" by the oyster knife still held in the hand. Ed Hazelton describes the oysters as being the size of your hand and most delicious. Log Creek was a small tributary of Cedar Creek, a short distance north of the Bay Side Inn. When he went for oysters, Mr. Cranmer pushed his boat through the water by hand with a setting pole. (Courtesy James Estelle.)

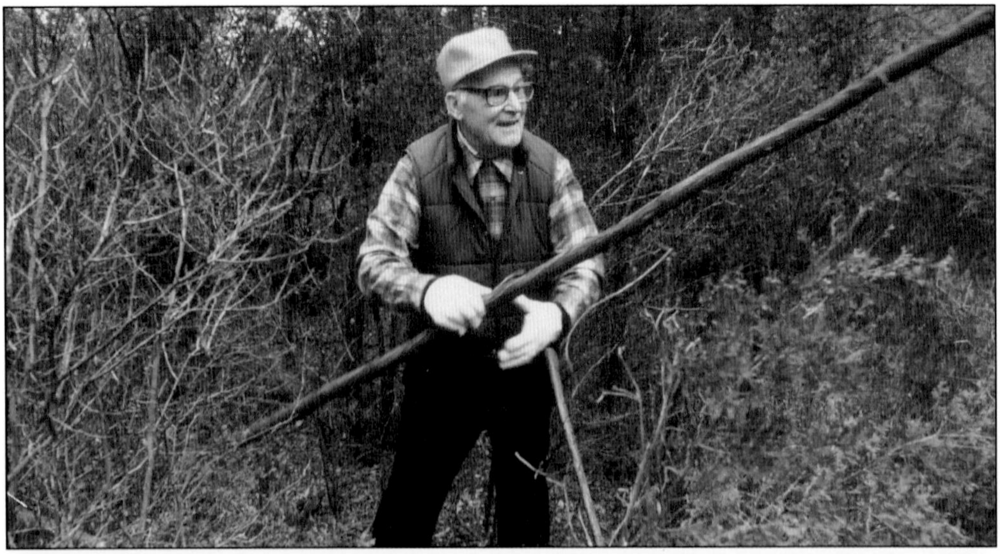

Jack Cervetto vacationed in Manahawkin as a boy and had fond memories of those summers. During the Depression he moved to the Warren Grove section of Stafford Township, where he built a sawmill and cut white cedar. His life was an example of community service: he was founder and member for forty years of the Warren Grove Fire Company; a member of the New Jersey Forest Fire Service, the Warren Grove Methodist Church, and the Tuckerton Lodge No. 4, F & AM; the district game warden; and the recipient of the Hurley Conklin Award from the Barnegat Bay Decoy & Baymen's Museum. Mr. Cervetto was eighty-six when he died in 1995. (Courtesy Pearl Cervetto.)

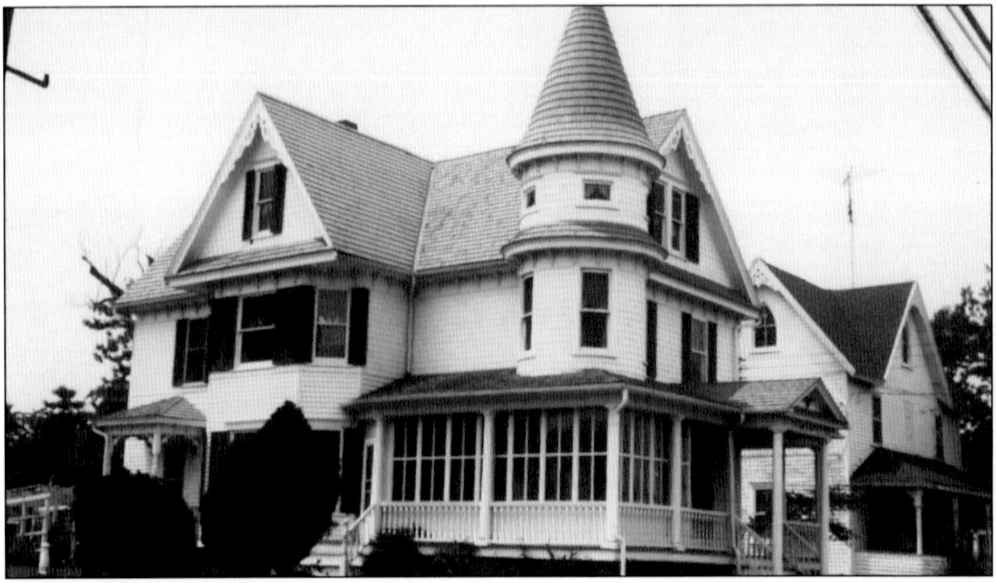

The Hazelton family began in Stafford Township in 1743 when Jarvis Hazelton and Ann Haywood, his wife of three years, arrived. Their eldest son James married Sarah Birdsall, and through their son Jarvis, they became the progenitors of all the subsequent Hazeltons in Manahawkin. Jarvis and his wife Rachel Letts had six sons and two daughters. This Hazelton house was the home of Edward Hazelton, who, along with his two sisters Edna and Irene (both deceased) were well-known and respected citizens of the community. (Courtesy OCHS.)

Roger "Doc" Cramer of Manahawkin, the best baseball player to come from the semi-pro teams along the Jersey shore, moved up to the major leagues in the 1920s and played with Philadelphia, Detroit, Boston, and Washington. He had a career batting average of .296 and has been proposed for the Hall of Fame. His nickname "Doc" came from his chauffeuring Dr. Hilliard on his rounds just so he could drive his Oakland Roadster. On "Doc Cramer Day," most of Manahawkin entrained for Philly, but it was Dr. Hilliard who presented their gifts to his young "assistant." (Courtesy James Estelle.)

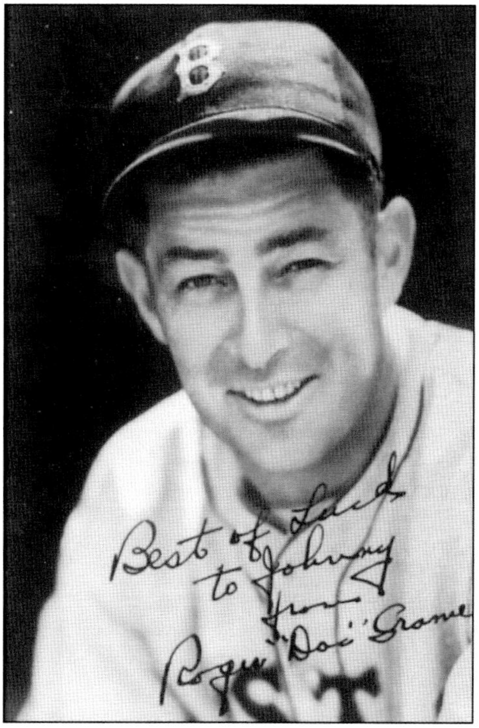

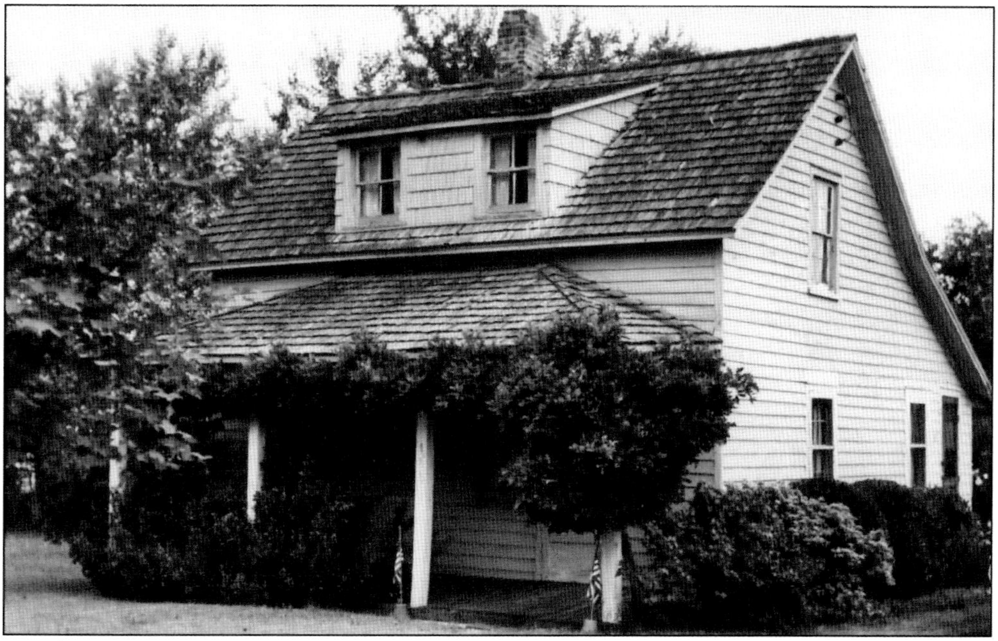

Cavalry Cottage, reputed to be the oldest residence in Manahawkin, was built *c.* 1760. Brigadier General Grier, a cavalry officer in the Civil War, lived there in the late 1800s and named it Cavalry Cottage. The original two-story building had two rooms on the first floor. About one hundred years later a stairway was built, dormer windows were installed, and two rooms were finished upstairs. The original part of the present Shinn Funeral Home may be as old or older than Cavalry Cottage. (Courtesy Burrell Adams.)

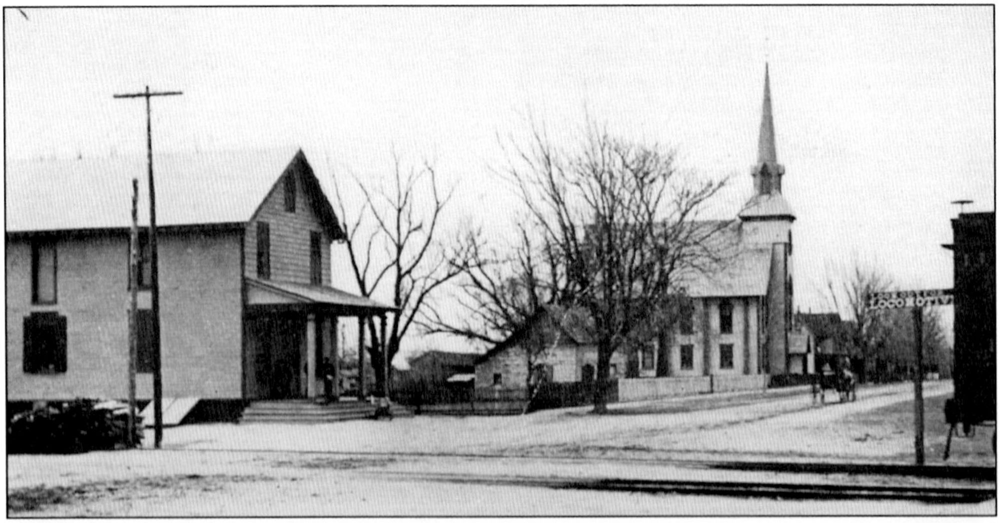

This is an early 1900s view of the Methodist church, which was erected in 1874 on Stafford Avenue to replace an 1803 building which was too small. To the left is the Manahawkin Post Office, which was located in Tom Sprague's store. He was the postmaster and was thus handy to the train station, where the mail arrived each afternoon. A crowd collected daily to wait for the mail to be sorted into boxes and to catch up on the latest news and gossip. (Courtesy James Estelle.)

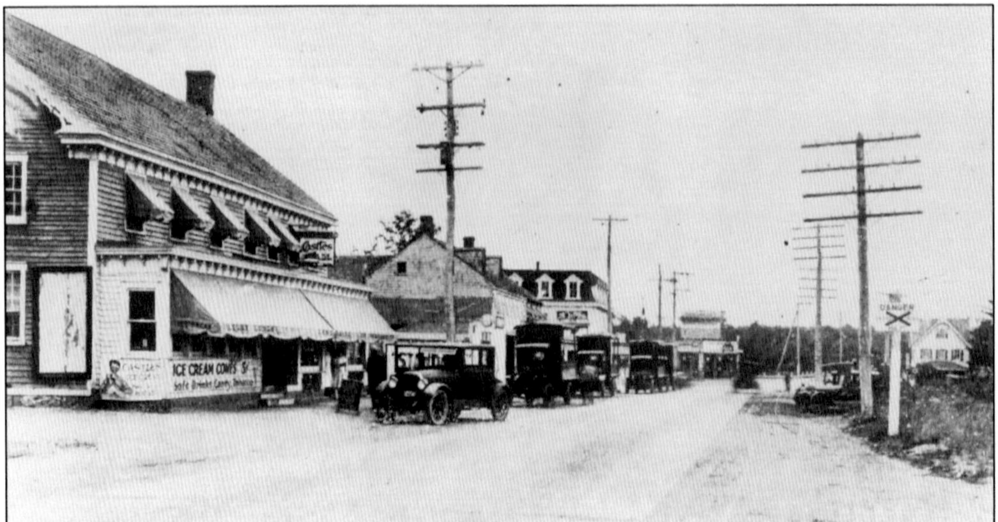

From north to south on the east side of North Broadway is the Lake House (with awnings), owned by C.H. Cranmer and rented for commercial use; a barely visible garage; the National Hotel; and Emma Hall, the large building with the mansard roof which housed stores, a lunch counter, and at one time, the ACME market. (Courtesy OCHS.)

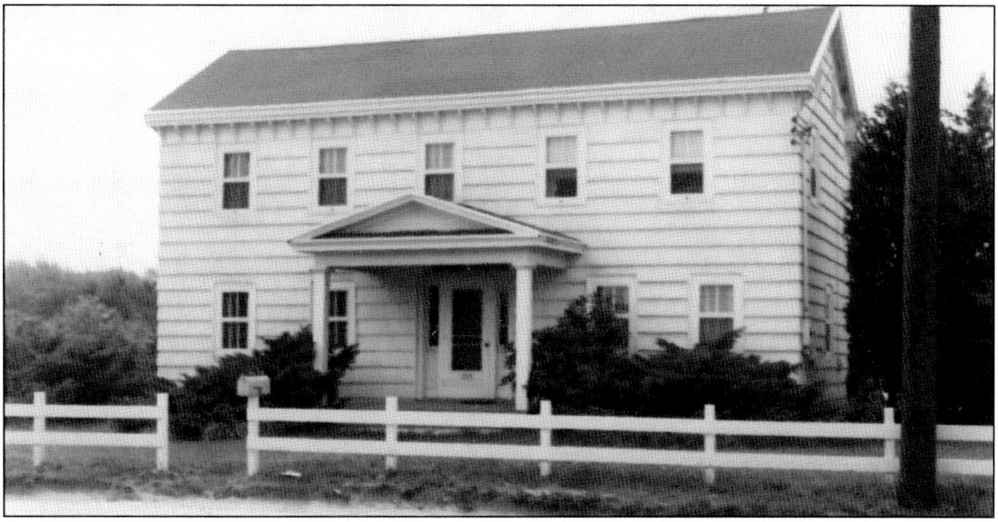

Stephen Inman built this house with pure colonial lines on East Bay Avenue in Manahawkin c. 1850 when he "came ashore" from Long Beach Island. He descended from a long line of whalers who worked "off the beach" with small boats at what was then known as the Great Swamp—now Surf City. The first Inman was Aaron of Rhode Island, who had "followed the whales south" early in the eighteenth century, since their numbers were depleted close to the New England shore. This house shows very little change from its original design. (Courtesy Elaine I. Pope.)

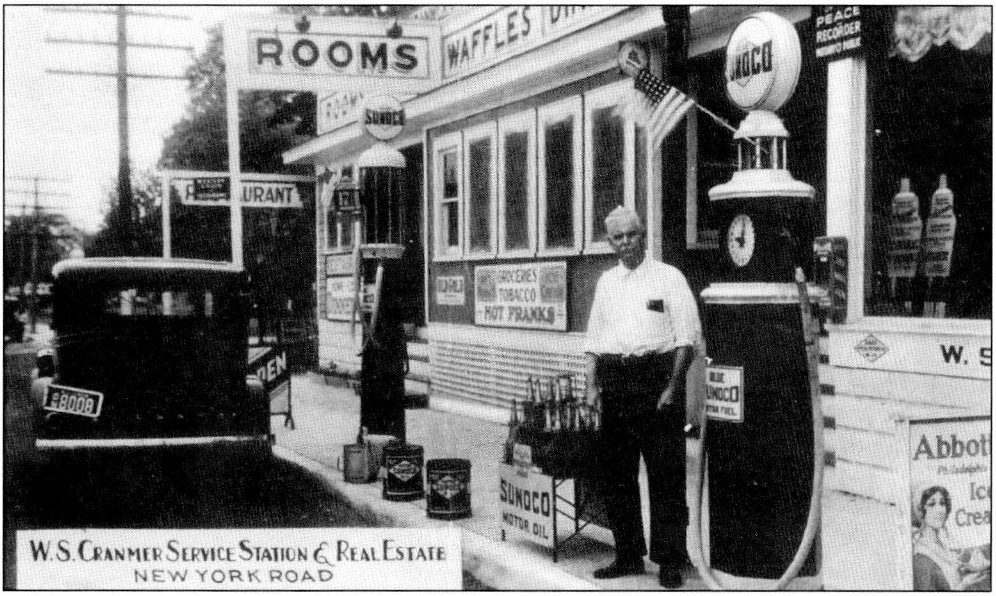

W.S. Cranmer was the owner of this combination inn, gas station, grocery store, restaurant, and Western Union office in Cedar Run. He was also the justice of the peace, recorder, and notary public. Very appropriately, this community once went by the name of Cranmertown. In 1880 Leah Blackman wrote, "There were at least four original branches of Cranmers of Ocean and Burlington Counties whose descendants are so numerous and so mixed up by intermarriage that at this late date there is no such thing as untangling the intricate web of their kinship." (Courtesy James Estelle.)

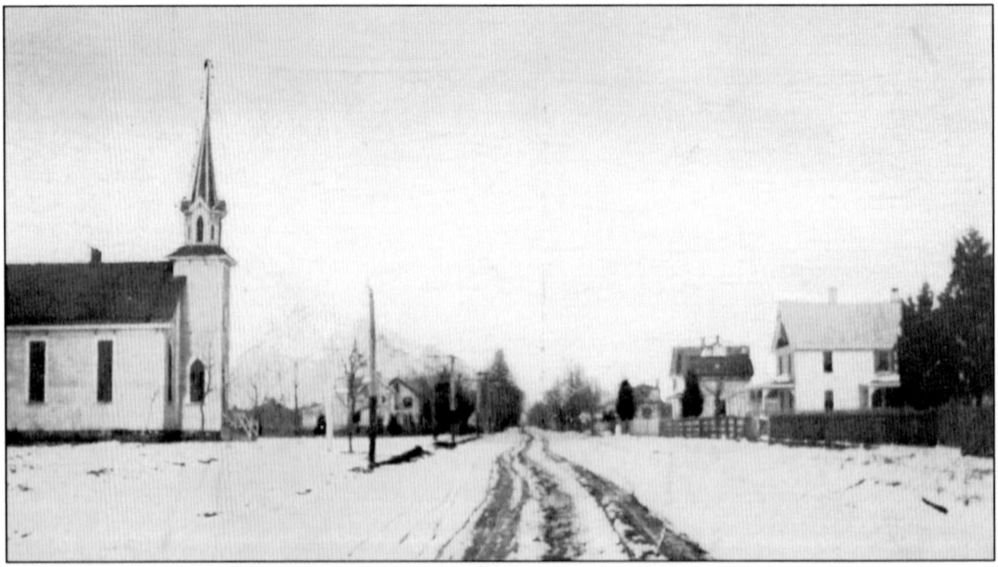

Cedar Run owes its development to its location between Mill Creek on the south side of Manahawkin and Cedar Run, which was named for its course through cedar swamps. There was an attempt to call it Unionville in the 1870s, but the town's name remained unchanged. Both the railroad and Main Shore Road passed through Cedar Run just a few hundred yards apart. The corner stone of the Methodist Episcopal church was laid November 20, 1874, with the Reverends Ballard, Graw, Parker, and Clark assisting. The church was dedicated December 15, 1880. (Courtesy James Estelle.)

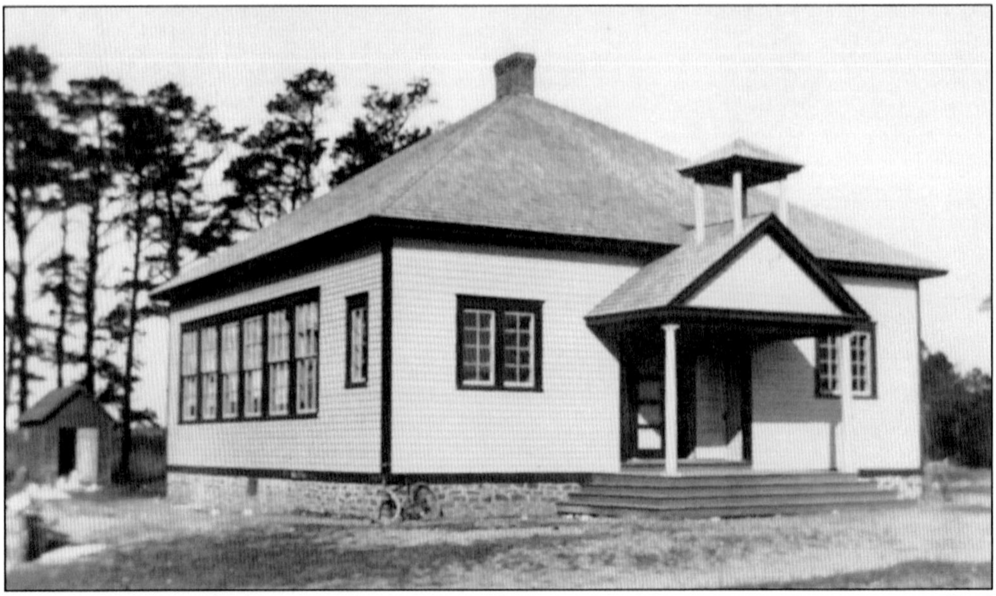

This Cedar Run schoolhouse, with two rooms but sometimes just one teacher, was a Stafford Township school built in 1901 and closed in 1927. The first school was across the street near a little stream. The second, which was behind this two-room school, was moved to Mayetta to be used by an auto parts store. Today it is covered with hub caps. This one, the third, has been well preserved and now serves as the Assembly of God Church. (Courtesy James Estelle.)

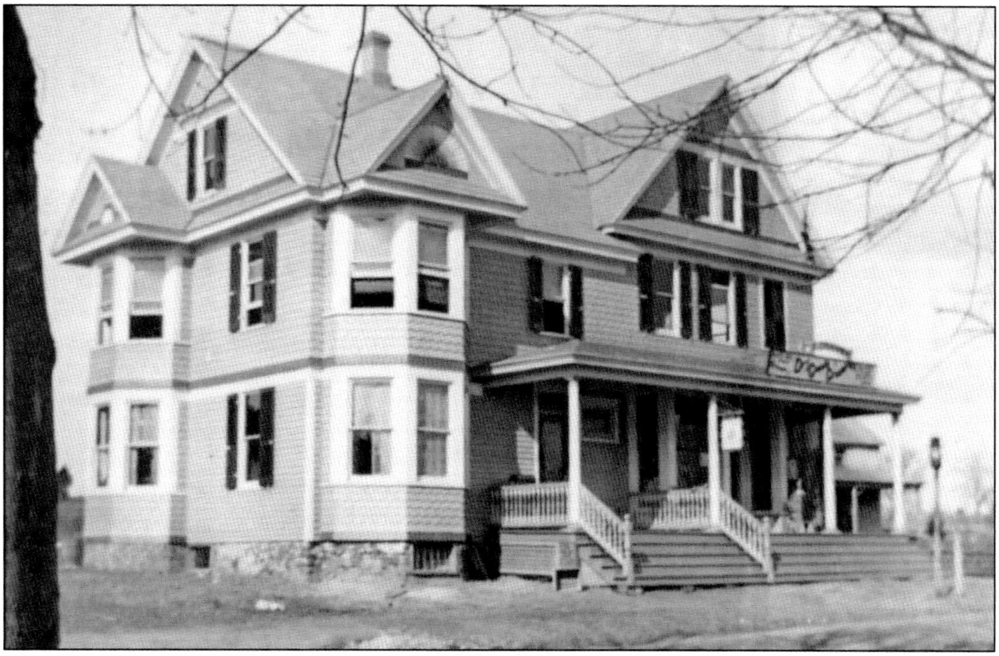

The post office was important to a community. The location of an office in a community gave it status and a listing among recognized towns. Often, as in Cedar Run, the post office was in a private home with the man or woman of the house as the postmaster or postmistress. (Courtesy James Estelle.)

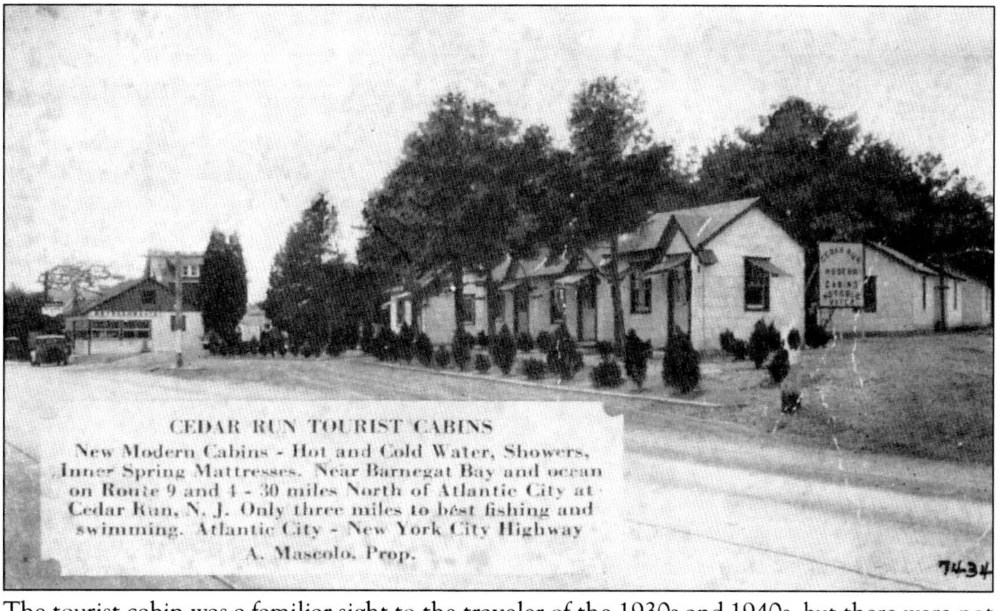

The tourist cabin was a familiar sight to the traveler of the 1930s and 1940s, but there were not many along Route 9 between New Gretna and Manahawkin. These cabins at Cedar Run were owned by A. Mascolo. They had hot and cold water, showers, inner spring mattresses, a nearby refreshment stand, and "were only three miles from the best fishing and swimming along the Atlantic City-New York City highway." (Courtesy James Estelle.)

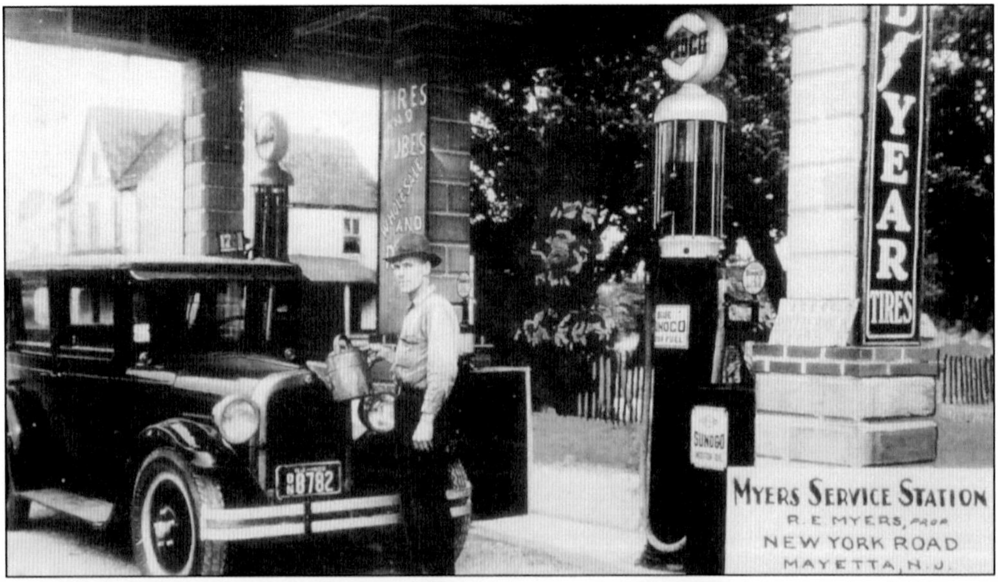

Myers Service Station was on New York Road, the present Route 9, in Mayetta. It sold Sunoco gasoline and Good Year tires as well as ice cold buttermilk for 5¢ per bottle. The car bears a 1932 license plate with O/N8782, which indicated Ocean County. Route 9 was the only north-south route along the southeastern part of New Jersey until the Garden State Parkway opened in the 1950s. (Courtesy James Estelle.)

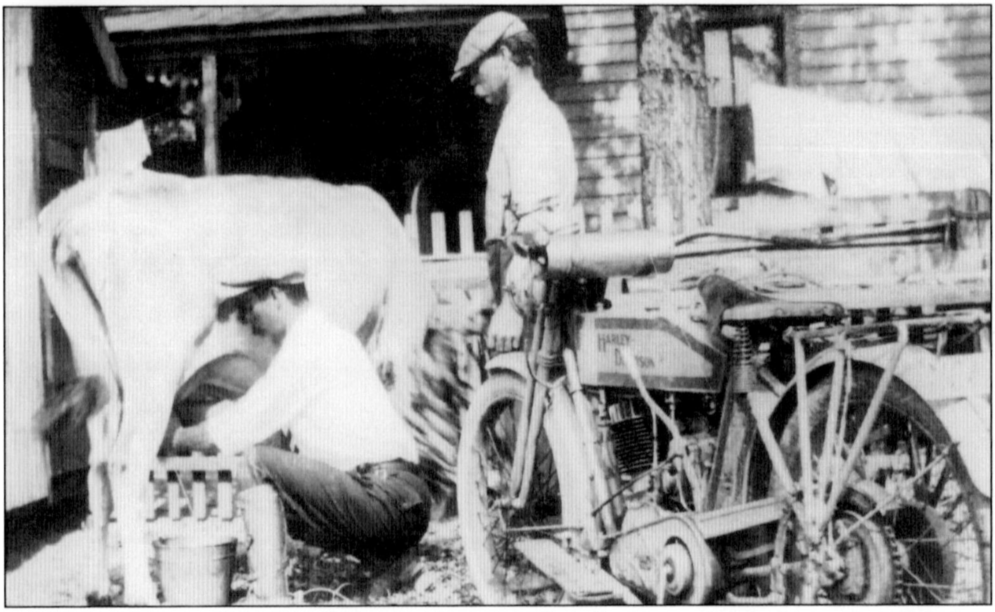

Bradford Salmons's life illustrates the diversity of skills so many inhabitants of this area possessed and which they used to support their families. Mr. Salmons was noted as a boat builder and designer of boats, including sneakboxes and catboats which were built in his back yard in Staffordville. He was also a decoy carver, carpenter, painter, farmer, salt-hay farmer, and surfman during the winter at the life-saving station in Ship Bottom. Here he "supervises" the milking of a cow by son, J. Earl. A 1914 Harley motorcycle stands by. (Courtesy Donald Salmons.)

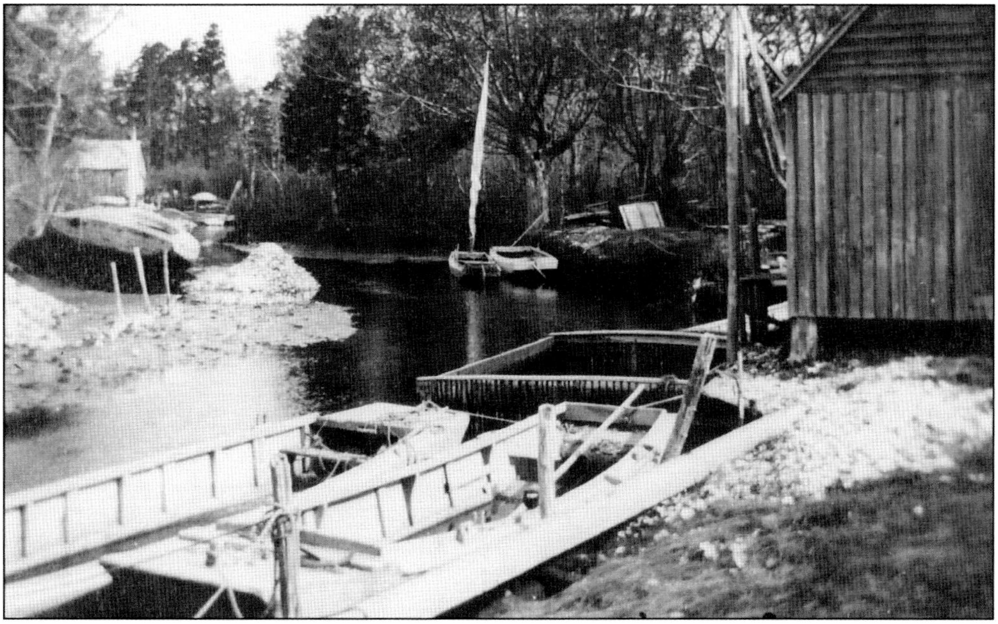

James P. Ward, a Civil War veteran of West Creek, wrote the following on a wintry January morning in 1874: "The boy on the shore is skilled almost as he begins to wear trousers, embarks in his fishing-skiff; and soon learns to handle her in all weather with a dexterity unknown to city lads. By the time he reaches the age of ten or twelve his character is half formed and a few voyages at sea and experience does the rest." It was in a setting like this on Cedar Run that little boys got their start. (Courtesy James Estelle.)

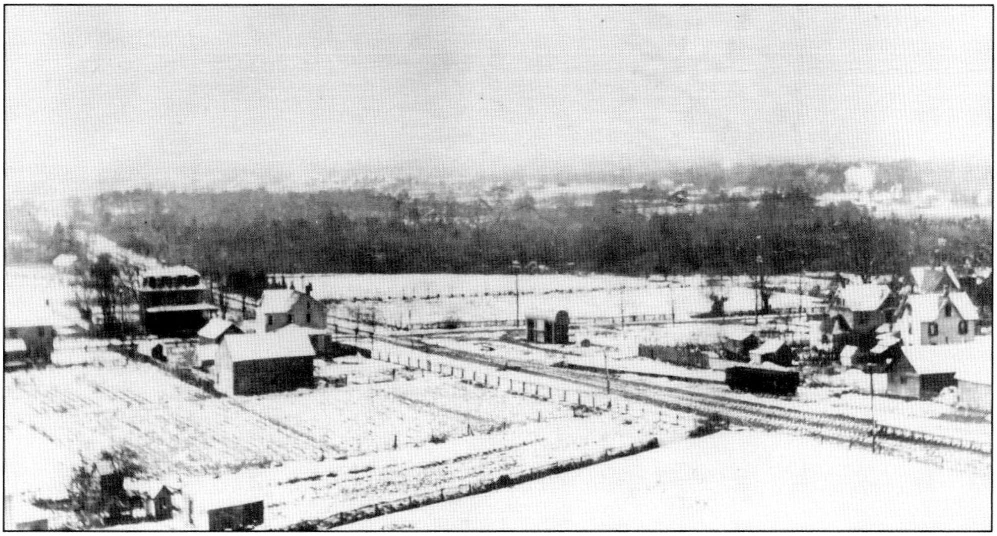

This bird's eye view of Manahawkin and Cedar Run was one of three taken between 1910 and 1915. From the steeple of the Methodist church, the cameraman shot to the north, west, and south. Unlike the other views, this shows many fields under cultivation in the Bay Avenue area. Cedar Run is in the distance. The Main Shore Road, which would be to the west, ran parallel to the Tuckerton Railroad tracks. The house with the mansard roof (to the left) still stands and oil is still stored diagonally across from that house on Bay Avenue. One tank is visible (lower center). (Courtesy OCHS.)

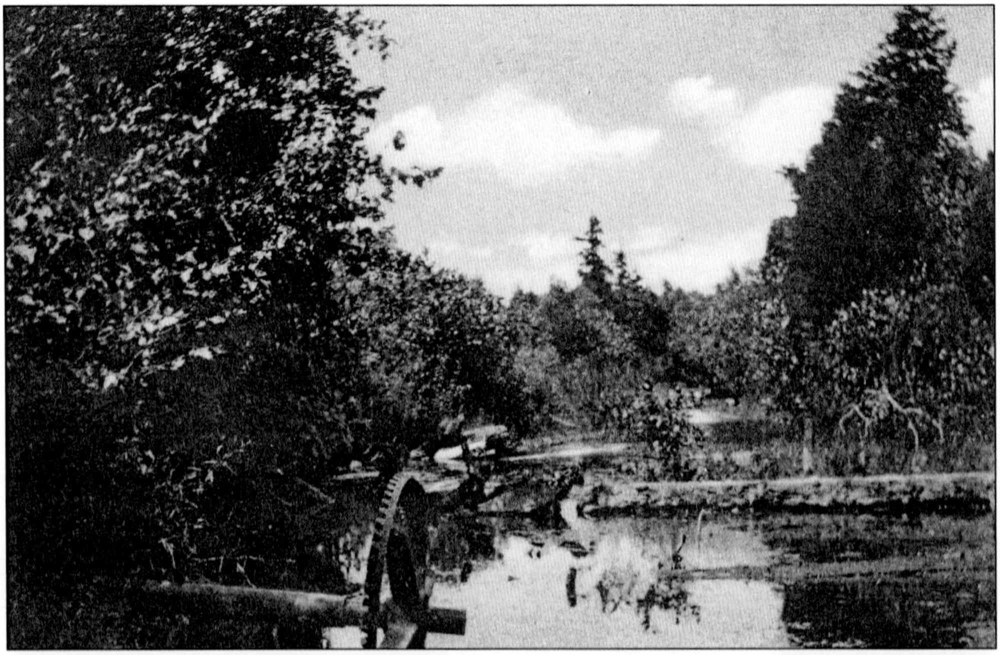

The old mill wheel on Westecunk Creek is a nostalgic sight. The sawmill was built around 1706, when the green forests of pine and oak and swamps of cedar drew some of the first settlers to this area. The wood and lumber they produced met their own needs and provided a trade item for the big cities and the West Indies. It was here that Jarvis designed and built the garvey. Much of the lumber used for local homes, garveys, row boats, and sneakboxes was milled here. (Courtesy EHS.)

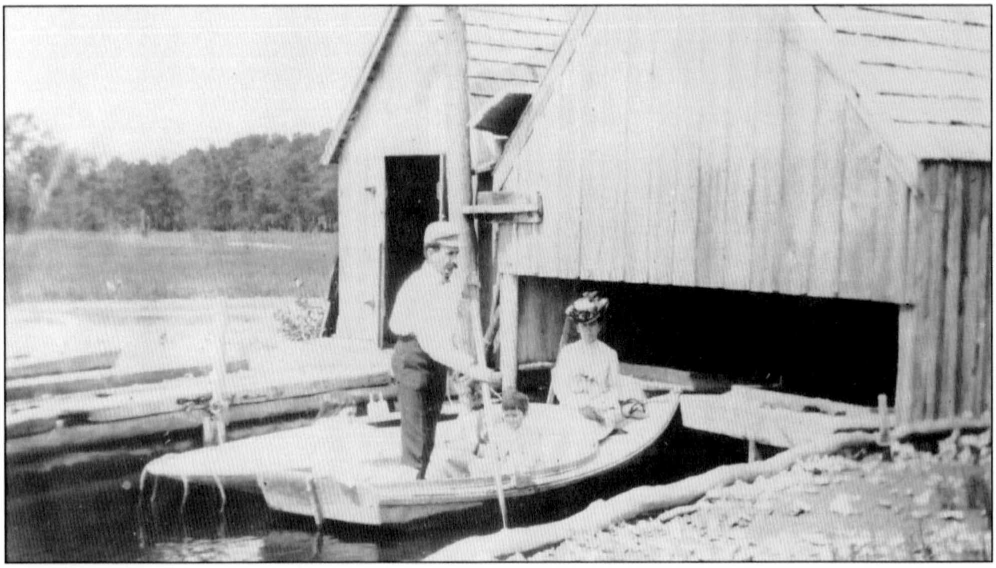

A man is about to take his wife and young children for a gentle ride in a sneakbox. The boat and equipment sheds behind them are doubtlessly privately owned. Much of the sedge and waterfront were privately owned in the early years. This allowed the owner to cut salt hay, which was used for stable bedding and also insulation, which was tied into the walls of houses and plastered with mud. (Courtesy A.W. Kelly, Esq.)

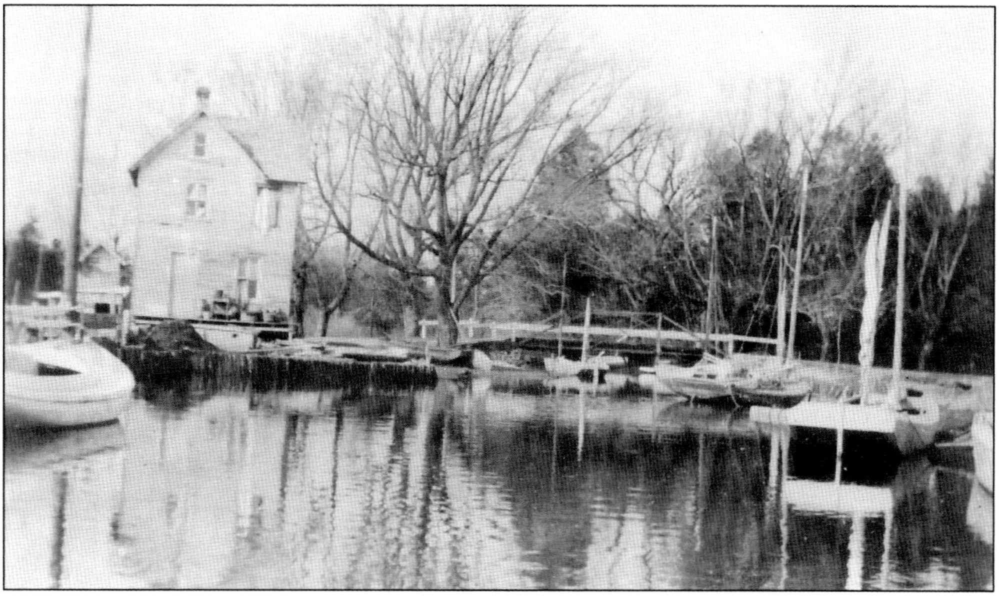

Hazelton Seaman's boatyard stood at the above site just downstream of the bridge over Westecunk Creek. Here he created the famed sneakbox for his personal use as a portable duck blind in the late 1830s. It became popular among gunners immediately, and sneakboxes were in demand. Countless numbers have been built by J. Howard Perrine and David Beaton as racing craft in the twentieth century. (Courtesy A.S. Kelly, Esq.)

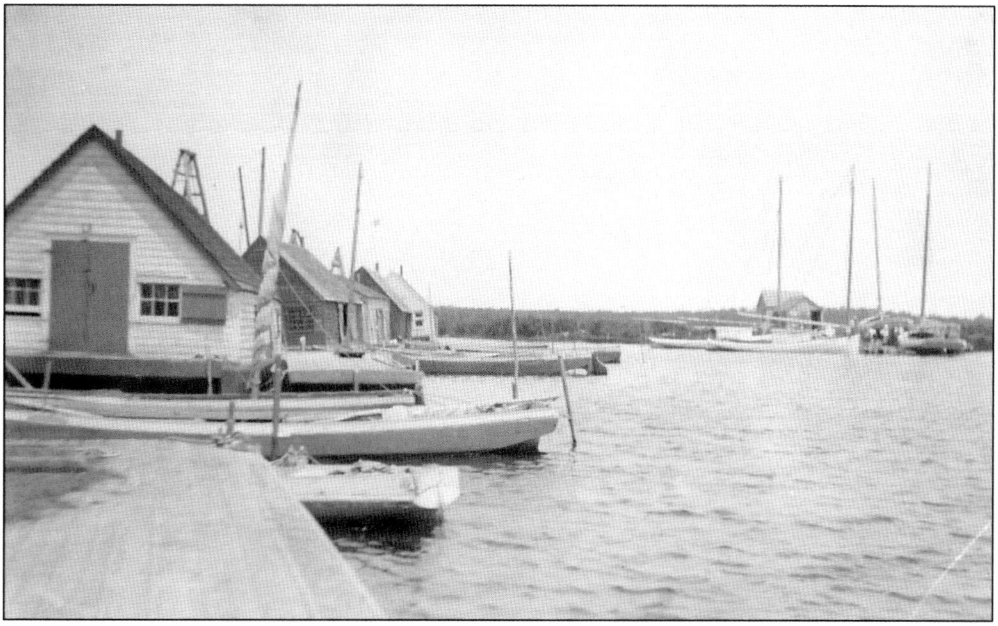

No activity and no people in sight indicate a Sunday on this normally busy stretch of Westecunk Creek. Visible are the stern of a sneakbox at the dock, oyster and clam packing houses, the tops of cranes to hoist the loads of clams and oysters, and catboats with sails furled. Napoleon Kelly and Edward Shinn were owners of some of these sheds on the north bank of the creek. Other oyster and claim dealers were R.F. Rutter, C.D. Kelly, George Kelly, Henry Cowperthwaite, Harper Rulon, and Al Kennimore. (Courtesy EHS.)

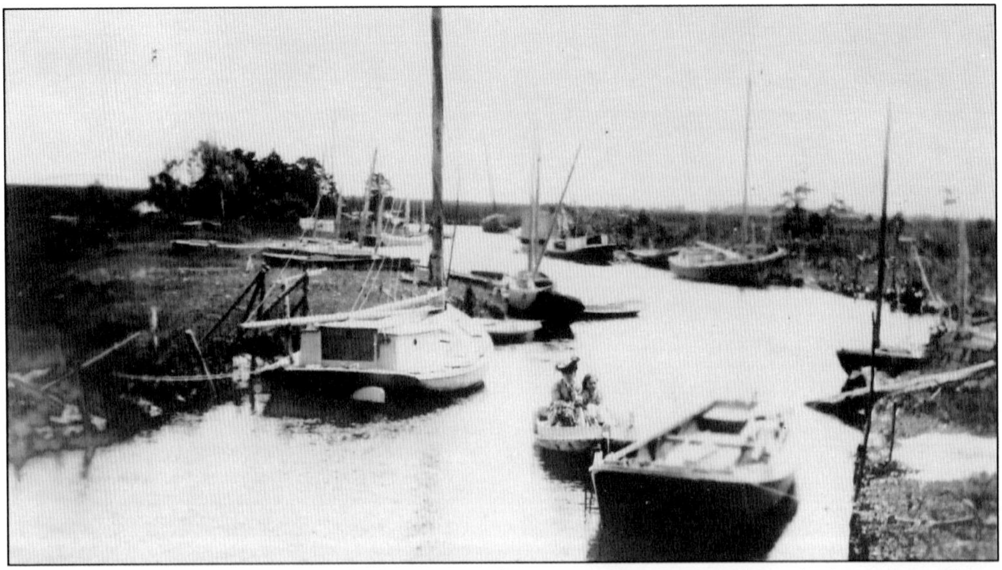

Downstream of the commercial docks, the creek runs a mile or more through the sedges where salt hay was cut. Here a variety of craft were moored along its banks. In the foreground is an early motorized garvey. At left is a broad-beamed cat-rigged sloop with a huge sail. The sloop carried 50-pound bags of sand which had to be shifted manually on each tack to balance the boat. Thus, the sloops were called "sandbaggers." (Courtesy A.W. Kelly, Esq.)

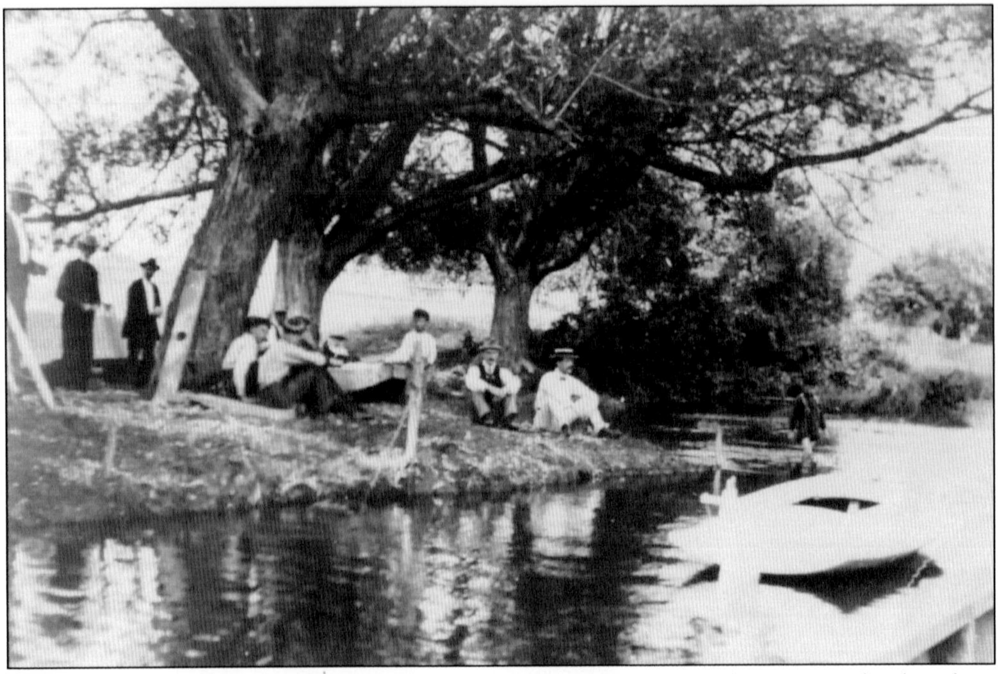

This tree-shaded bank of Westecunk Creek was doubtless the coolest spot to be found on Sunday, August 3, 1903, when these men, attired in their Sunday best, sought refuge here after church. A young boy was wading upstream of the sneakbox with his best breeches carefully rolled above his knees. Wives and mothers were no doubt at home slaving over hot dinners! (Courtesy A.W. Kelly, Esq.)

These sneakboxes are "at rest" not far from the boatyard where the first one of its kind was designed by Hazelton Seaman c. 1836. Its intended use was a duck blind that could be moved easily from place to place and covered with marsh grass. A distinctive feature of this beautifully shaped boat was the rail around the stern of the boat inside which decoys could be stored as they were taken to and from the gunning sites. (Courtesy EHS.)

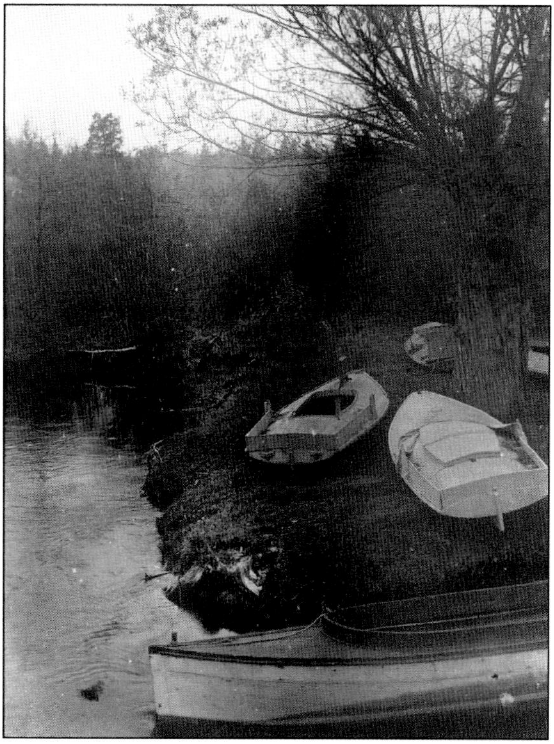

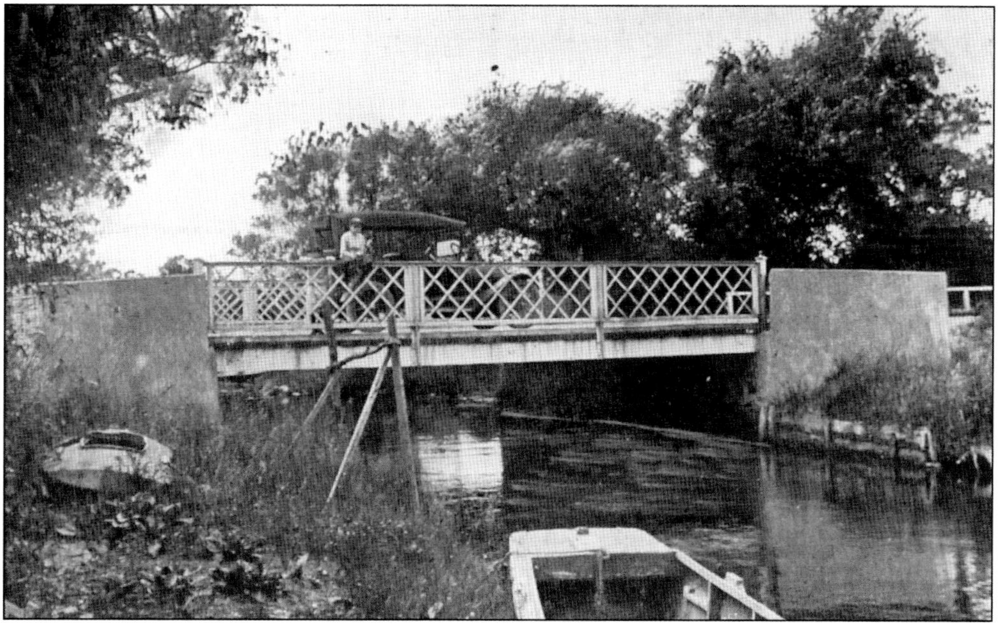

This wooden bridge spanned Westecunk Creek on the Main Shore Road, a stagecoach route which tended to follow the firmer ground just to the west of the marshes. Elsie, the sender of this 1919 card, advised Mr. Charles Stevens of Philadelphia, "I am learning how to run a car." This bridge site was a popular gathering place for local residents, a swimming hole, a place of baptism, and a launch site for small boats in the early years. It was at the head of the navigable portion of the creek. (Courtesy EHS.)

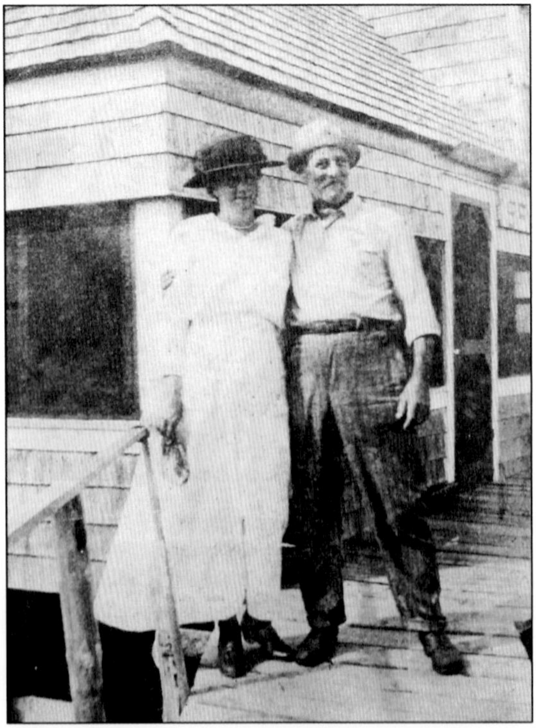

John Will Rutter, born in 1857, married Mary Amelia Truex from Cedar Run. They had four sons and two daughters. John was a member of the Lifesaving Service. Three sons, one grandson, and one great grandson have followed in his footsteps by serving in the U.S. Coast Guard. Two of John and Amelia's granddaughters, active today in the local historical society and the Methodist church, are Helen R. Wisner and Gladys R. Loveland. (Courtesy EHS.)

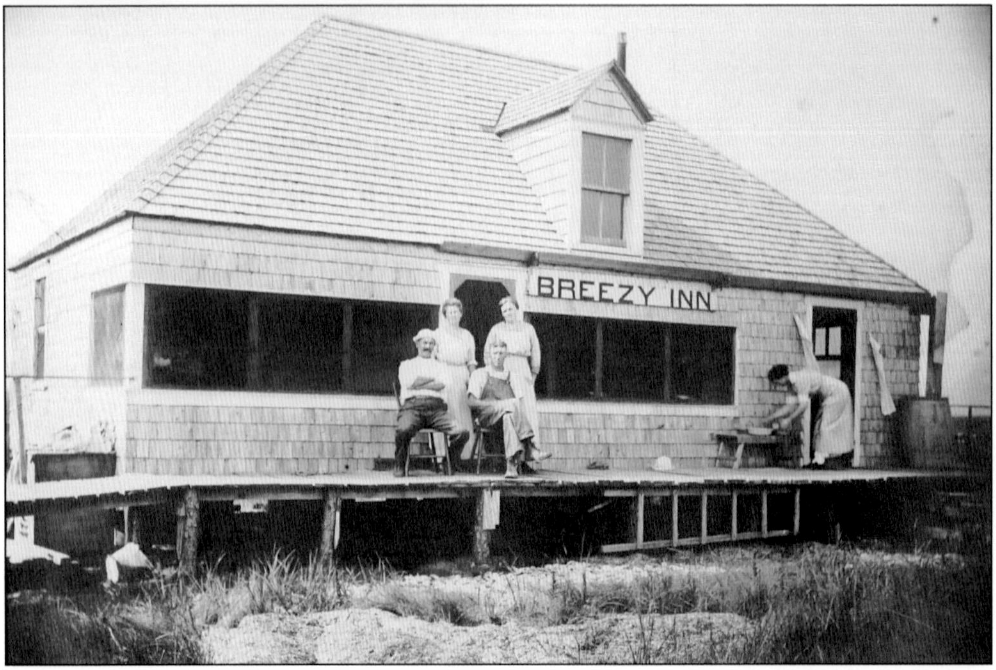

Breezy Inn was a boarding lodge for gunners and fishermen in the early 1900s. It was located at Long Point on Parker's Run at the southeast end of the present Dock Road. The inn burned down on January 20, 1921. People pictured are, from left to right, John W. and Mary Rutter and owners Frank and Julia Holman, parents of Stella Kelly Wegst. An unknown lady is on the right. (Courtesy EHS.)

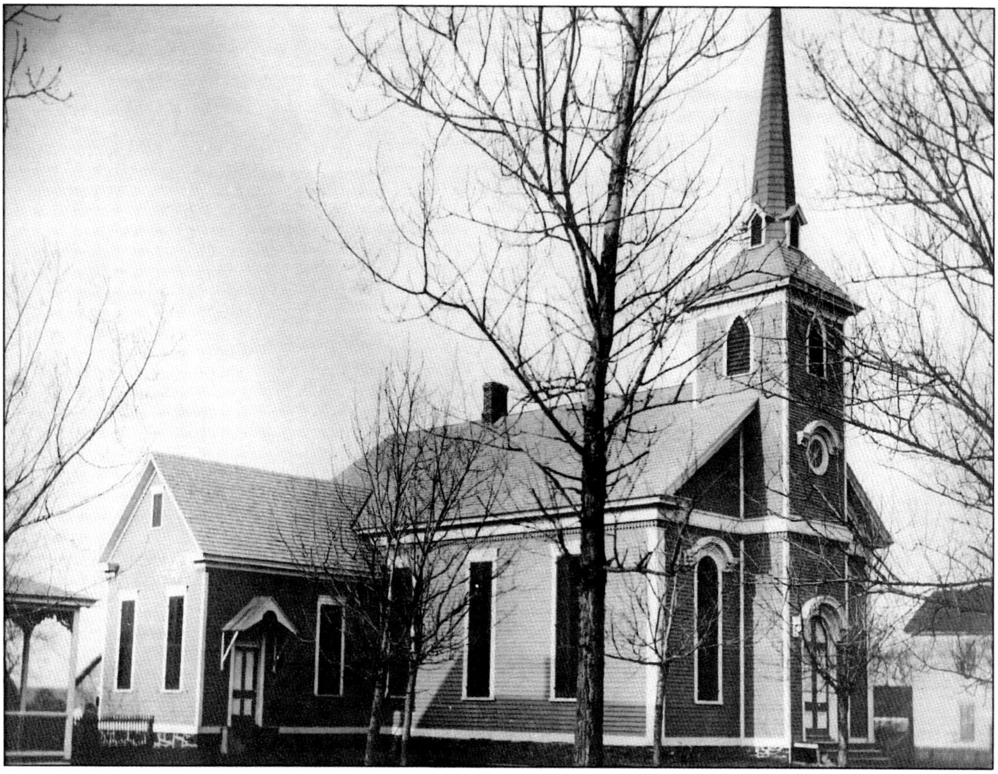

This is the United Methodist Church, built c. 1869 with its annex on the left added in the 1890s. The porch of the parsonage is at the left. The original church, built in 1819 and later sold to the Baptists, was located in the northeast corner of the cemetery. Some of the money for the building was raised through a lottery or raffle. Among the many prizes offered were a 30-foot sailing yacht, a "fall top" carriage, and four gold hunting case watches. The crowd which attended on July 4, 1868, quickly exhausted the ladies' picnic supplies. (Courtesy EHS.)

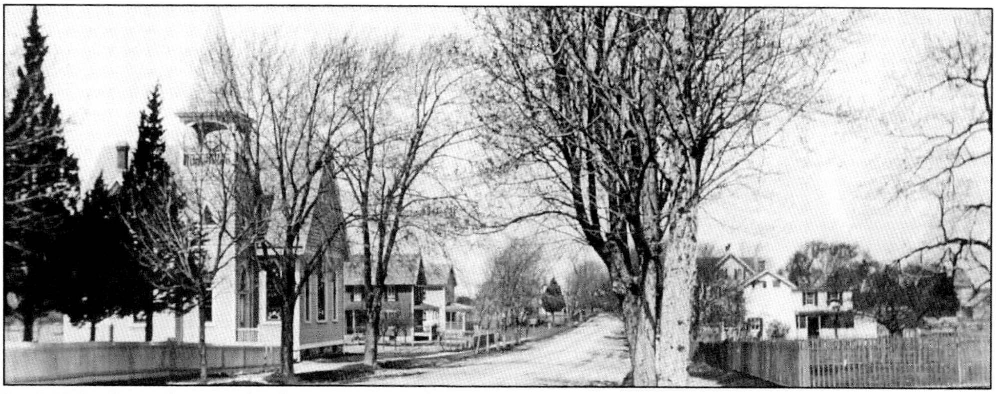

In 1875 when the Methodists were ready to sell their old church, there were but two known Baptists in West Creek, Dr. T.T. Price and Pastor Reverend C.A. Mott. Both men, members of the Manahawkin Baptist Church, were interested, but no purchase was made. Joseph Haywood planned to buy it for personal use, but then $400 was raised by Jonathan Shinn, Charles Budd Pharo, and others who wanted to purchase it for church use. Since then, there have been several moves and some new construction. The building now houses the Calvary Baptist Church of Parkertown. (Courtesy EHS.)

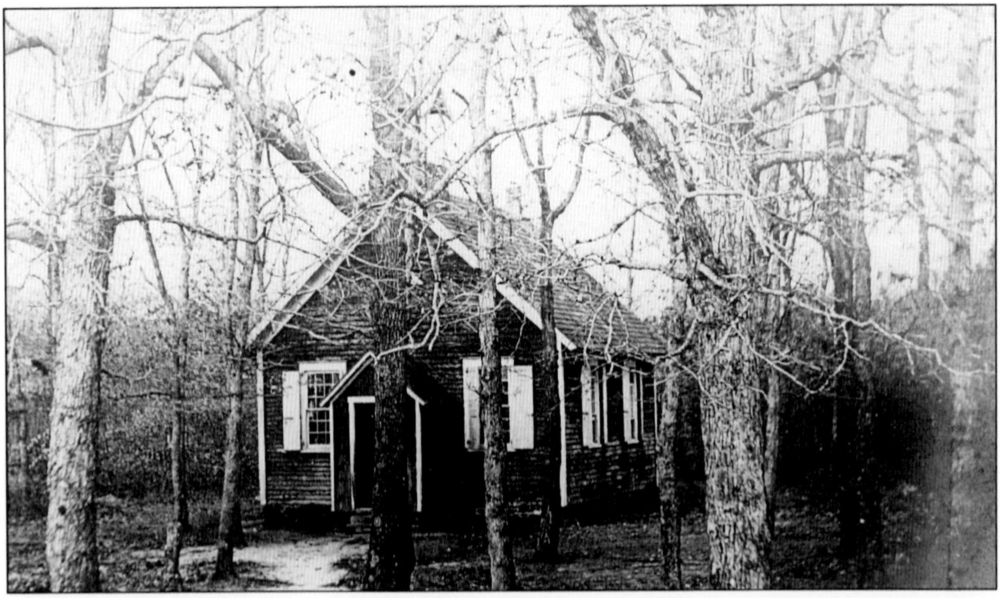

In 1885, when there were too many pupils for the school on Church Street, a lot with a stand of oak trees was purchased from John Bartlett for $43.75. John Jones, the builder of the school, charged $541.95. Carrie Cranmer (Kelly) was the teacher in 1917 when some pupils who disliked her burned the school to the ground. She continued to teach in the school on Division Street and then in Tuckerton in both the high school and grade eight. James and Joyce Bartlett now live at the old school site. (Courtesy EHS.)

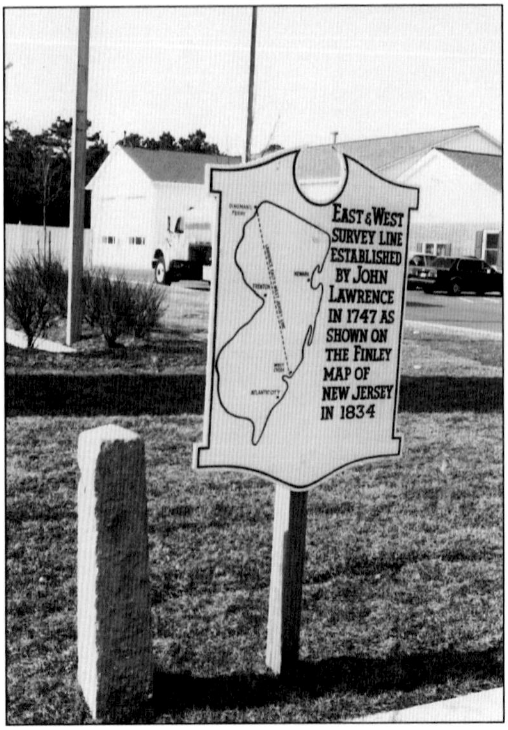

In 1747 engineer/surveyor John Lawrence ran a series of granite markers about 5 miles apart diagonally across New Jersey from Dingman's Ferry on the Delaware to Tucker's Island. This line separated East Jersey from West Jersey. East Jersey was controlled by a board of proprietors, which still acts today upon land matters in dispute in New Jersey. The West Creek marker is located on the west side of Main Street north of town. Tucker's Island Monument disappeared when the island washed away. (Courtesy EHS.)

Ruth Kelly Penn was one of many outstanding teachers who were products of the local schools. Others included: James Ward, Sue Salmons, George S. Shepard, Carrie C. Kelley, and Stella Wegst. Mrs. Penn, wife of Russell Penn, a mail clerk on the railroad, taught in the West Creek School from 1923 to 1957. In bad weather the boys would take her by sled from her house to the school. She allowed skating on the bog at recess. Both her father George Gaskill Kelly and grandfather Theodore Kelly were oysterman and cranberry growers. (Courtesy EHS.)

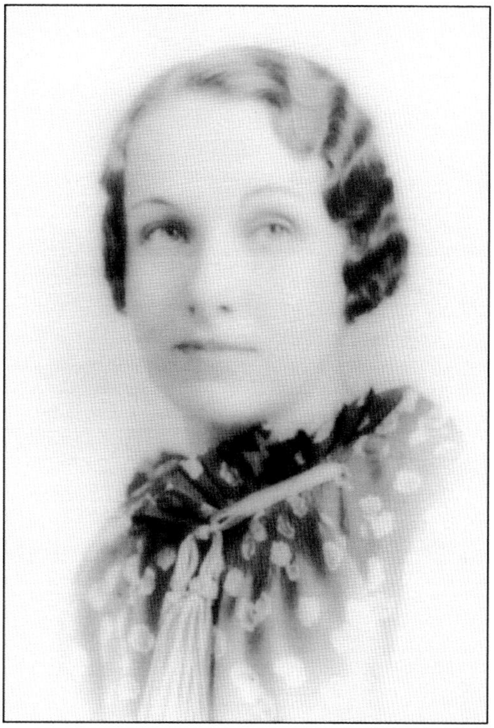

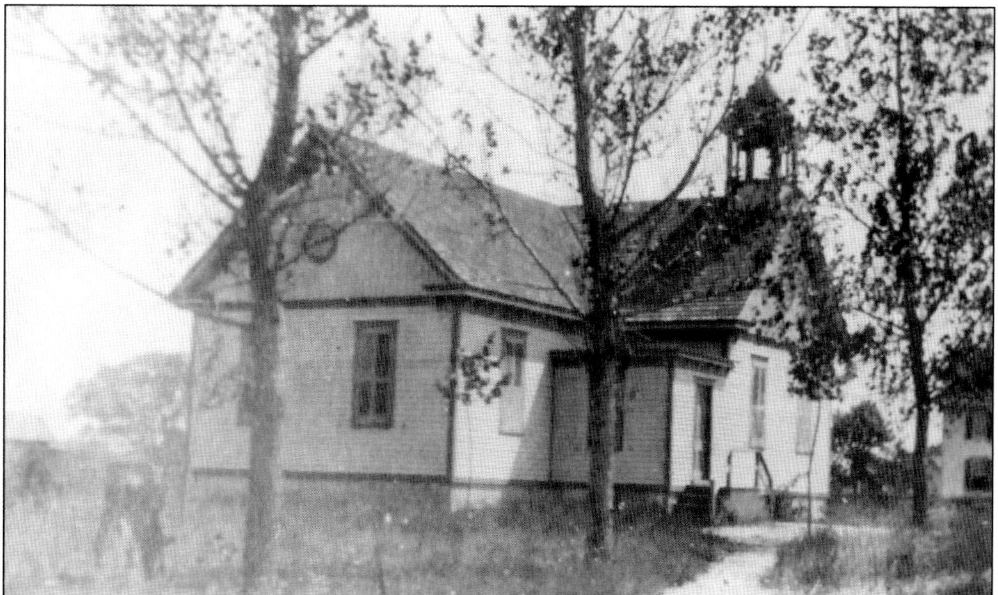

Residents of West Creek have always shown a keen interest in education. This school, the fourth one in town, was preceded by a log school, the "company school" on Church Street that was financed by local men, and the Oak Grove School. Built as a two-room school in 1888, this building on Division Street continued as the Eagleswood Township School, with a third room added, until 1968. It is now the township's municipal building. (Courtesy A.W. Kelly, Esq.)

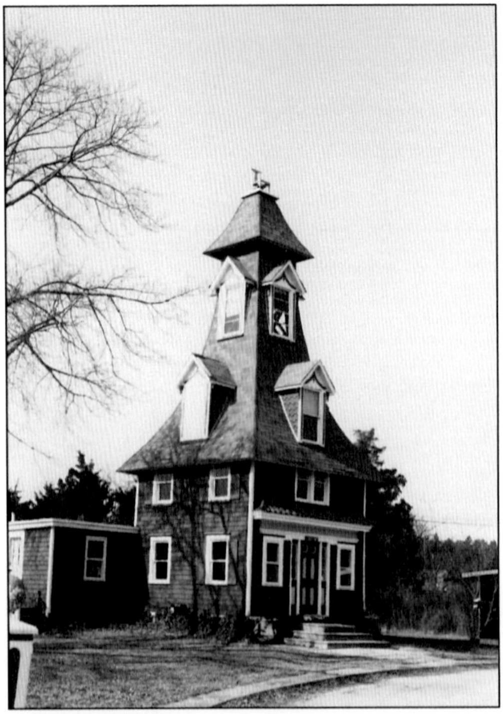

This unusual structure was originally used as a water tower on the southern end of Long Beach Island. It was moved to West Creek in pieces by boat and reassembled by Alvin Lindholm in the 1930s. A chair was placed on its top as a curiosity. Occasionally, Santa Claus sits up there at Christmas time. It is located on Route 9, north of the center of West Creek. (Courtesy EHS.)

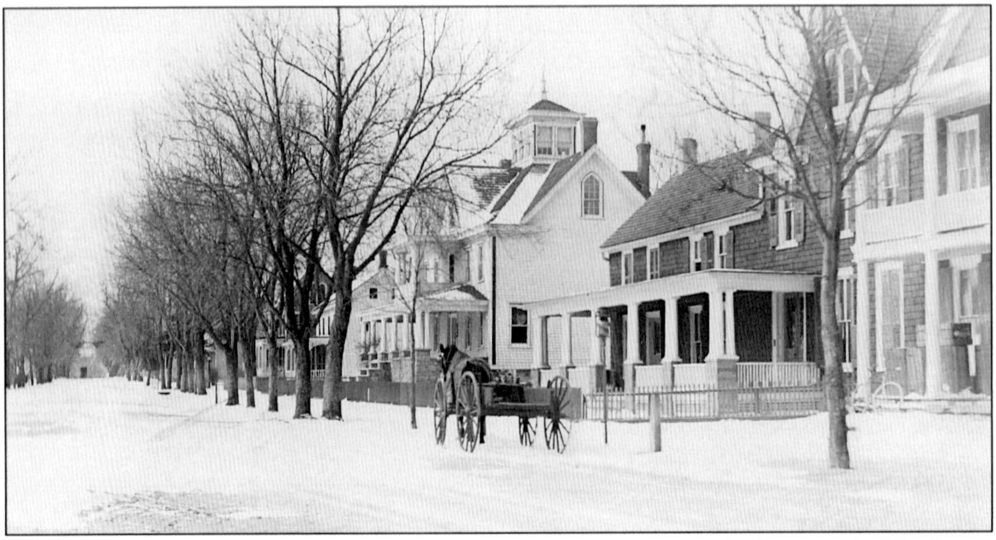

This is an 1800s view of the west side of West Creek's Main Street looking south. The house with the cupola, the home of Oscar Parker, later became apartments and then a retirement home. It was finally destroyed by fire. The home to its right is that of Joseph B. Cox, with the house that served as their store next door (far right). (Courtesy EHS.)

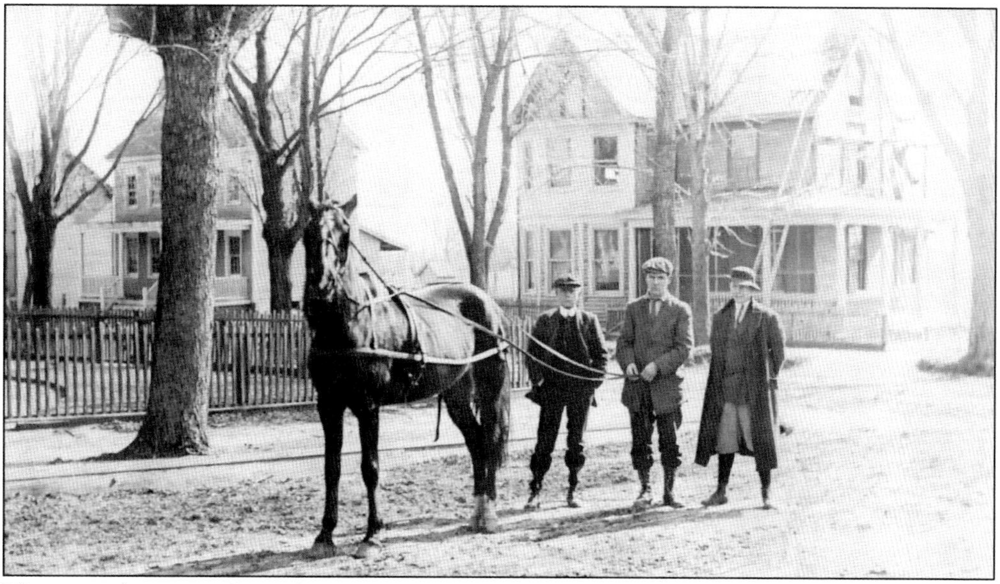

These gentlemen in the early 1900s are getting ready to hitch the horse to a buggy or wagon. The location is the east end of Thomas Avenue, with Main Street/Route 9 running left and right behind them. Note the unpaved roads, wooden curb, neat circular drive behind the picket fence, and the house behind the men either being repaired or built. (Courtesy EHS.)

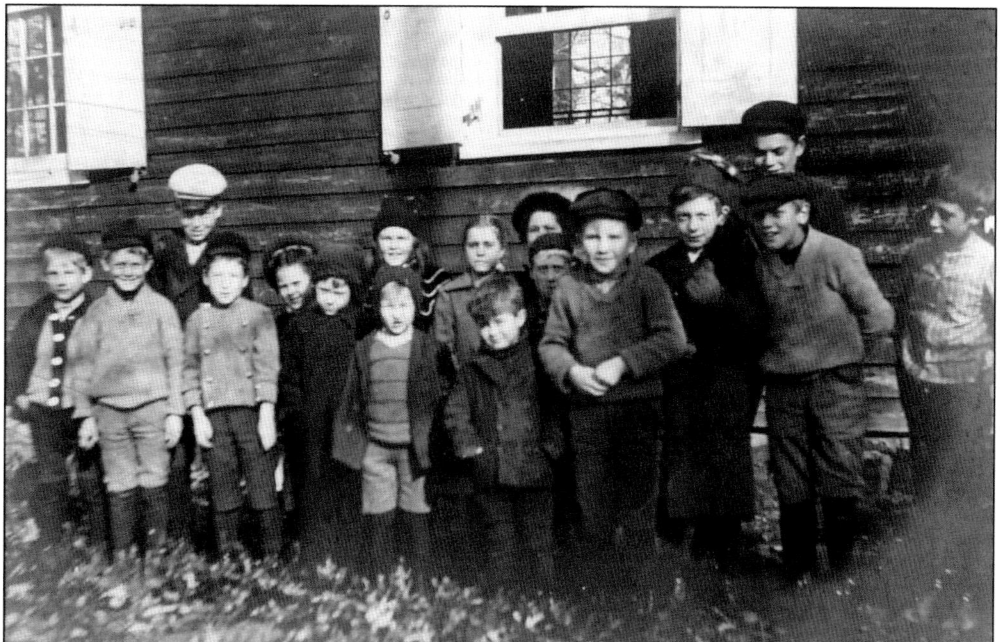

The eagerness of these children was captured on film at the school on Division Street c. 1910. They are symbols of the link between the past and the future. Their intelligence, ambition, values, and creativeness were inherited from their ancestors. Hopefully, they would find success and happiness in the service they would give to their community in the future. Most of them would remain in the area in which they were born, find themselves related to most of the people in town, marry locally, and make their living near home. (Courtesy EHS.)

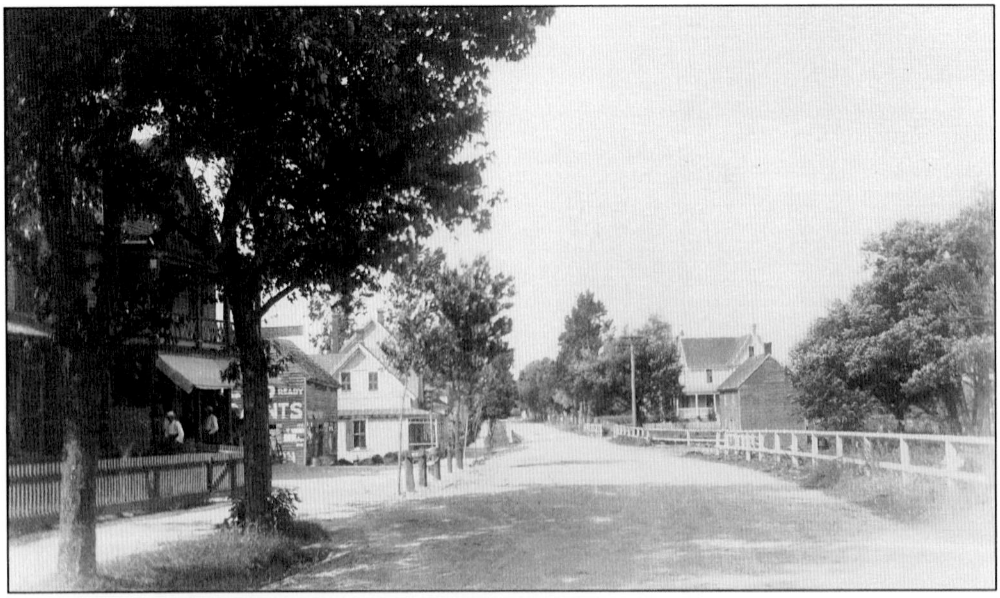

This tree-lined street of the early 1900s was West Creek's Main Street. On the left can be seen the J.B. Cox General Store. Mr. Cox was a large landowner in the late nineteenth century. His large farm extended behind a dozen Main Street homes on the right. He owned a cranberry bog that was across the road from the store, plus additional property to the north of the bog. The large house on the right with a porch was the home of Eugene and Carrie Cranmer Kelly. It was built in late 1800s. (Courtesy EHS.)

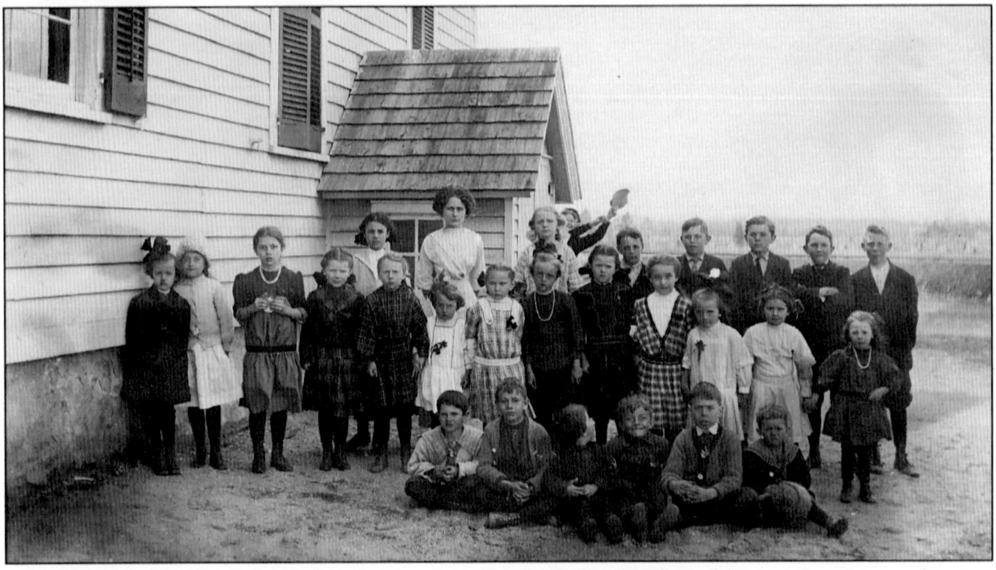

The Division Street School during the first third of the 1900s held two classes, one having grades one through four and the other grades five through eight. Emma Leigh and M. Emma Jones divided the teaching duties just prior to and following World War I. This very nicely dressed group of children includes Lester and Chester Rutter (third and fourth from the right in the back row). The teacher is identified as Miss Jones, who taught the upper grade group, although these youngsters were probably in the lower class. Note the two arms holding a ball and glove. (Courtesy EHS.)

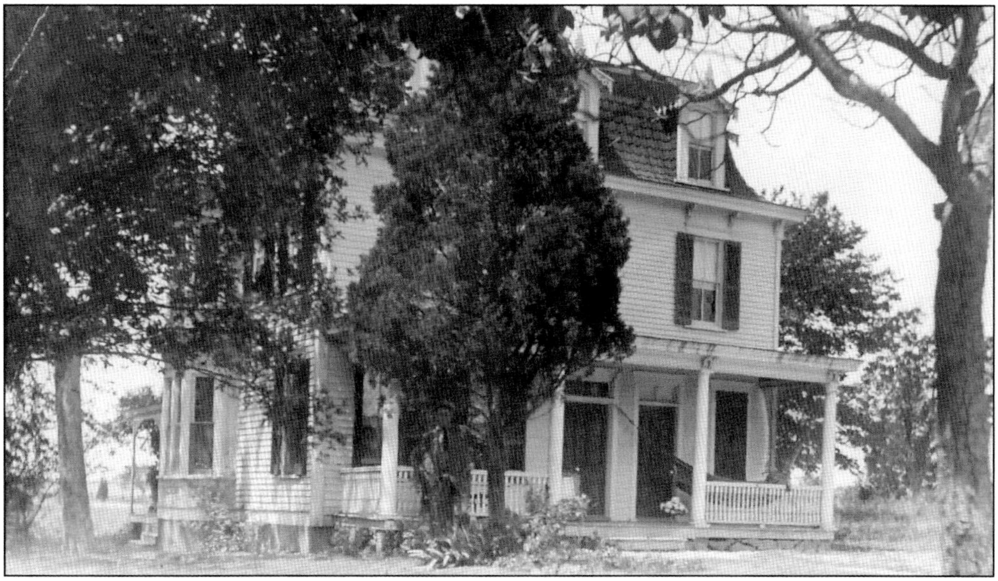

Note the mansard roof on this house on Main Street and Thomas Avenue. It was built about 1795 by Thomas W. Haywood. Thomas's son Joel added eight bedrooms in 1850 to accommodate his twelve children! This was the same Joel Haywood, who as a member of the Whig party in 1849, was responsible for getting a new County of Ocean created from the lower part of Monmouth County. The house eventually became a branch of the Ocean County Library. (Courtesy June Methot.)

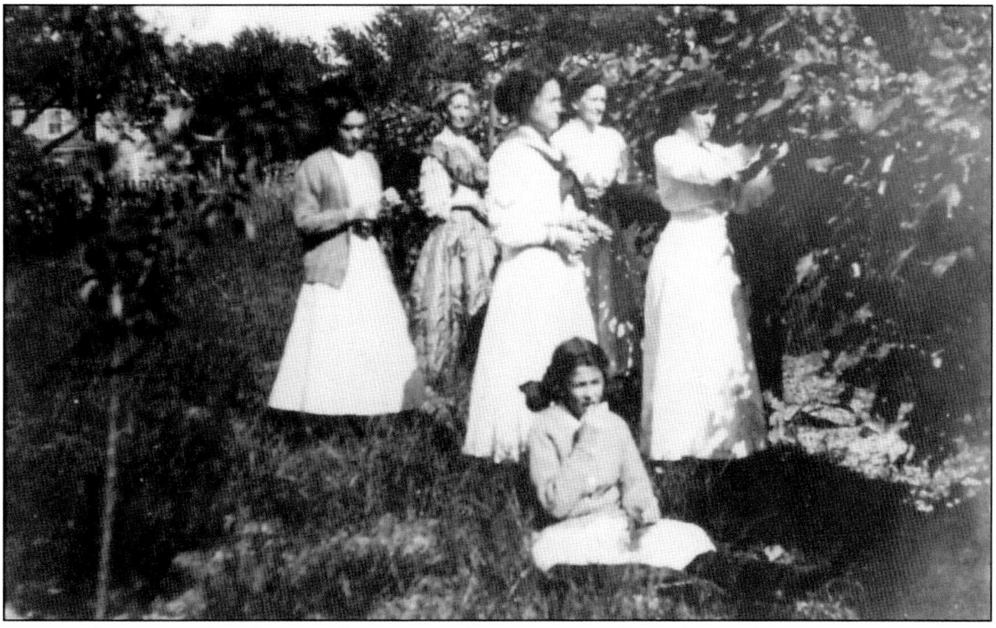

Grape arbors were found in nearly every yard in years gone by. Above, three generations check on the ripeness of the grapes in the Willits arbor. From left to right are as follows: Helen Kelly, Helena (Willits) Westcott, Nina Kelly, Rebecca (Willits) Kelly, and her daughter-in-law Annie (Haywood) Kelly. Marjorie Kelly (seated on grass) and her sisters, Helen and Nina Kelly, were daughters of Annie Kelly. (Courtesy A.W. Kelly, Esq.)

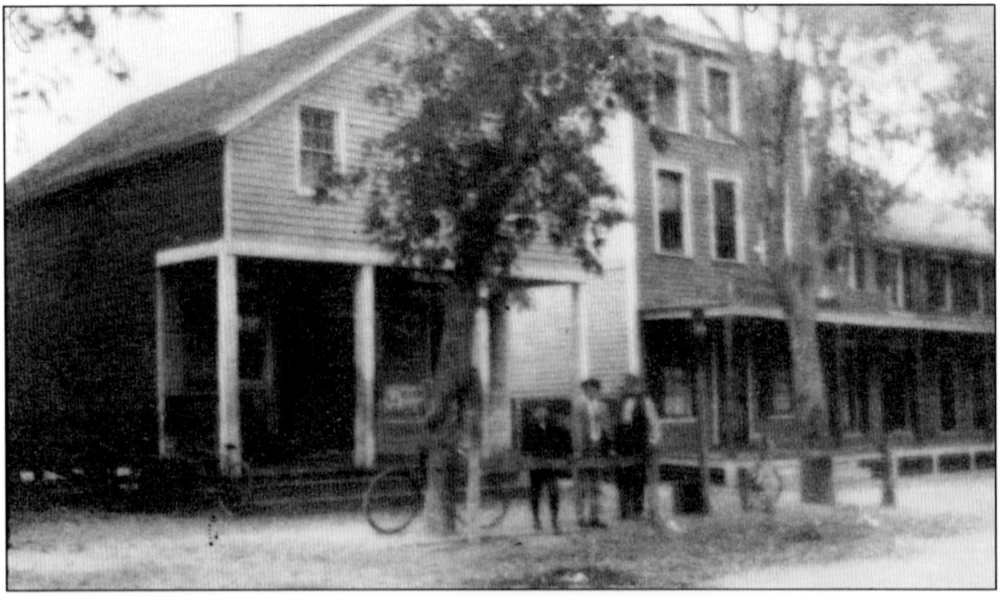

These buildings are on the west side of the Main Shore Road between Thomas Avenue and Division Street. The combination post office and general store (on the left) was first founded by John Willits and then owned by son Arthur T., by W. Homer, and by the Holloways. Beyond it is the West Creek Hotel and Bar. The hotel was probably the original Westecunk Tavern, a stagecoach stop run by Cornelius Kelly in the 1820s and later by his son William. (Courtesy EHS.)

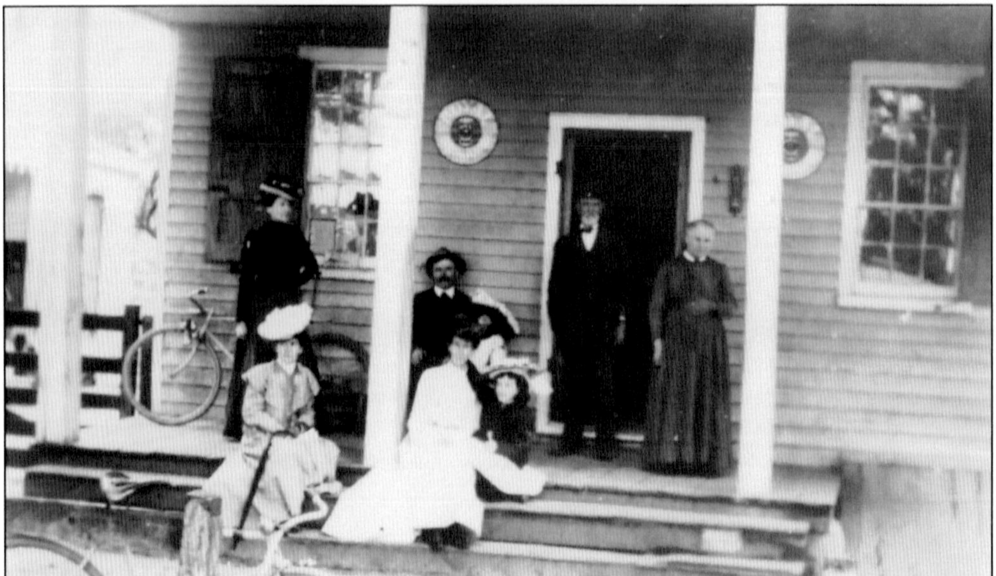

Willits' Store, founded by John Willits about 1825, stood just south of the West Creek Hotel on the Main Shore Road. In the doorway are his son Arthur "Pop" Willits, his second wife Ann Eliza Sprague, two daughters (to the left of the post), his granddaughter-in-law and two of her children, and Oliver Pharo (center). After "Pop" Willits' death in 1904, this store was purchased by the Holloways. (Courtesy A.W. Kelly, Esq.)

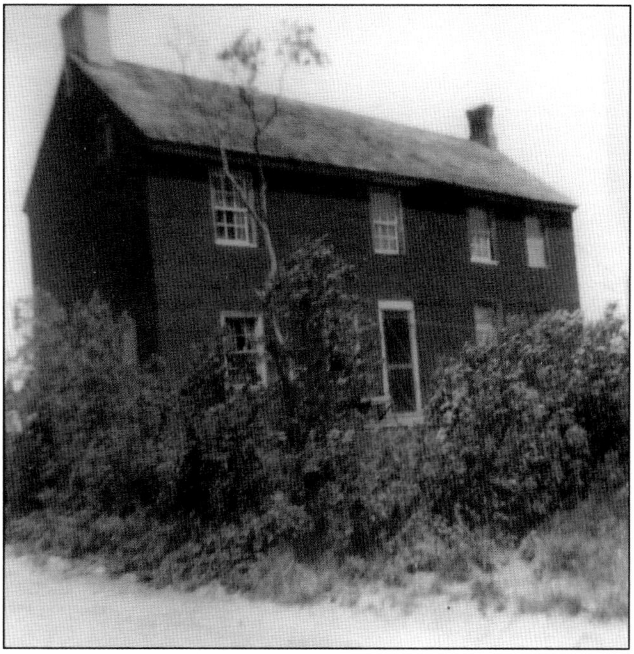

This home was built in 1705 by Gervas, or Jarvis, Pharo. He was born in England and came to America in 1678 and settled along Westecunk Creek in the early 1700s. He built and operated a sawmill nearby. A section of this house has been removed. It contained a large chimney and baking oven used by local families as a community center to bake and pass the time of day. A trapdoor is located in the floor of the house and is said to have been a place to hide in the event of privateer attacks. The house is reported to be one of the oldest in Ocean County. (Courtesy EHS.)

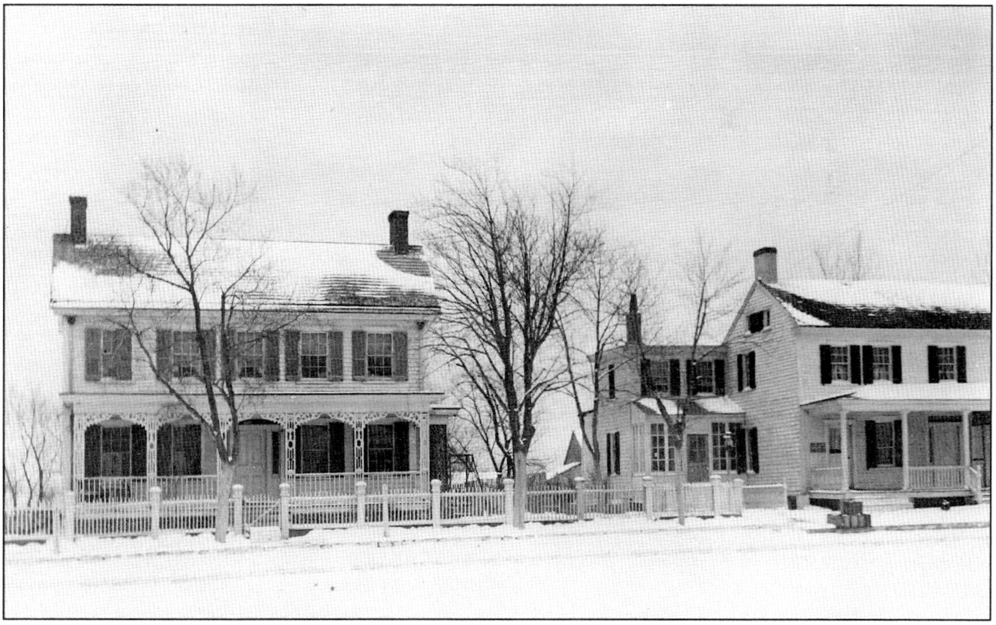

Two Shinn homes appear on the 1878 map of West Creek on the east side of Main Shore Road, a short distance south of Westecunk Creek. One belonged to E. Shinn and the other to C.L. Shinn, in whose home the post office was located. This lovely home with its beautiful wrought iron work still stands along Route 9 opposite Mill Street. (Courtesy EHS.)

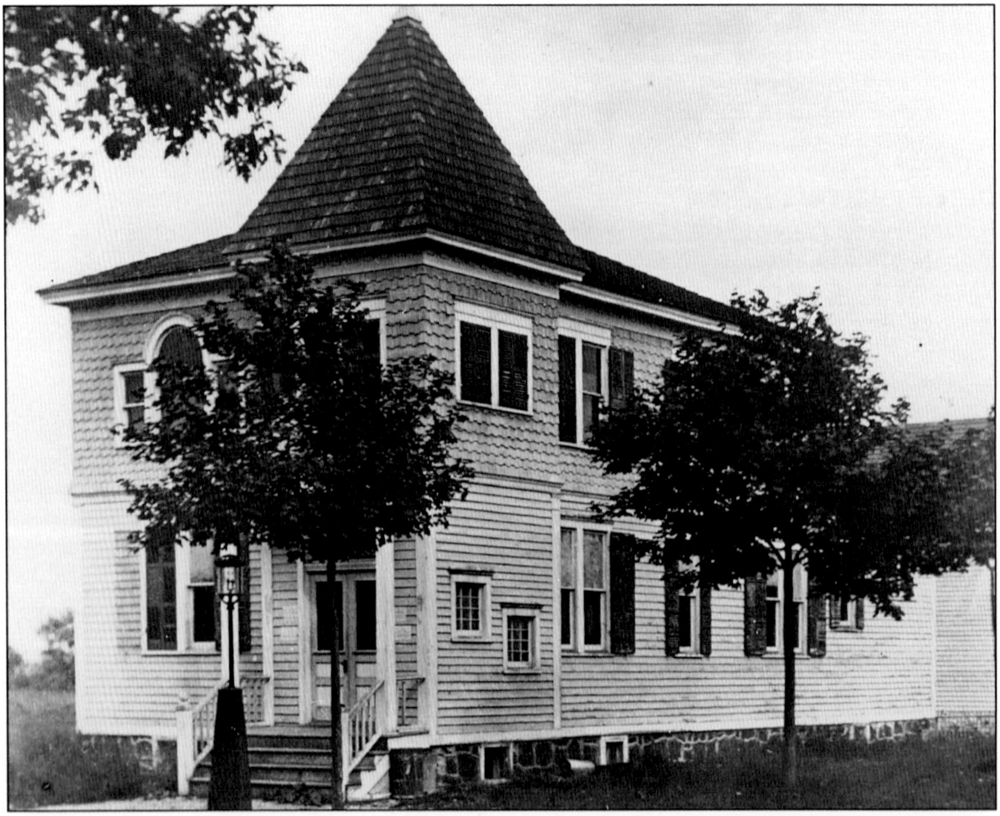

Many township functions, as well as lodge meetings of the Order of United American Mechanics (OUAM), were held in this OUAM Hall. Frank Holman, father of Stella Kelley Wegst, hand-dug the cellar of the building for $20 to pay for his daughter's birth around 1900. (Courtesy EHS.)

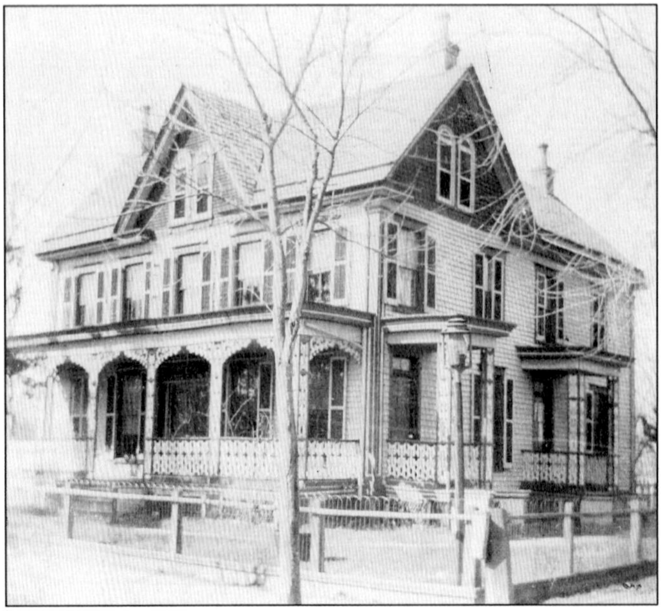

This was the home of Captain James Cranmer, who was listed as a boatman and age thirty-seven in the 1850 census. Captain Cranmer's home was built c. 1830 on the southwest corner of Main and Division Streets. Many of the original details of the home remain, as well as outbuildings. The home is now occupied by Chester Purves, the great, great-grandson of Captain Cranmer. (Courtesy EHS.)

The Tuckerton Railroad Company, which existed from 1871 to 1936 and which also operated the Pennsylvania and Beach Haven Railroad, was important to West Creek for shipping oysters, clams, and salt hay. There was a flurry of activity on Thursdays to get seafood ready for shipment to Philadelphia for weekend restaurant supply. The salt hay was used in numerous ways, including packing materials for the glass and china trade. (Courtesy EHS.)

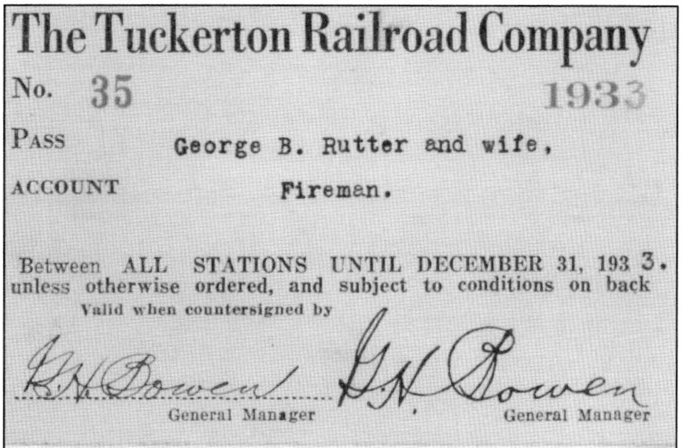

The Tuckerton Railroad Company

No. 35 1933

PASS George B. Rutter and wife,

ACCOUNT Fireman.

Between ALL STATIONS UNTIL DECEMBER 31, 1933. unless otherwise ordered, and subject to conditions on back

Valid when countersigned by

G.H. Bowen General Manager G.H. Bowen General Manager

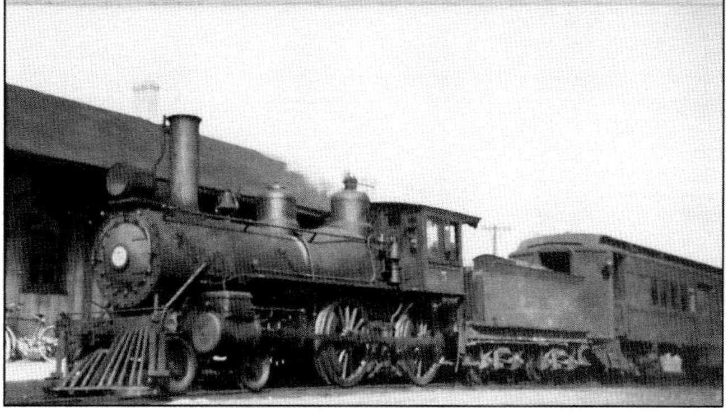

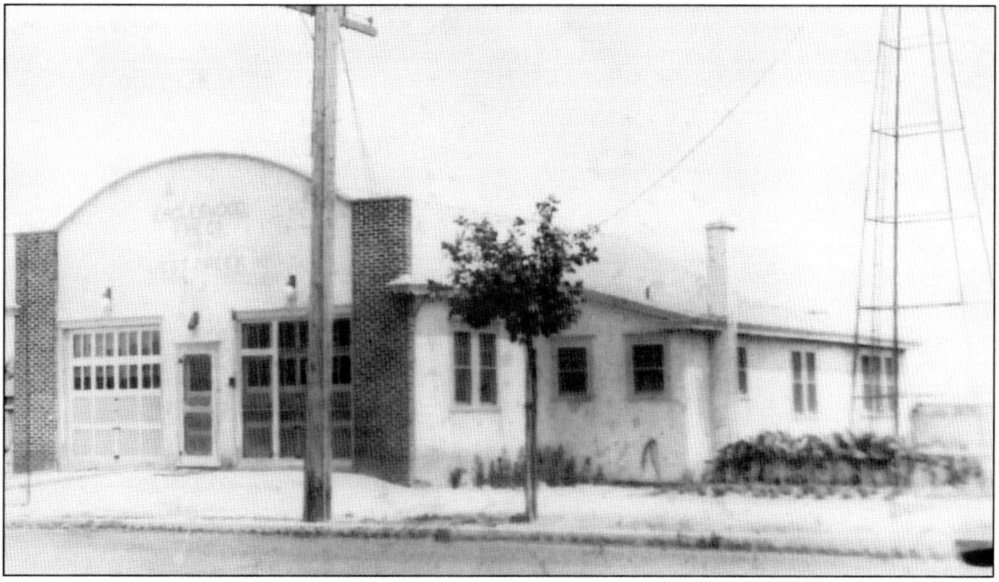

The Eagleswood Fire Company organized in 1927 and immediately ordered a motorized firetruck, although that truck wasn't delivered until a year later. That engine still appears today for special occasions and parades. The building now houses Tip's Hardware Store. The owner was Stanley H. "Tip" Seaman, the beloved politician who served the area faithfully for many years and to whom Tip Seaman Park in Tuckerton was dedicated in 1981. The Fire Company is now located on Railroad Avenue. (Courtesy EHS.)

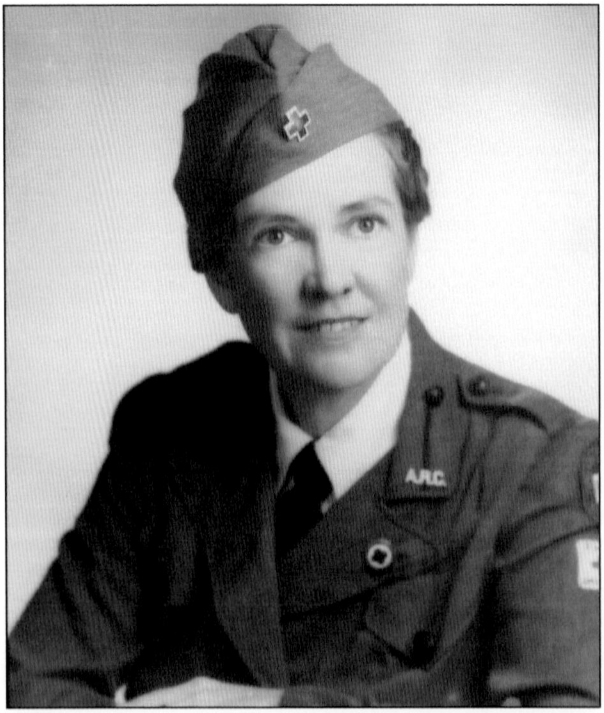

Marion Haywood Brown was active in all community organizations and was recorder of deeds at the Ocean County Clerk's office. She was the daughter of Ezra and Bella Haywood Brown and the great-granddaughter of Joel Haywood, the founding father of Ocean County and a native of West Creek. She was especially active in the American Red Cross. (Courtesy EHS.)

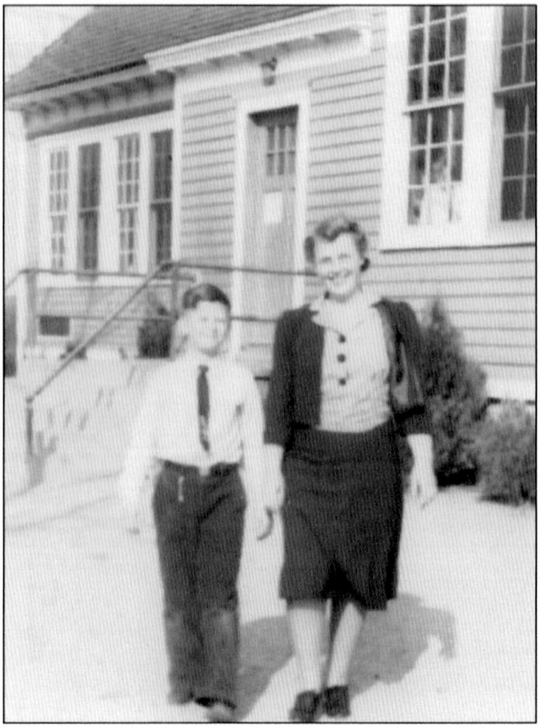

Stella Wegst, daughter of Frank and Julia Holman, is one of the oldest residents and a leading citizen of West Creek. A graduate of Tuckerton High School (1917) and Trenton Normal School (1919), she taught in Egg Harbor, Beach Haven, West Creek, and Bayville. After the death of her first husband, Chester Kelly, she married Edward Wegst. She has a son, William Kelly. Among her many accomplishments can be listed the founding of the Eaglewood Historical Society, recovery of the huge iron hammer from Stafford Forge, and documentation of the Lawrence Line. (Courtesy Stella Wegst.)

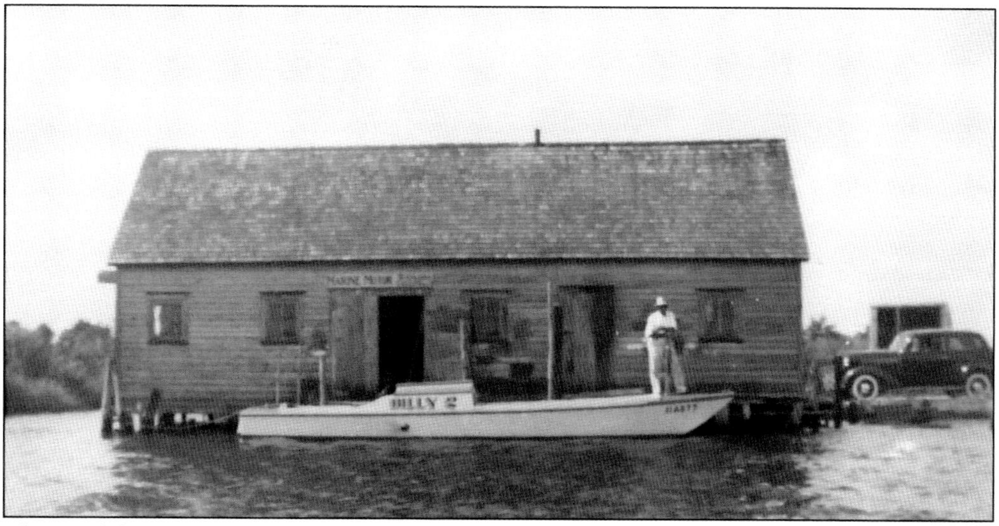

The need for a working boat that could be used for fishing, clamming, and oystering spurred Jarvis (or Gervas or Garvey) Pharo to design an all-purpose boat called a garvey. It could be towed, powered by the wind, or motorized. A simple small cabin or shelter from the wind gave adequate protection. Lots of open deck could be filled with the "catch." From the dependable work boat which plied the bay waters for generations has evolved the sleek racing craft of today. John Will Rutter stands on the bow of this garvey at a dock on Westecunk Creek. (Courtesy EHS.)

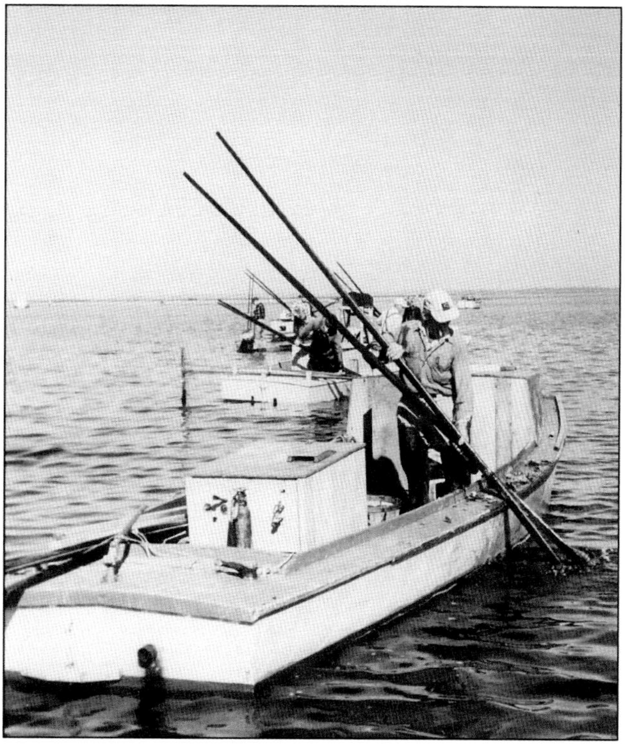

The clammer and his garvey were a common sight on the bay. He usually worked alone using long-handled tongs to dig the clams from the mud. A variety of clams was available to the tonger. There were quahogs, cherrystones, little necks, top necks, and chowder clams. (Courtesy of BBD & BM.)

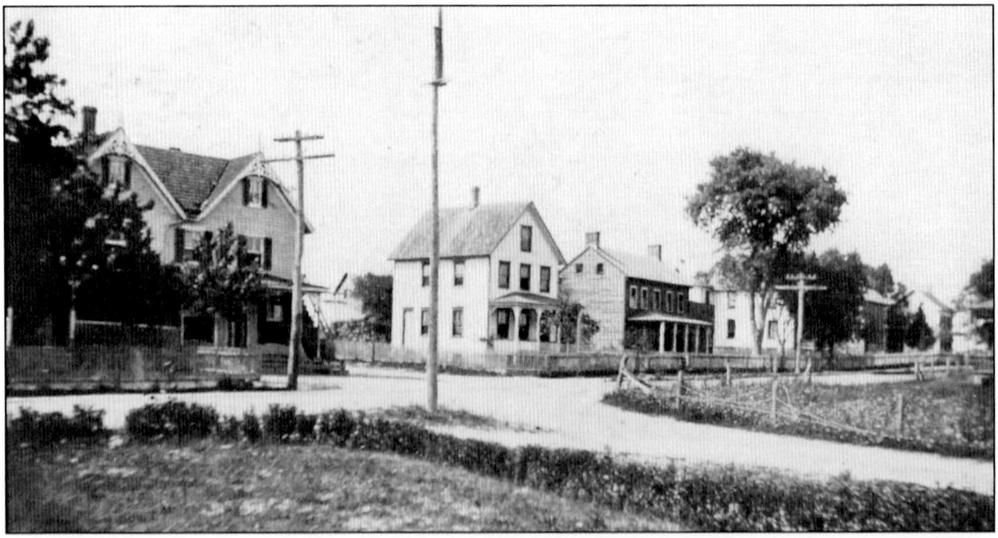

This intersection, seen *c.* 1908, is at the corners of the Main Shore Road, Walnut Street, and Dock Road. Parkertown is a small community between West Creek and Tuckerton. Its very existence is due to Parker's Run, a short stream that flows to the bay, thus providing settlers with a sheltered creek for their boats and access to the riches of the waters of the bay. Parker is one of the very old and very numerous names in this downshore area. Early families settled along Parker's Run and became true baymen. (Courtesy EHS.)

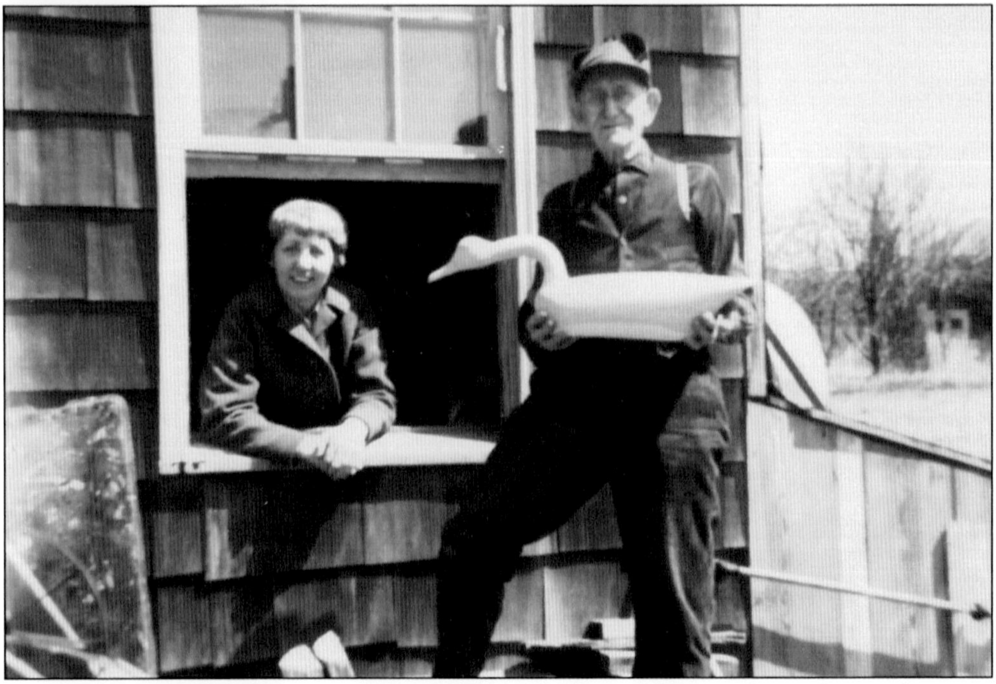

Jay C. Parker (1882–1967) was a pioneer bayman, who was born and raised in Parkertown. He was a noted decoy carver and outdoorsman. He is shown here holding an unfinished goose decoy. Parker sailed the schooners *Friar Tuck* and *Virginia* along the Atlantic seaboard. He was also a charter boat captain aboard the *Evelyn*. Parker served as Beach Haven's first lifeguard and as a cook at the Engleside Hotel. (Courtesy BBD & BM.)

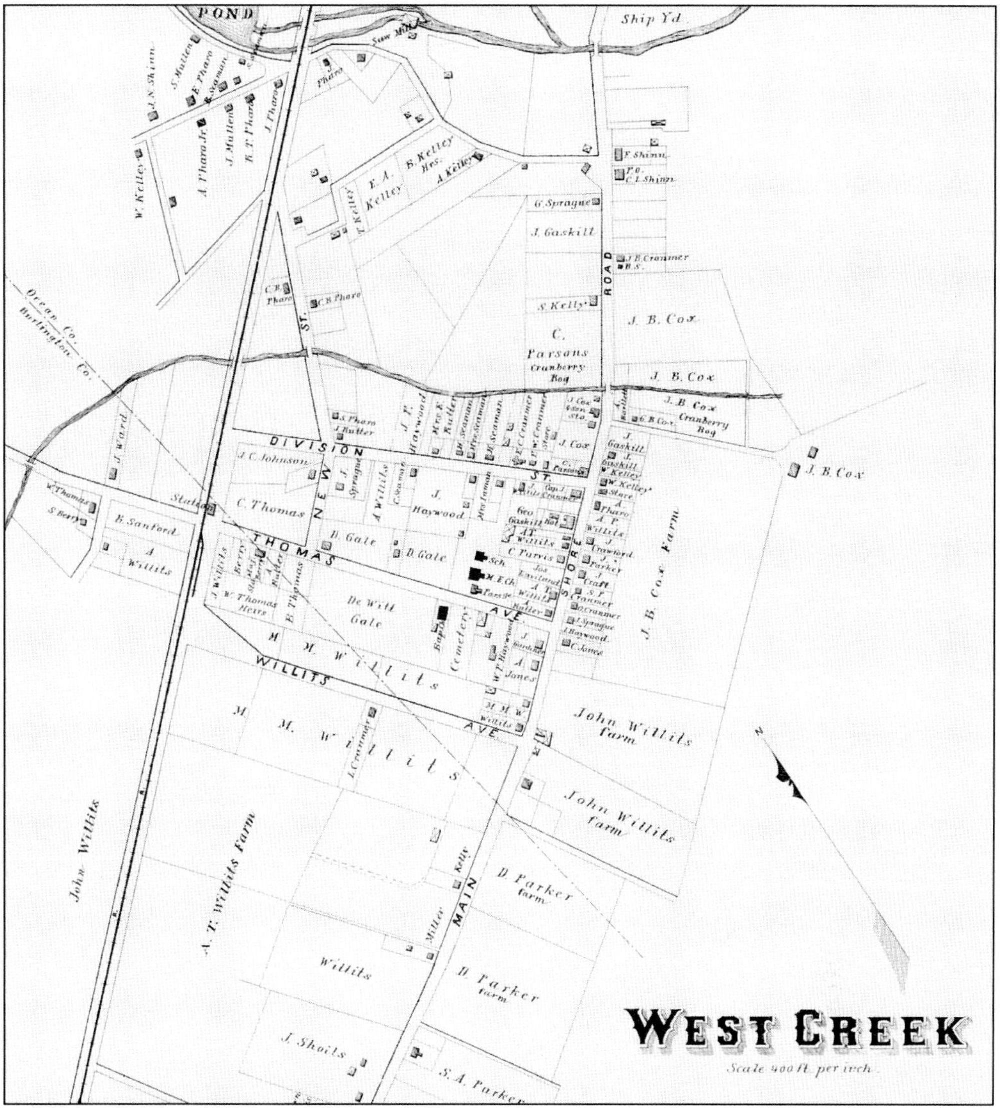

West Creek is an early Ocean County village which has retained its charm. It was part of Stafford Township in 1749 but became part of Eagleswood in 1874. It was named Westecunk from the Native American language and means "place of good meat." The principal north-south road through the village was Main Shore Road, and Route 9 follows the identical route today. A road to the east (Dock Street today but not designated on the map of 1878) just a short way south of the bridge winds along the "crik" to "The Landing" on Little Egg Harbor Bay. The area along the creek became the most important economic section of town with all the water-related businesses located there. The Tuckerton Railroad almost paralleled the Main Shore Road. Church Street today extends from Thomas Avenue to Division Street. The school shown next to the Methodist church on what is today's Church Street is the "company school," West Creek's second school. Many people had farms on the east side of Main Shore Road, even though the land was not the most productive. The farms probably extended to the edge of the marshes. The county line, which divided this area in the 1800s, existed until 1891 when Little Egg Harbor Township was transferred from Burlington County to Ocean County. (Courtesy OCHS.)

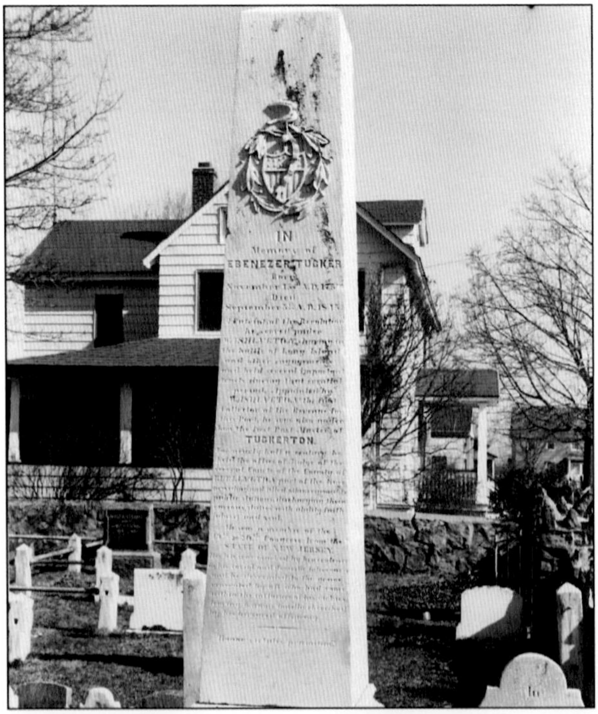

This monument honors Ebenezer Tucker (1757–1845), a leading citizen of Tuckerton. He was the town's first postmaster (a position he held for fifty-four years), collector of the port of entry (his commission was signed by George Washington), a member of Congress (1825–1829), and a freeholder for twelve years. His business ventures include the Union Hotel which he built in 1800, trade with the West Indies, shipbuilding, timber, and merchandising. His fellow citizens chose to rename Clamtown in 1798 to Tuckerton in recognition of his service. (Courtesy THS.)

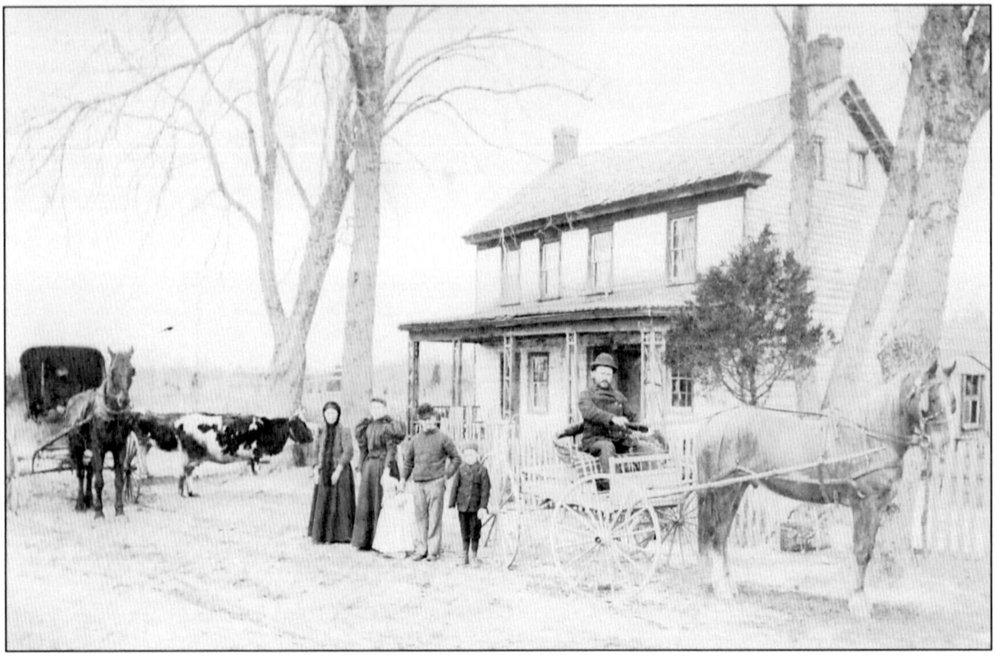

The residence of Nathan Gerber was on Nugentown Road in Tuckerton. Gerber was one of the best known merchants in the shore. He arrived here from Russia in 1882. At first he became an ordinary pack peddler. By 1886 he had opened a department store in Tuckerton, which eventually had several branches. Gerber died in 1912, but his family, consisting of his wife Rebecca and three sons, Abram, Lipman, and Louis, carried on the business for many years. (Courtesy THS.)

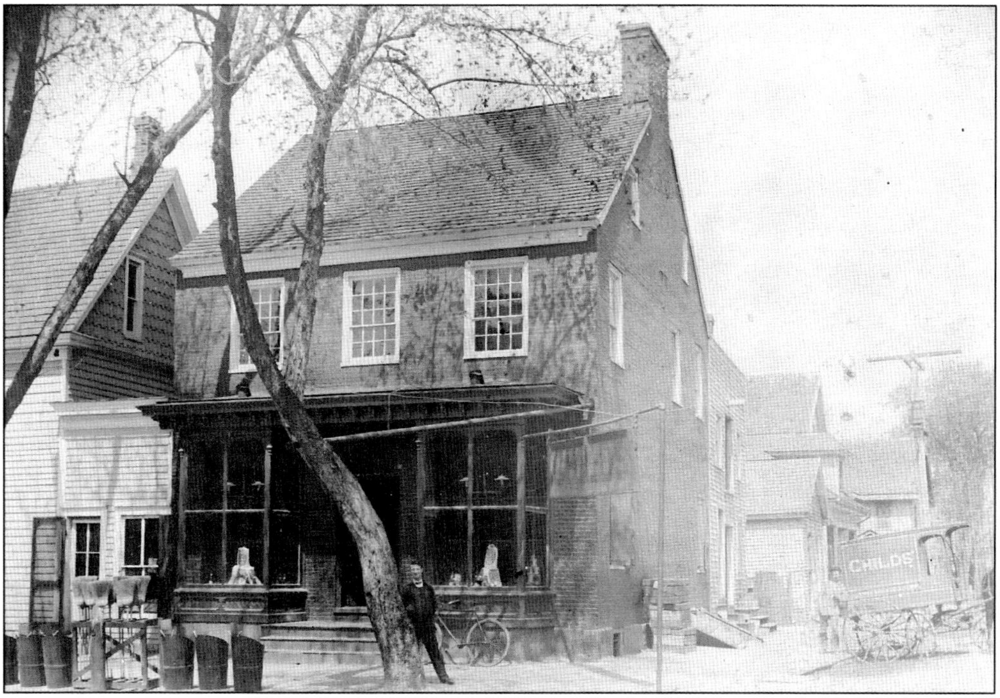

Childs's store, part of a chain of grocery stores, was located on the southwest corner of Main and Green Streets. Though we don't know the exact date for it, another in this chain was in Toms River in 1885. The American Store followed Childs's which, in turn, was followed by Morey's Meat Market. Located at the busiest intersection in Tuckerton, the building was the only remaining brick structure of the period that still has many of its original features. (Courtesy THS.)

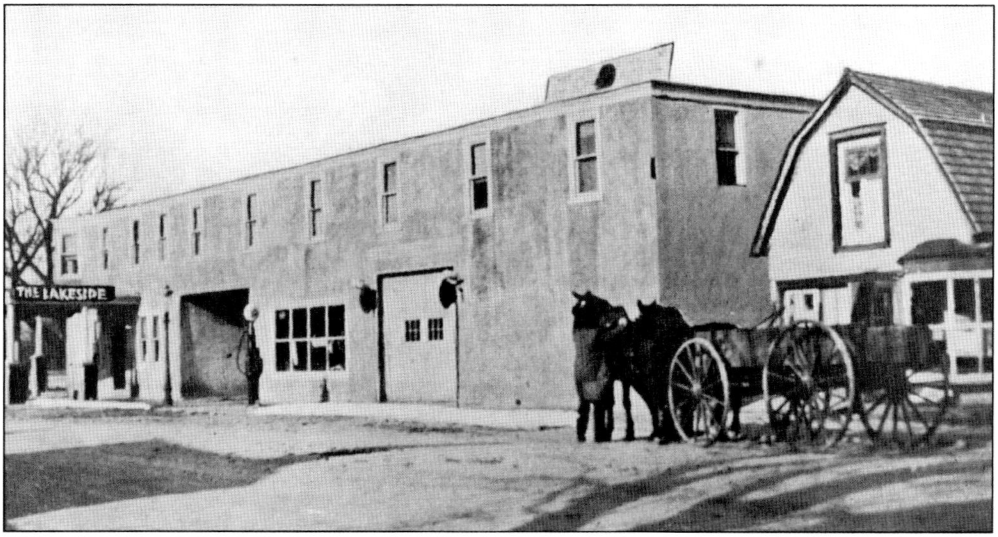

The Lakeside Hotel stood on the north side of Main Street by Lake Pohatcong. It was owned by Job Smith, the village mortician, *c.* 1920. The hotel and garage at the east end of the lake were on the site of the present Shell Service Station. A monument listing World War I veterans was at the west end of the building; it is now located in Greenwood Cemetery. (Courtesy THS.)

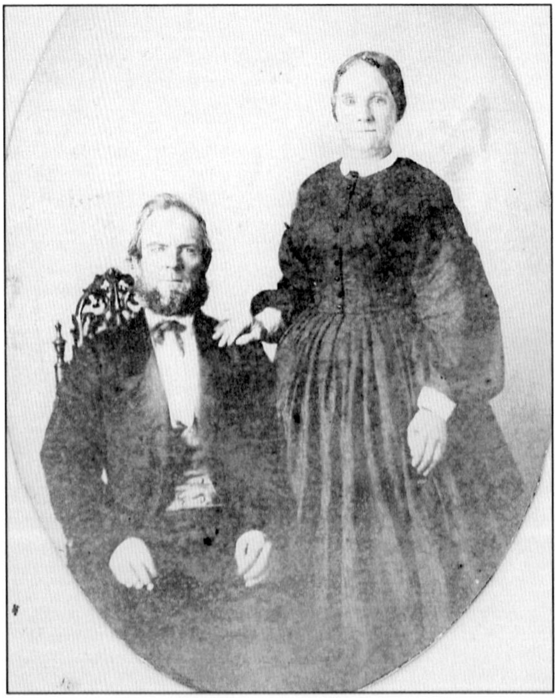

In 1840 Leah Mathis, descendant of Great John Mathis of New Gretna, married Ezra Blackman, whose ancestors (Sculls) purchased land in the area as early as 1694. Leah's father, Elihu Mathis, was a surveyor, a tax assessor, and served in the state legislature. Leah's formal education was limited, but her thirst for knowledge was never quenched. A notable achievement of hers was the publication in 1879, at age sixty-eight, of *History of Little Egg Harbor Township*, which includes a wealth of genealogical information. (Courtesy THS.)

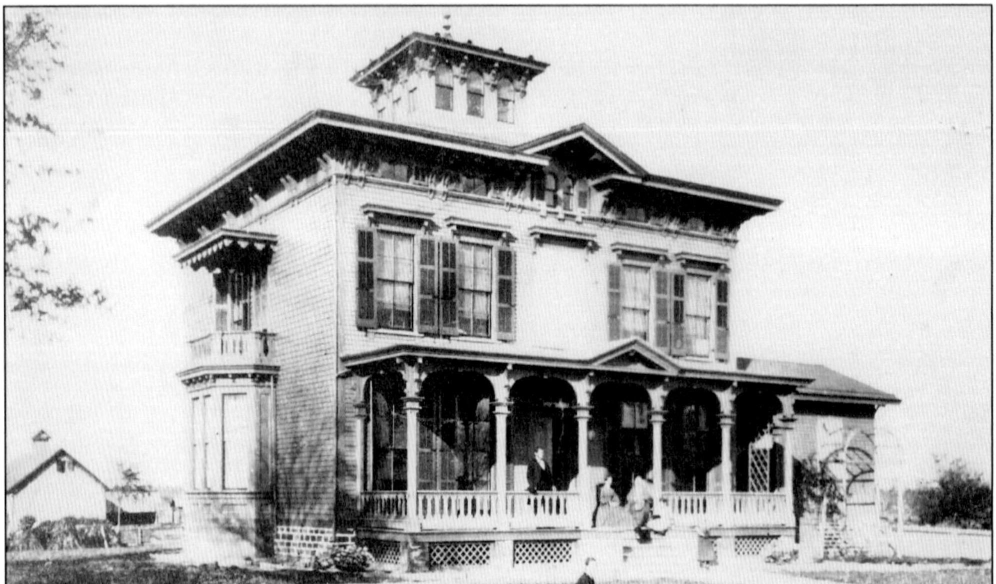

Dr. Theophilus Townsend Price, owner of this imposing residence built during the years 1867 to 1869, was a busy man on both the local and state scenes in the late 1800s. He graduated from Pennsylvania Medical College in 1853, married Elisa, the daughter of Archelaus R. Pharo, and settled in Tuckerton. He was town superintendent, postmaster, legislative member, and surgeon at the U.S. Marine Hospital in Tuckerton. He helped to secure the charter of the Tuckerton Railroad and wrote the historical narrative for the *Woolman and Rose Atlas* of 1878. (Courtesy THS.)

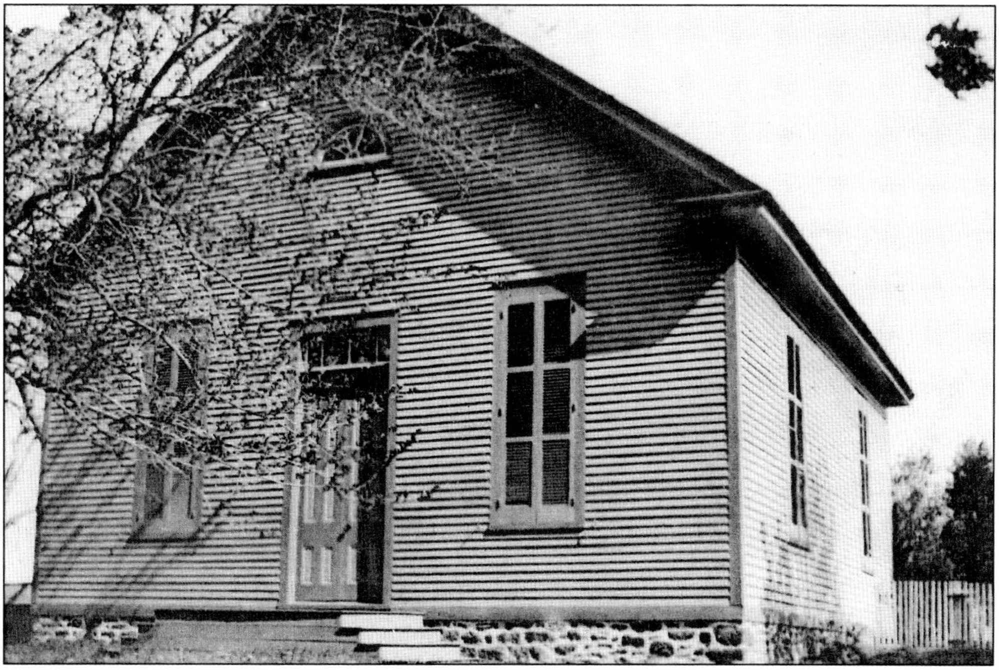

This Little Egg Harbor Meeting House, established by Edward Andrews (1704) and built (1709) on land which he donated, was the only one between Cape May and Shrewsbury. It had leaded windows, which were taken out during the Revolutionary War and hidden so as not to be confiscated for their lead. This first house was replaced in 1863. The new house was a large room with a 3-foot high partition down the center of the seats. A sliding partition was pulled down to meet the lower one to separate the men and women during business meetings and the disciplining of members. (Courtesy OCHS.)

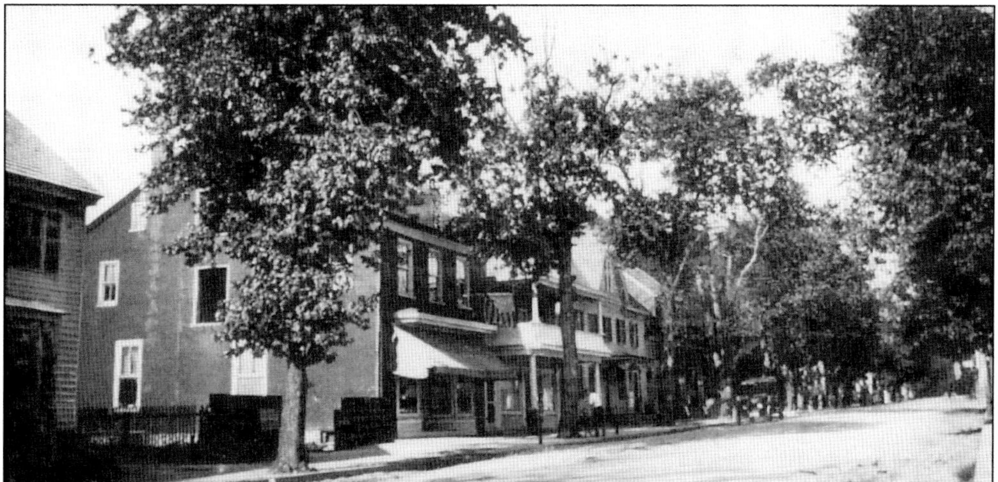

Beyond the Gerber store, which is the building with awnings, was Blackman's Ice Cream Parlor. This view is toward the Green Street intersection. After Nathan Gerber's death in 1912, his son Lipman S. Gerber assumed full control of the business. He was a graduate of the University of Pennsylvania and the Wharton School. Gerber was a director of the Tuckerton Band and a member of the board of education. (Courtesy THS.)

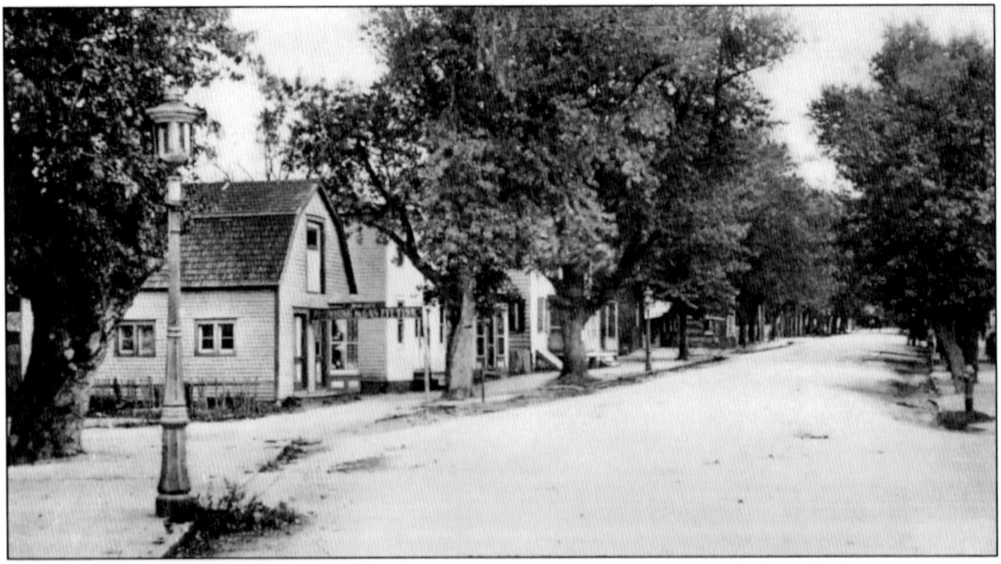

This view to the east along Main Street from the old mill was taken after 1904 when Mayor Frank Austin and council voted to introduce gas streetlights. The first of seventy-three was placed on North Green Street. The first building beyond the gas light was William Pitt's "plumbing and gas fittings" store which later became a tavern. Nathan Gerber's clothing, dry goods, and notions store was located beyond the plumbing store. He bought Timothy Pharo's store next to the alley, which led to the Quaker church. (Courtesy THS.)

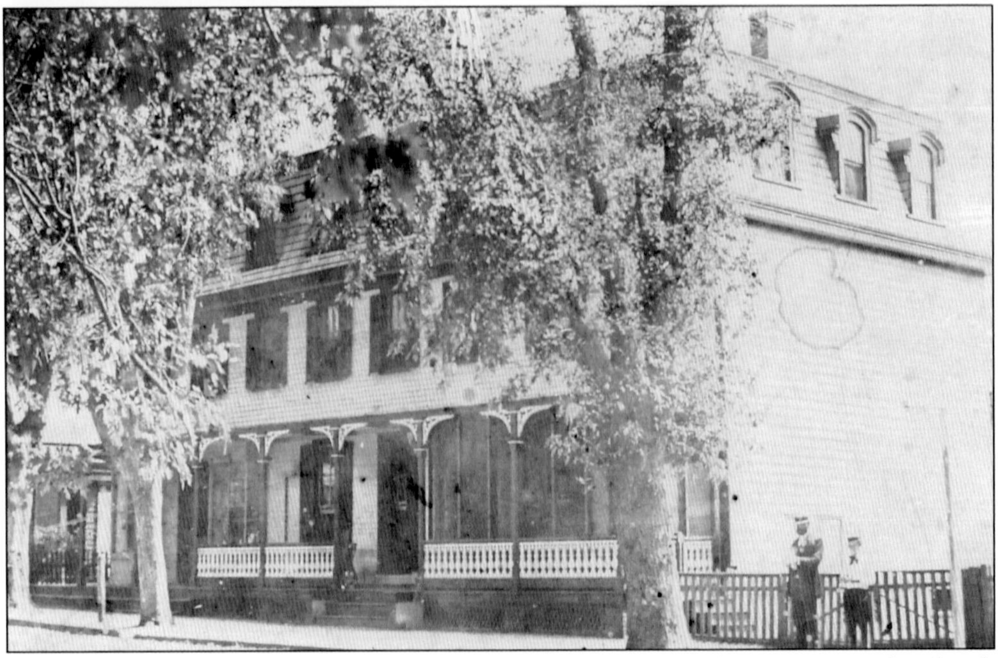

The Everett House, built in the 1870s by George Adams, was a first-class temperance hotel with a clean caterer and excellent rooms. Board was provided for transient guests by George Leek. Numerous hotels and boarding houses existed in Tuckerton in the late nineteenth century to accommodate the number of people brought to the area by railroad. The Everett House was midway between Green and Water Streets on the south side of the block. (Courtesy THS.)

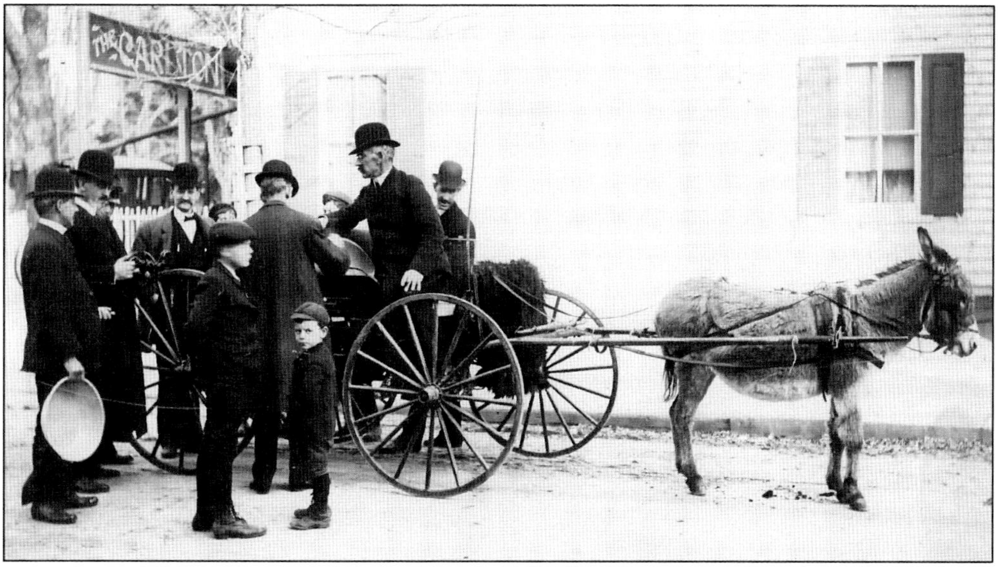

What could be of such interest in this wagon stopped in front of the Carlton Hotel? Snow covers the ground and the donkey. A warm robe has been folded and draped over the wheel. The man standing at the front of the wagon seems to be the dispenser of whatever goodies just arrived. At least two men brought large round pans in which to carry the treasure home. Men and boys look as if they've donned their Sunday best. If you have answers, please contact the authors. (Courtesy THS.)

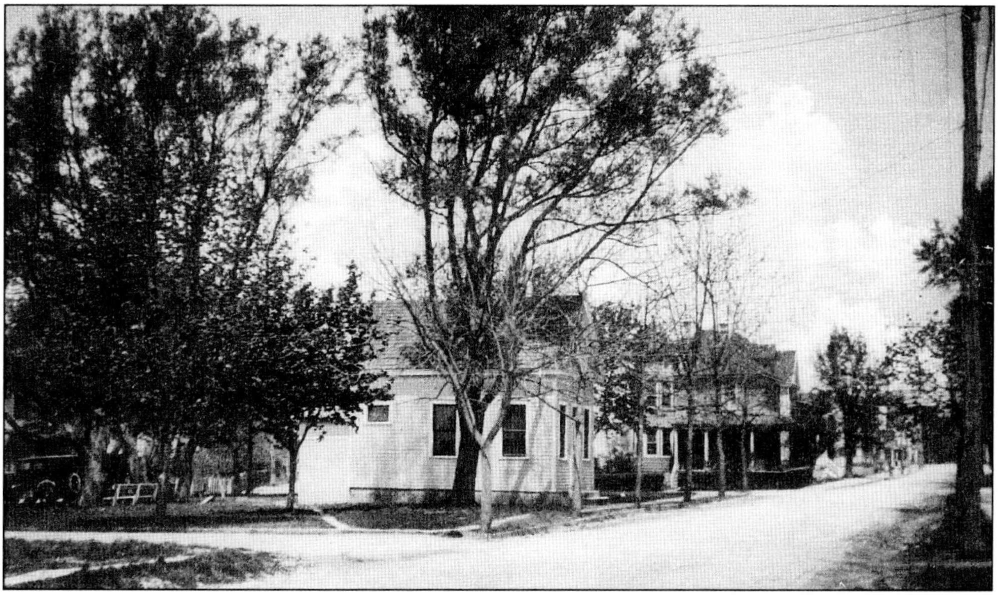

Little Egg Harbor Township was annexed by Ocean County in 1891. Ten years later the borough of Tuckerton was created. This "Little Borough Hall" was completed in September 1906 at a cost of $545, plus $112 for a two-cell attached jail. The first meeting in the building took place on October 15, 1906, and court sessions began in 1907. In 1934 a new firehouse was built, which the borough then used for meetings. This hall between Willow Landing and Green Street was in a very busy part of the community when numerous ships docked here. (Courtesy THS.)

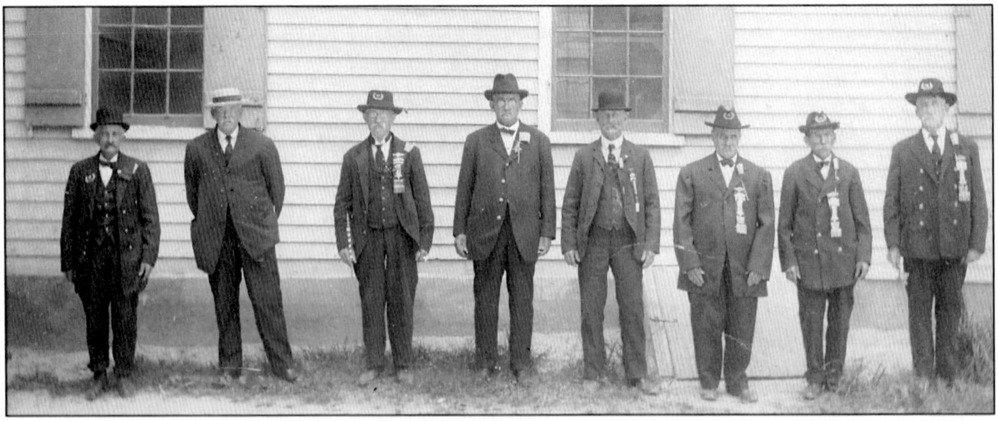

Of 135 men from Little Egg Harbor who fought in the Civil War, these eight members of Ryerson Post, No. 74, G.A.R., remained to be photographed in the early 1900s. John H. Austin and James H. Nugent, the first two enlistees from this area walked to Weymouth to enlist for three years in the 4th New Jersey Infantry, on August 17, 1861. In 1890, J.H. Austin, Q.M., urged the members to bring any old muskets they might have so they could drill for one hour before the meeting. Thomas C. Blackman (1843–1912) is fifth from the left. (Courtesy THS.)

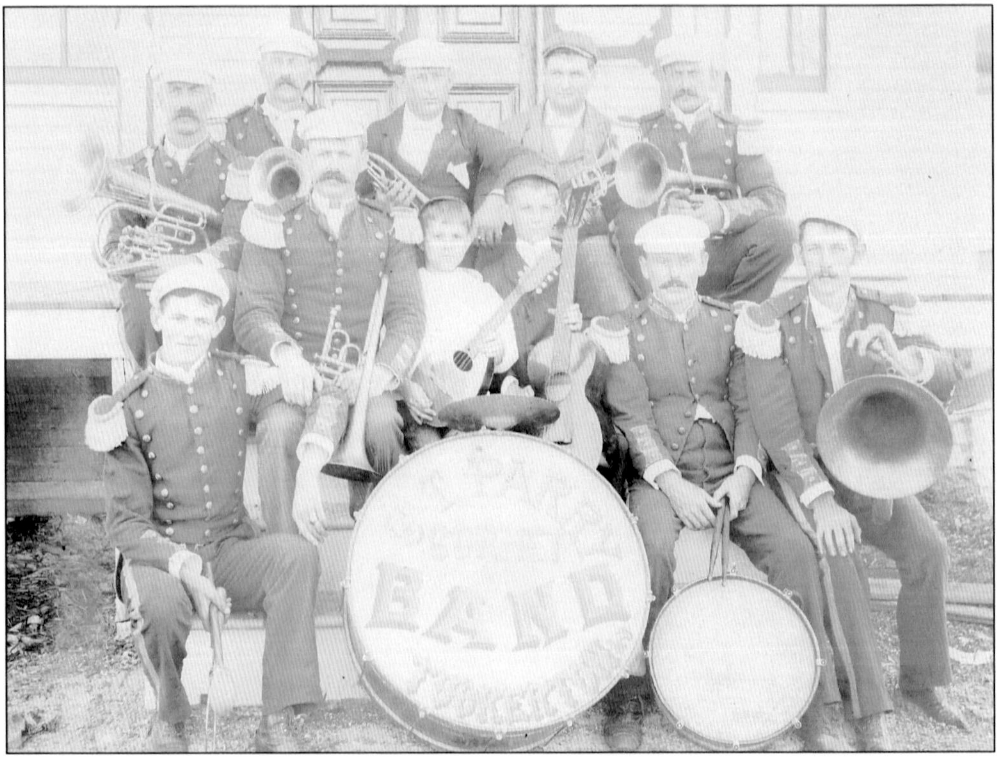

Many Tuckertonians and visitors to the area, who traveled across Little Egg Harbor Bay on the *Barclay* and *Pohatcong*, paddlewheel boats, enjoyed the music of the Charles T. Parry Band. Mr. Parry, of the Baldwin Locomotive Works, was the principal stockholder of the Tuckerton and Long Beach Improvement Association. The paddlewheelers were also used to tow barges with construction material to be used on the island. Travel by boat was the only way to reach Long Beach Island until the railroad connection from Manahawkin in 1886. (Courtesy THS.)

In 1778 Governor Livingston became alarmed by British activity in the Chestnut Neck area south of Bass River Township. Congress sent Polish Count Casimir Pulaski and his Foreign Legion to defend Little Egg Harbor. A hostage gave away Pulaski's location on the west side of Tuckerton Creek on Osborn Island, causing many of his troops to be massacred. Pulaski engaged the British, who retreated in good order and returned to New York. This monument on Radio Road tells the story of the battle. (Courtesy THS.)

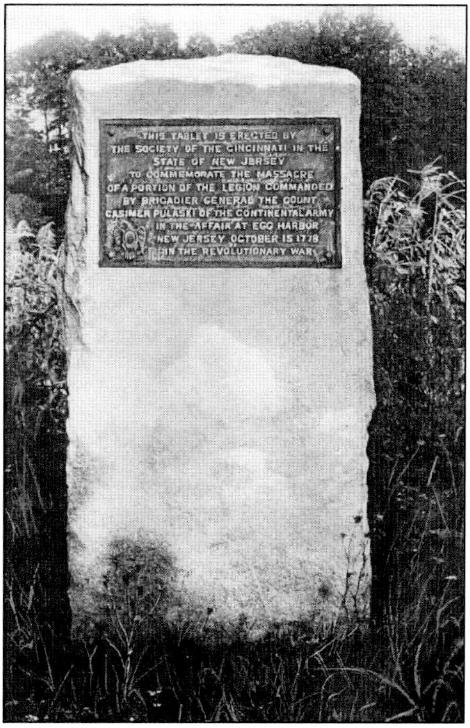

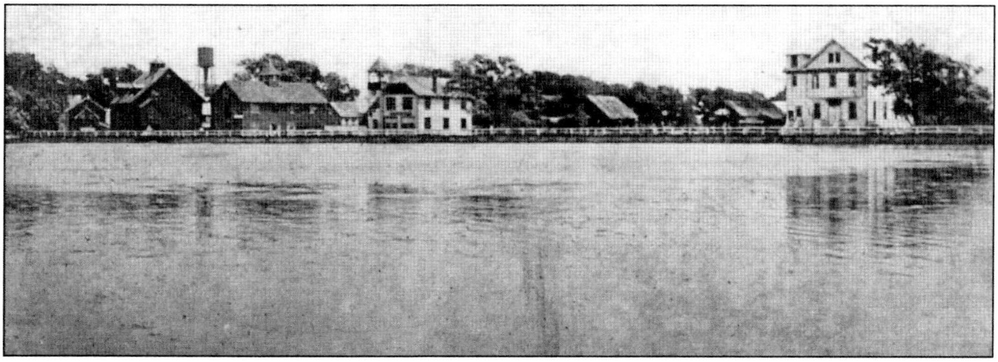

These four large buildings are, from left to right, the old mill built in 1704; the Tuckerton Manufacturing Company, owned by T. Frank Pharo, maker of window sashes; the Fire Company, built 1894; and the YMCA, 1904. They were built on the dam, which created Lake Pohatcong. Proximity to the creek was a priority in the early days because the creek was the "main highway" of the time. The YMCA building was first used for entertainment and then by the Moray Manufacturing Company, maker of army tents. Fire destroyed it in 1918, but all fifty female employees escaped. (Courtesy THS.)

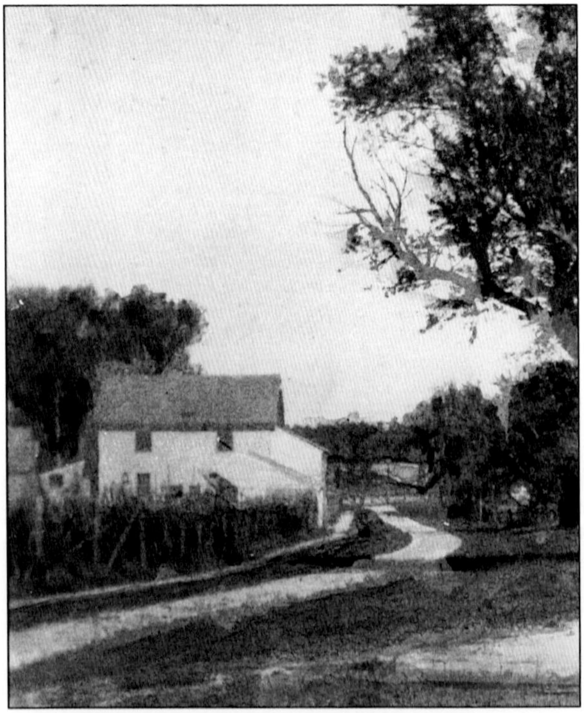

In 1812 John Hallock, a Quaker minister, bought a 278-acre farm on a site now known as the Bartlett tract. He planted castor beans and began harvesting and shipping the beans. He received two patents for bean presses and began producing castor oil. He sold half his interest in the operation to Nathan Bartlett in 1823, and in 1826, being unable to pay his debts, he filed for bankruptcy after purchasing a mill on Wading River at Harrisville. (Courtesy THS.)

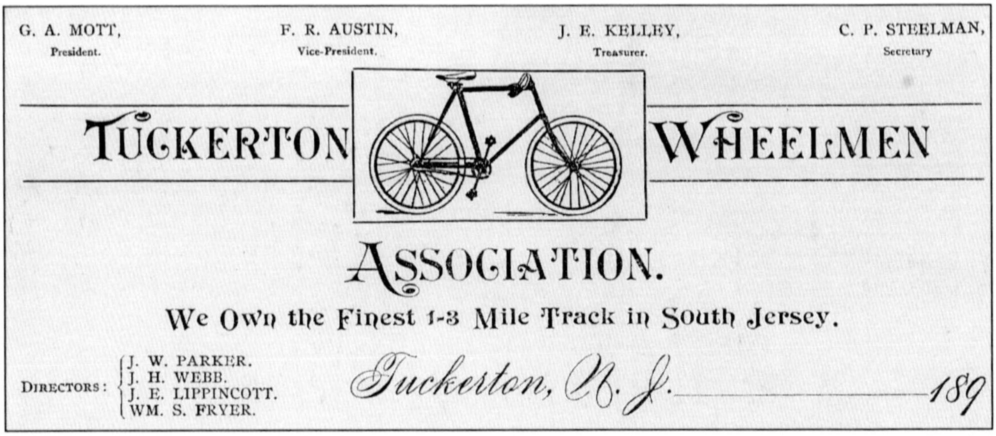

G. A. MOTT, President. F. R. AUSTIN, Vice-President. J. E. KELLEY, Treasurer. C. P. STEELMAN, Secretary

TUCKERTON WHEELMEN ASSOCIATION.

We Own the Finest 1-3 Mile Track in South Jersey.

DIRECTORS: J. W. PARKER. J. H. WEBB. J. E. LIPPINCOTT. WM. S. FRYER.

Tuckerton, N. J. ______ 189

The Tuckerton Wheelmen Association organized with thirty-two members in 1896 under the auspices of officers G.A. Mott, F.R. Austin, J.E. Kelley, and C.P. Steelman. Membership cost 50¢ and dues were 10¢ per month. Their track was near the site of the radiomarine station on E. Main Street. A race held on October 18, 1894, had six entries: Charles Conrad, Amos Birdsall, and Edward Bennett of Barnegat; Roy Austin of Tuckerton; Ashbrook Cranmer of Mayetta; and Edward Hand of Manahawkin. The 1/4-mile race was run in five heats. Conrad won the race and the gold medal. (Courtesy THS.)

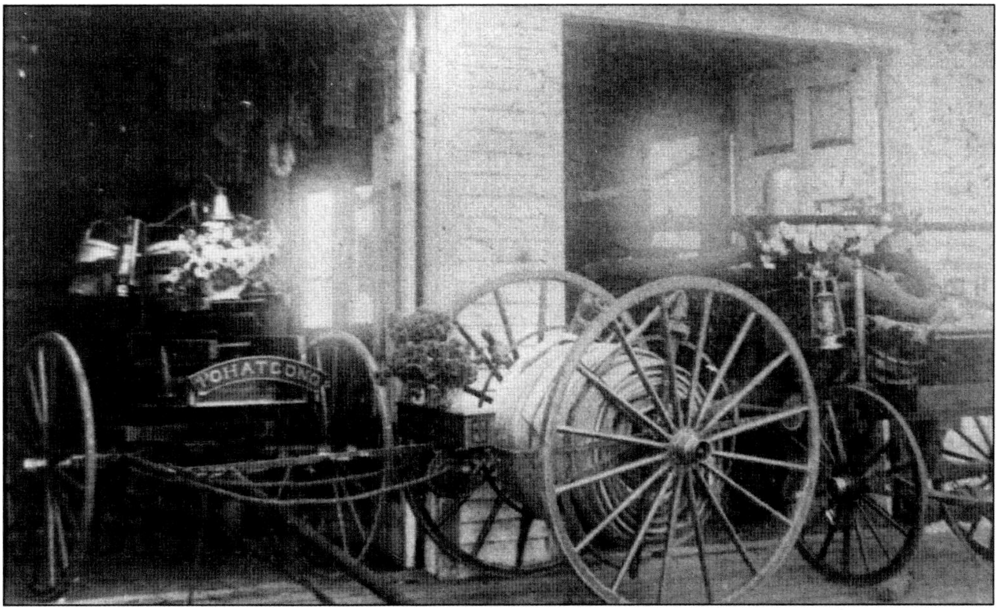

The Tuckerton Fire Company No. 1 was organized in 1894 when fires were fought with bucket brigades. They "modernized" in 1899 with the purchase of a large chemical truck, which was used until 1915. Thomas A. Mathis was instrumental in obtaining a 1,400-pound bell and a hose unit. The Thomas A. Mathis Hose Company, as it was renamed, elected John C. Price (president), William C. Sawyer (vice president), Job Smith (secretary), C.M. Berry (financial secretary), and F.R. Austin (treasurer). The fire chief was T. Frank Pharo. (Courtesy THS.)

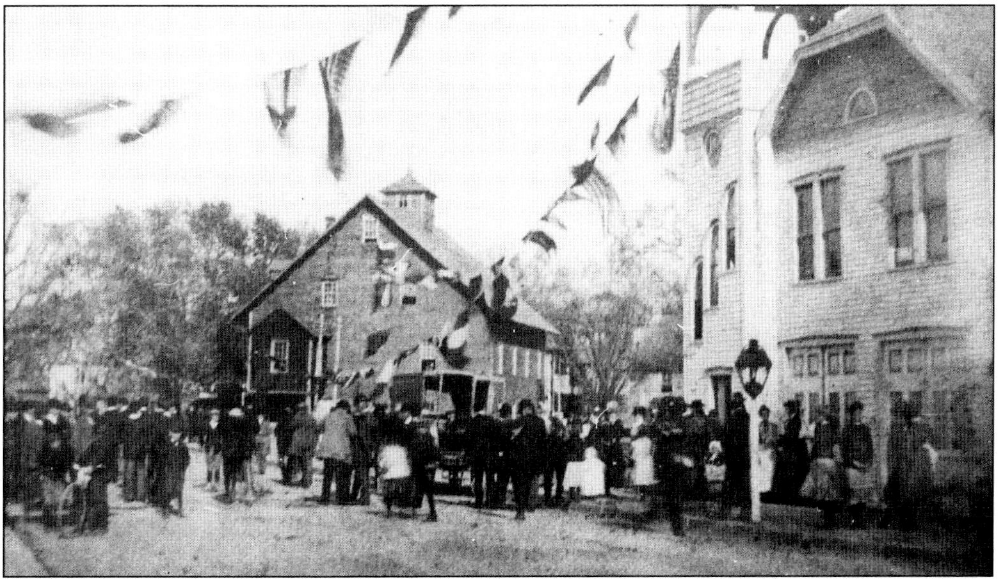

This is an interesting but puzzling photograph. The gas lights date it after 1904. The flags tell us it was a festive day. The crowds of people imply that it was a holiday or some very special occasion. Gentlemen are in suits, but women and children are not wearing coats, so it was a warm-weather event. The crowd has its attention focused to the west along the Main Shore Road. The old mill stands in the center and to the rear, a witness to this exciting event. What was going on? (Courtesy THS.)

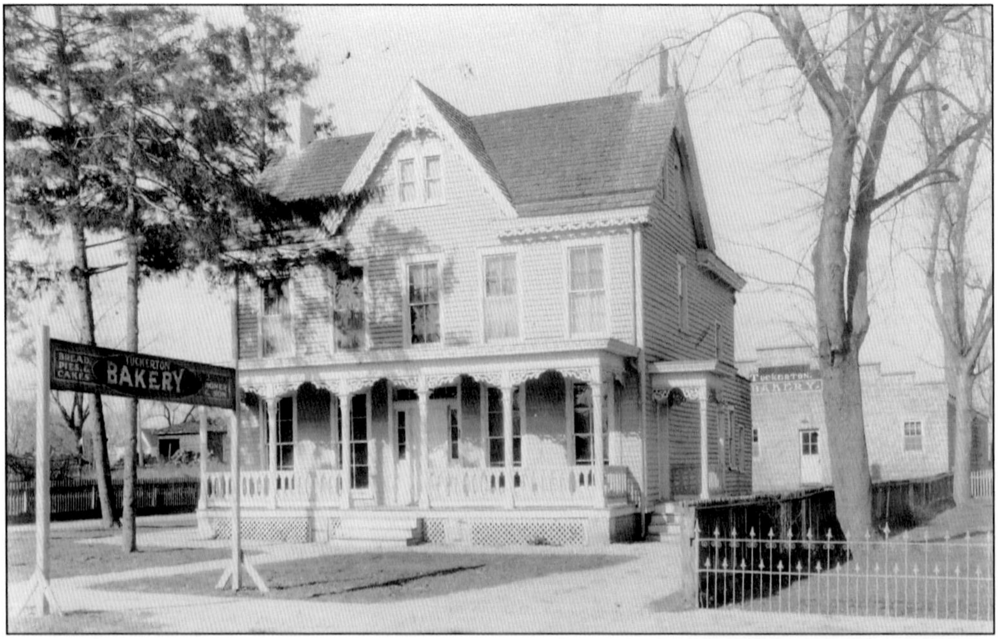

The owners of this Victorian house on East Main Street operated a bakery in a building behind the house. Howard J. Smith was the proprietor at the time of the 1910 census. The sign in front of the house indicates that Honer (probably Julius) and Son owned the business when the photo was taken. (Courtesy THS.)

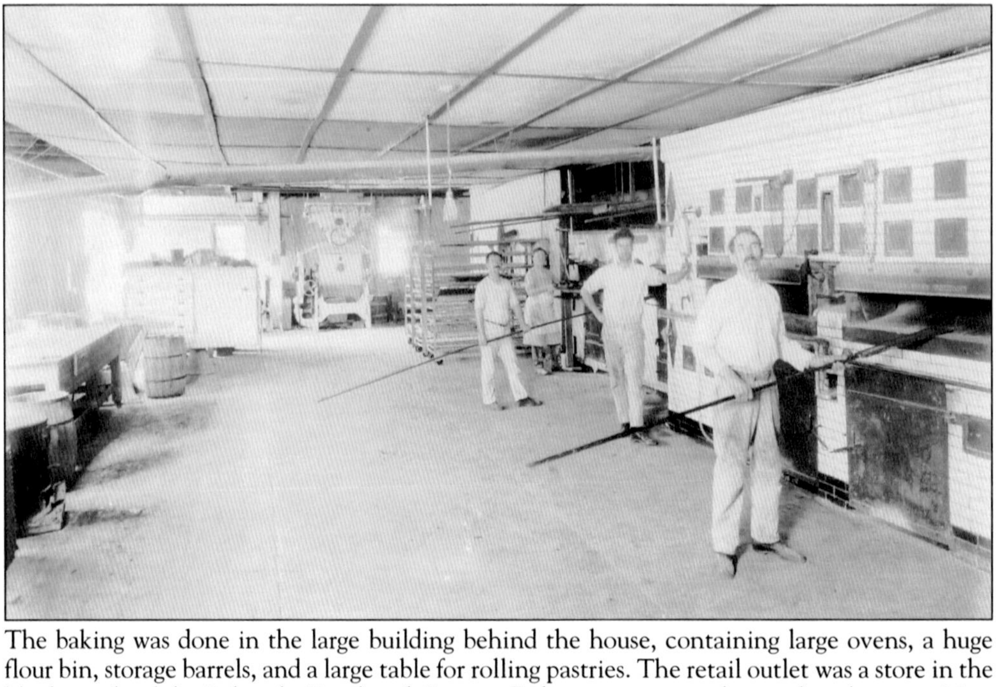

The baking was done in the large building behind the house, containing large ovens, a huge flour bin, storage barrels, and a large table for rolling pastries. The retail outlet was a store in the block north of the Lakeside Hotel and Garage. Deliveries were made anyplace between New Gretna and West Creek. According to the 1905 Tuckerton census, William W. Cranmer was a driver and Benjamin Ridgway was a baker. (Courtesy THS.)

The Tuckerton Methodist Episcopal Church began on February 4, 1797, when a certificate of incorporation for a chapel was issued. It evolved eventually into this beautiful Colonial-style structure with a slate-covered steeple, town clock, bell, stained-glass windows, and pipe organ. On May 7, 1979, a wind-whipped fire destroyed this church. On February 3, 1980, ground was broken for a new church, and on May 25, 1980, the first service was held. It was debt-free due to the sacrifice and efforts of many people. (Courtesy THS.)

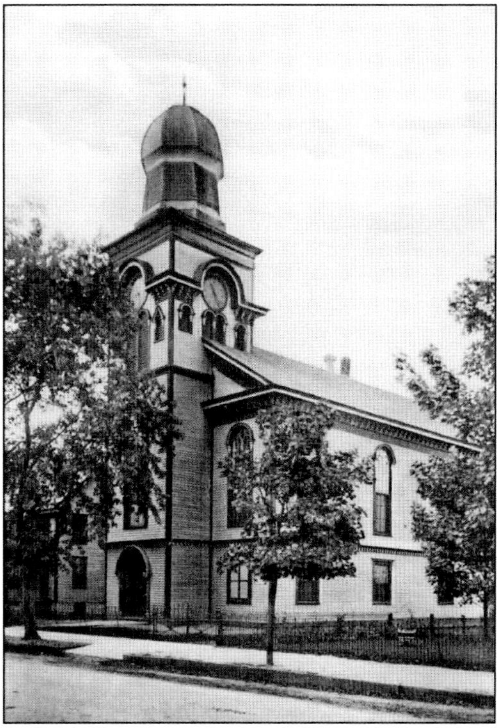

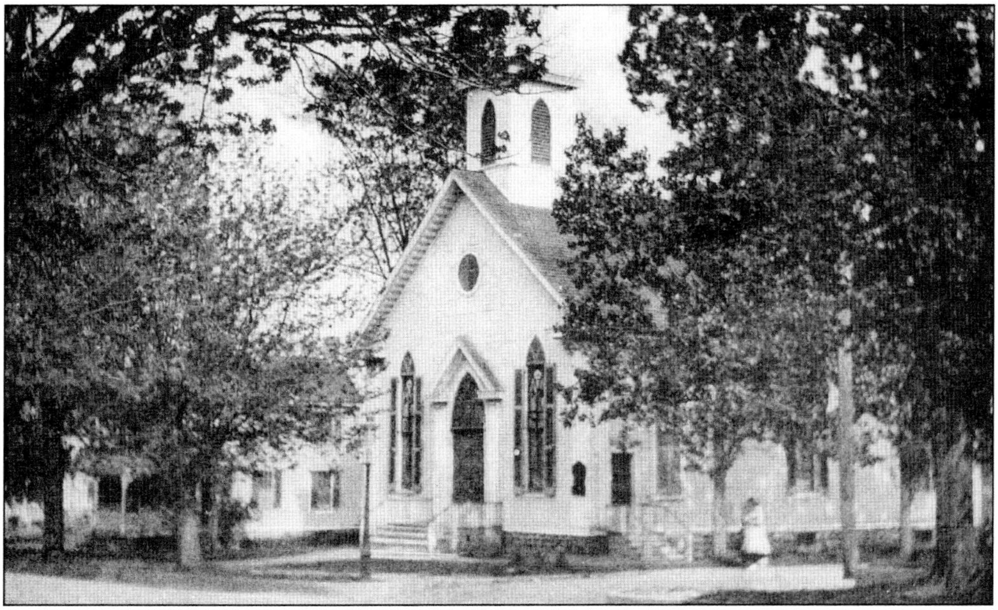

The First Presbyterian Church of Tuckerton was organized in the fall of 1843. Services were held in the Good Templars Hall until 1860, when a lot was purchased from Dr. T.T. Price. A church building was completed the next year and dedicated by the Reverend Samuel Miller. The frame structure, located at the corner of Main and Marine Streets, was built at a cost of $3,700. The original members were Mr. Joseph B. Sapp; Mr. George A. Sawyer; and elders, Mrs. Sarah Darby, Mrs. Mary Adams, and Mrs. Ann Mapps. (Courtesy THS.)

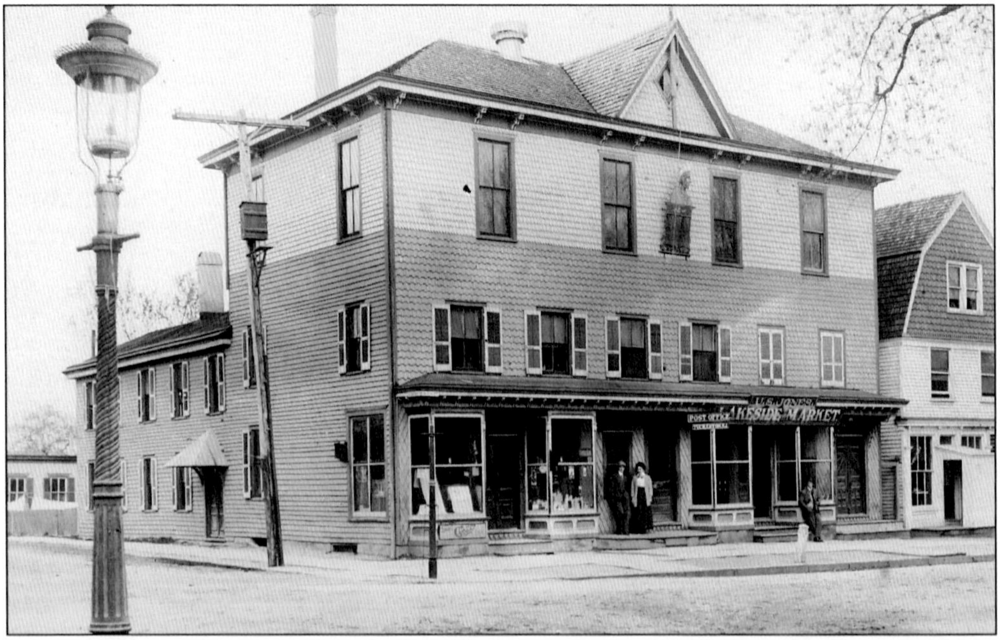

The Pohatcong Building was constructed in 1894 on the southwest corner of Main and Green Streets by the Pohatcong Tribe #61, Imp'd. Order of the Red Men. They met on the upper floor and rented the lower one, which was used as a pharmacy, meat market, post office, and by Nathan Gerber for clothing and dry goods at different times. A figure of a Native American projected from the face of the upper part of the building. Notice of a meeting in 1896 read, "Meets every Saturday sleep, 7th Run, 30th Breath. In Red Men's Wigwam." (Courtesy THS.)

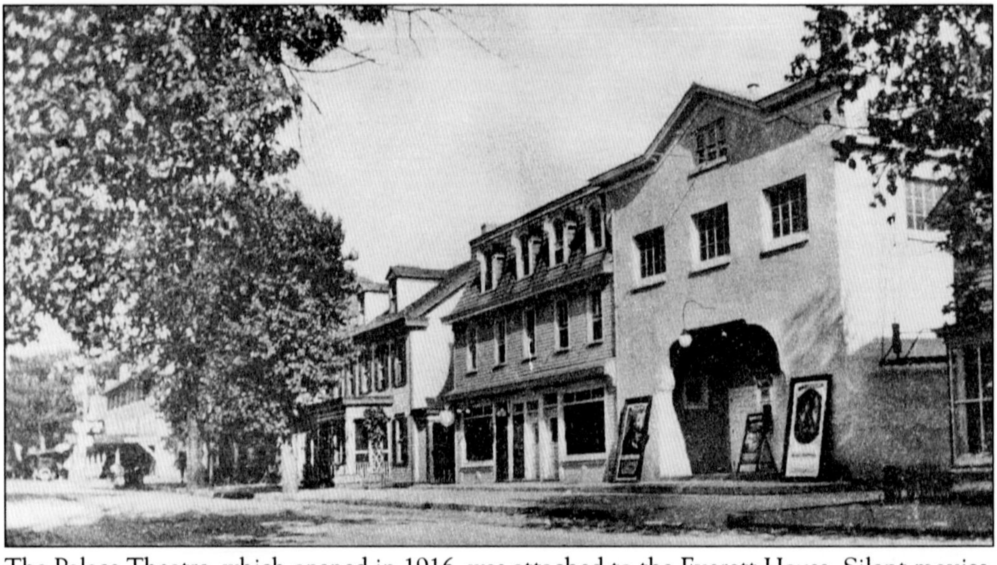

The Palace Theatre, which opened in 1916, was attached to the Everett House. Silent movies, accompanied by a piano player, had been shown previously at the YMCA. The Palace was later purchased by a group of men with experience in managing a motion picture house. The latest type screen, projection machines, and seating were introduced. The building was completely renovated and named the Community Theatre. It was owned by Isadore M. Hirshblond of Toms River. (Courtesy THS.)

Marion Leake, a lifetime Tuckerton resident, served as clerk in the post office for forty years, retiring in 1956. She was born in 1896 to Ann Eliza Burton and George Leek, who owned and operated the Everett House. As a member of the 1915 high school class, she graduated as the valedictorian. She was active in the Methodist church, fire company, library, and first aid auxiliaries. A news and social column for the *Tuckerton Beacon* bore her name for many years. (Courtesy THS.)

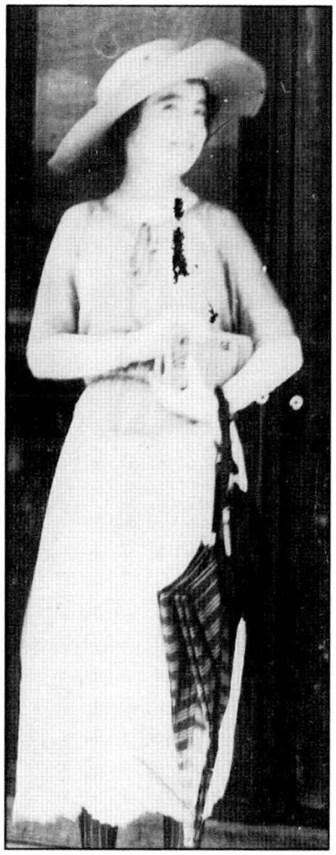

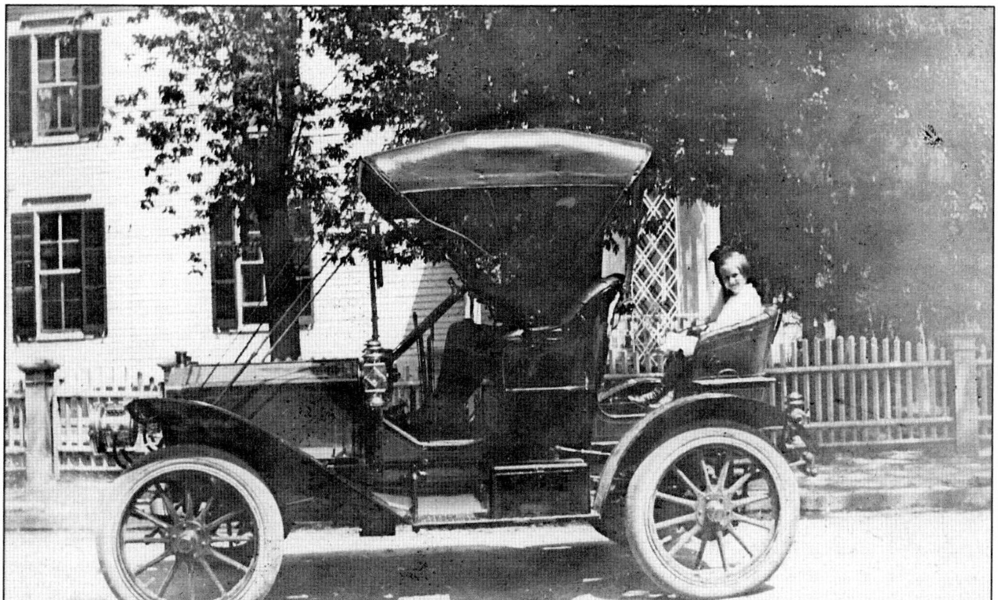

This 1906 Cadillac belonged to Dr. Charles H. Conover. It was "equipped with all modern conveniences." A neat buggy top with glass curtain front made it possible to travel in any kind of weather! Dr. Conover opened a pharmacy in the Pohatcong Building and practiced medicine in Tuckerton from 1899 until 1918, when he enlisted in the Army Medical Corps. He married Gertrude Olmstead, who was the principal of the school in 1898. (Courtesy THS.)

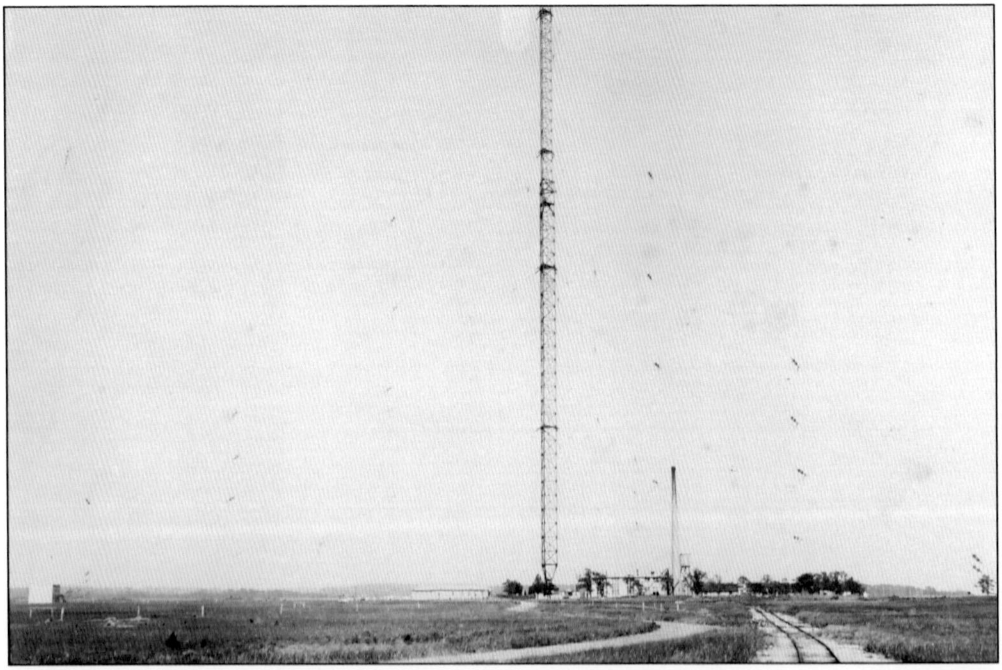

In 1912 the German government constructed the Goldschmidt Wireless Tower on Hickory Island near Tuckerton. The tower was 820 feet tall, topped with a 60-foot mast. It was the tallest structure in the United States at the time. The tower was assembled and tested in Germany before being taken apart and shipped to New York. It went by rail to Tuckerton and was trucked to the site. (Courtesy THS.)

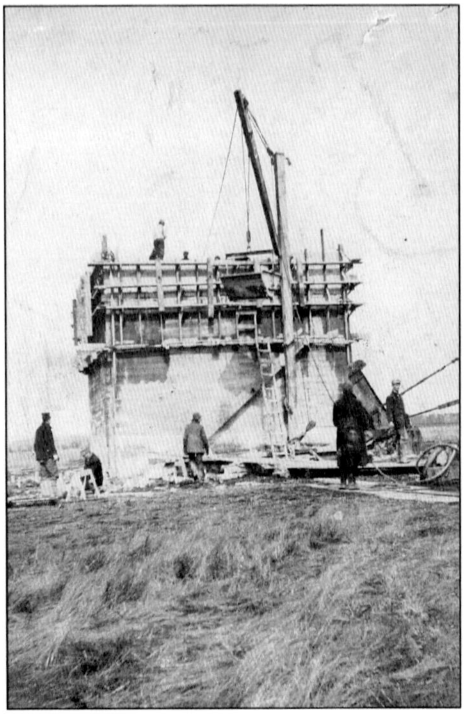

The tower was triangular in shape. Twelve cables were attached to three steel reinforced concrete blocks, each weighing 1,100 tons. Each huge block extended from 20 feet in the ground to 24 feet above the surface. These blocks still stand in the middle of the Mystic Island development. The tower maintained a half million volts. The base, standing on a solid steel ball, was completely insulated. The wires were protected by porcelain insulators, each weighing 1,800 pounds. (Courtesy THS.)

Most of the engineers who built the tower and some of the early laborers were of German descent. However, many of the workers at the Goldschmidt plant were Tuckerton townspeople. At times the work was quite dangerous. The type of wire used in the cables had to be greased by hand. The riggers used a bosun's chair to accomplish this feat. (Courtesy THS.)

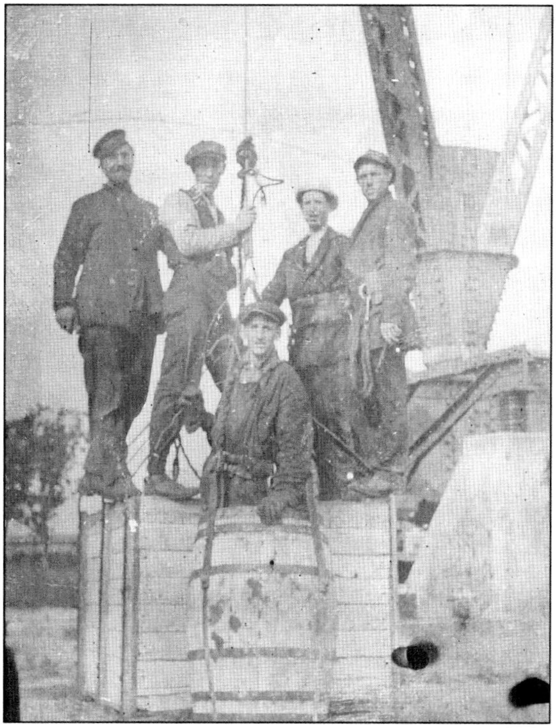

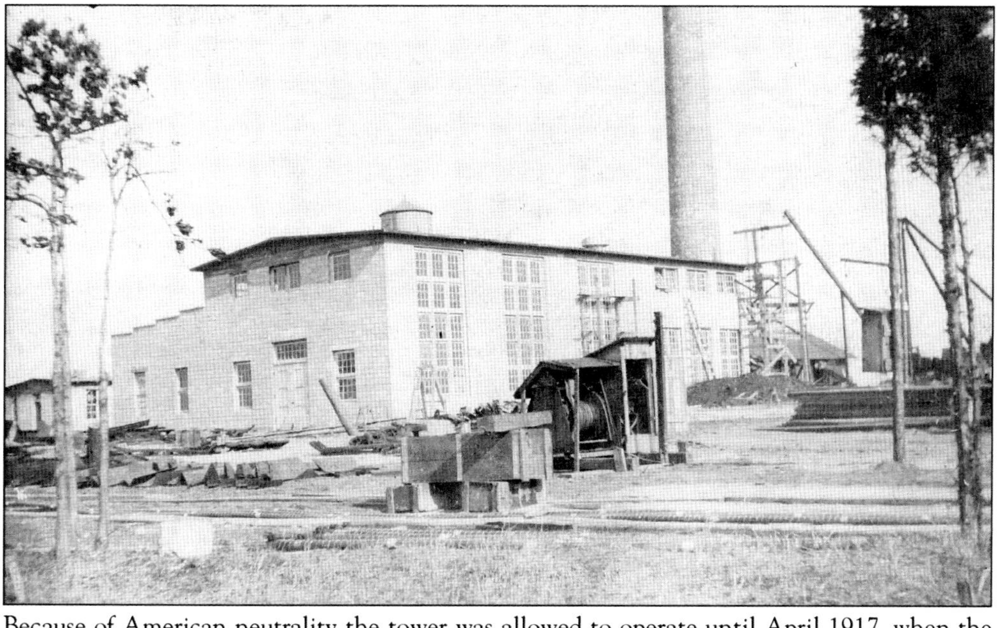

Because of American neutrality the tower was allowed to operate until April 1917, when the U.S. entered World War I. The American government then took over the operation and ran it for the duration. Later the tower was operated by RCA until seized by the military during World War II. The tower was closed in 1949 and was taken down and cut up for scrap in 1955. A receiving building contained five rooms with living quarters, and the transmitting building included the boilers, generators, and motors. (Courtesy THS.)

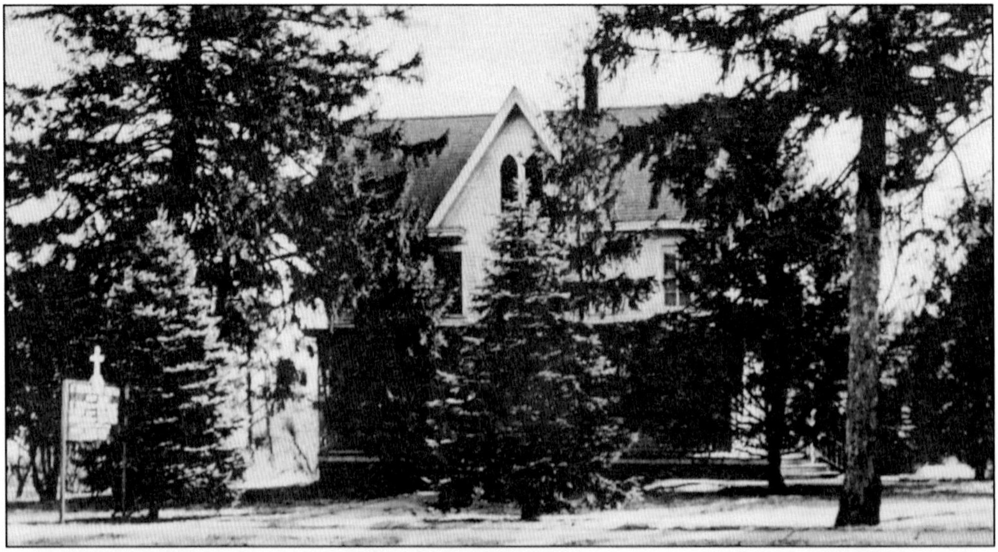

Tuckerton was almost exclusively a Quaker settlement for over a hundred years. The Presbyterians and Methodists followed in the 1800s, but there was no Catholic church in Little Egg Harbor until 1934, when St. Theresa's Church was begun as a mission of St. Thomas Aquinas Church in Beach Haven. Franciscan Friars said Mass in a rented store on W. Main Street until 1944 when the William S. Steelman home at Cedar and E. Main was purchased and used as a church. The present church was dedicated in 1953. (Courtesy THS.)

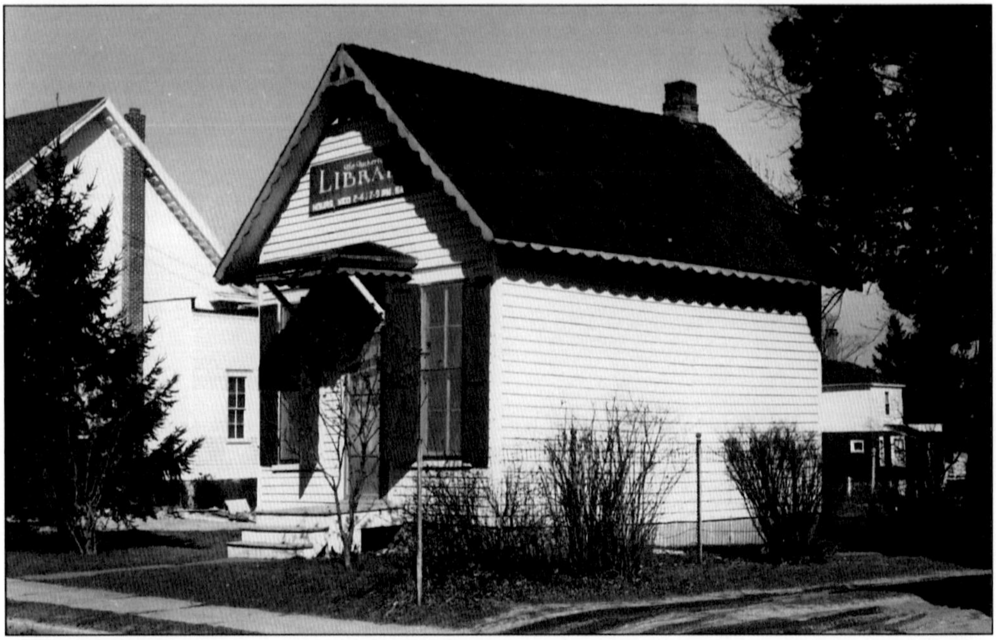

This tiny Tuckerton library, which claims to be the oldest in the county, was moved from Marine Street and attached to the new county branch, which opened in Tuckerton in 1972. It had been at the Marine Street site since the small building was moved from the Quaker meeting grounds about 1900. Incorporation and the sale of stock in 1875 provided maintenance funds as did the support of the Price family. For many years Eleanor B. Price, daughter of T.P. Price, served as librarian. (Courtesy THS.)

Gertrude Woodin Olmstead was the principal of the Tuckerton Grammar School in 1898, when the staff consisted of Lidie E. Stewart (intermediate), Josie E. Kelley (primary), and Barton Pharo (assistant). The graduates that year were Chester Headley, Jeanette Palmer, William E. Blackman, and Mary H. Ireland. Miss Olmstead had previously taught in Iowa and Oregon. The family was related to the Riders of Tuckerton who were lighthouse keepers in Sea Haven. Marriage to Charles Conover probably ended her teaching career. The Conovers had one daughter, Eleanor. (Courtesy THS.)

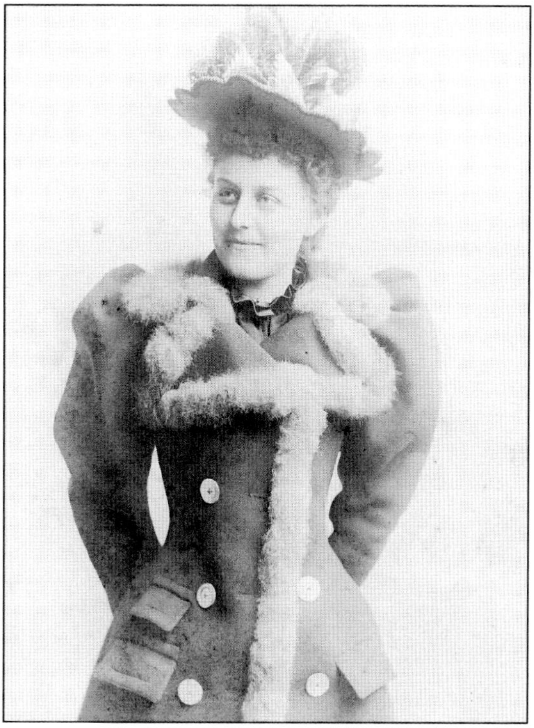

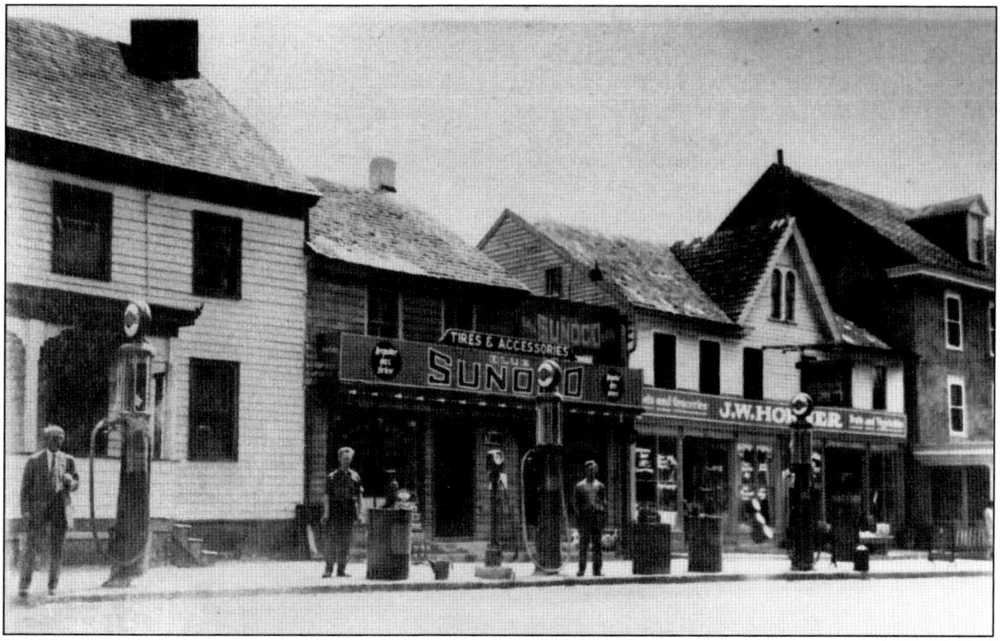

John Winfield Horner established a grocery store in Tuckerton in 1896. It was located on Main Street next to the Carlton House. Mr. Horner was said to be one of the most progressive merchants in the area. He was a cash dealer offering lower prices. His stock contained all types of canned goods, fancy groceries, and food supplies. The store also carried such items as toys, school supplies, souvenirs, and tin and enamel ware. (Courtesy THS.)

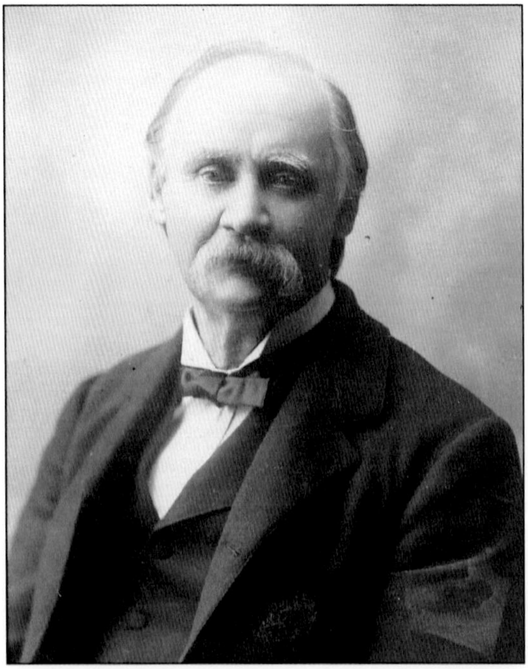

Joseph Beaumont Maugham, a native of London and teacher in the East Tuckerton School, was the first editor of the *Tuckerton Beacon*. At that time, the paper, founded in 1889, consisted of four hand-printed pages. The outer pages carried national news, while the inside pages were devoted to local news, features, and editorial material. In its earliest days, the paper had a circulation of three hundred. It continues today as part of the *Times Beacon* publications. (Courtesy THS.)

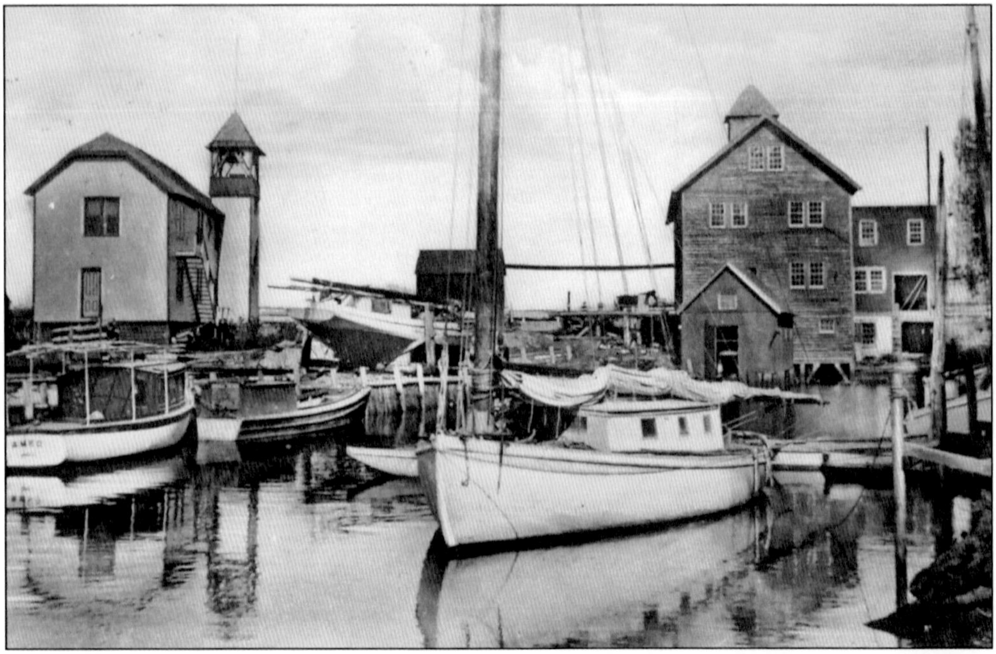

This is the head of Tuckerton Creek from which can be seen two buildings, the firehouse on the left and the mill on the right. They face the Main Shore Road and Lake Pohatcong. The numerous boats indicate the amount of activity on this stretch of the creek along Water Street between Main Street and Willow Landing. At a later date the Tuckerton Manufacturing Company would be built between the firehouse and mill. (Courtesy THS.)

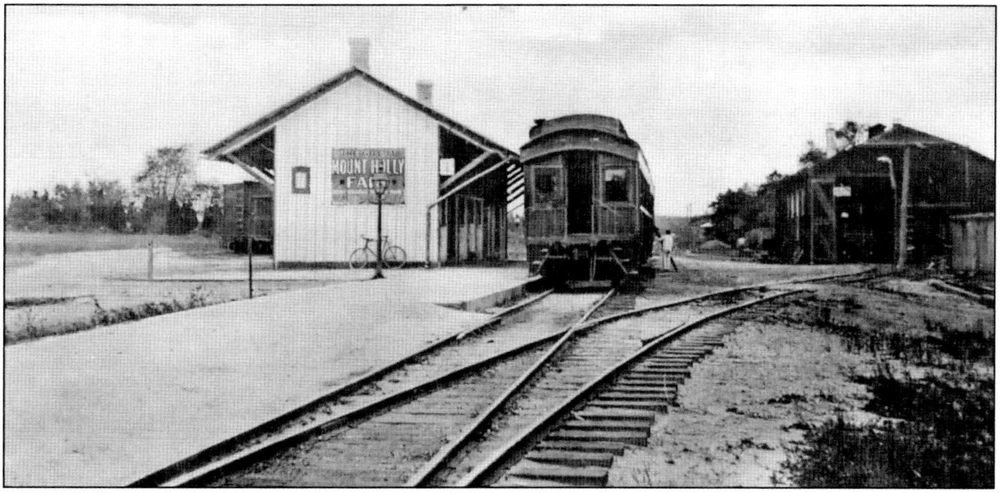

In this picture the train is near the Tuckerton station, the southern terminus of the Tuckerton Railroad (1871–1940). The northern terminus was Whitings, 29 miles northwest from Tuckerton. Two important backers of the Tuckerton Railroad lived in Tuckerton, Theophilus T. Price and Archelaus R. Pharo. They realized the importance of a railroad to link Tuckerton with larger railroads at Whitings for shipment of clams and oysters to New York City and Philadelphia. Tourists, hunters, and fishermen also had better access to Long Beach Island and vicinity with the advent of the railroad. (Courtesy Michael Mangum.)

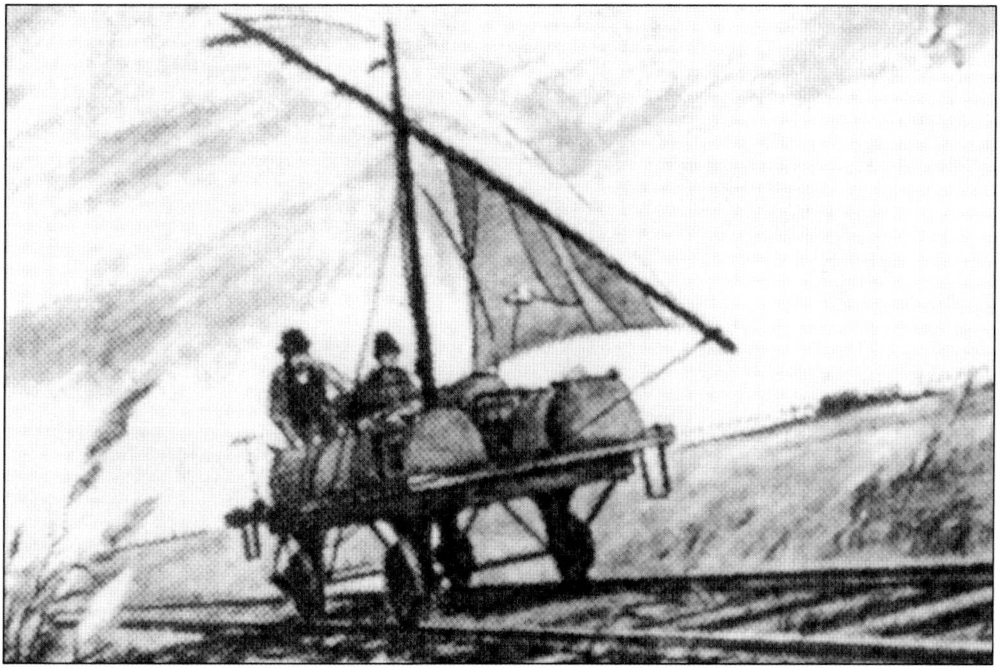

After the Tuckerton Railroad abandoned the short spur from the Edge Cove to the main line, it was leased to E.A. Horner and F.R. Austin for $1 per year for the transportation of clams. The "Clamtown Sailcar," a flatcar, was propelled by means of a sail, horse, or mule. Use of the rail continued until about 1915. The arrangement stipulated that all clams dug from Little Egg Harbor Bay be shipped on this 1.75-mile track to the Tuckerton Railroad Station. (Courtesy John Brinckmann, *The Tuckerton Railroad.*)

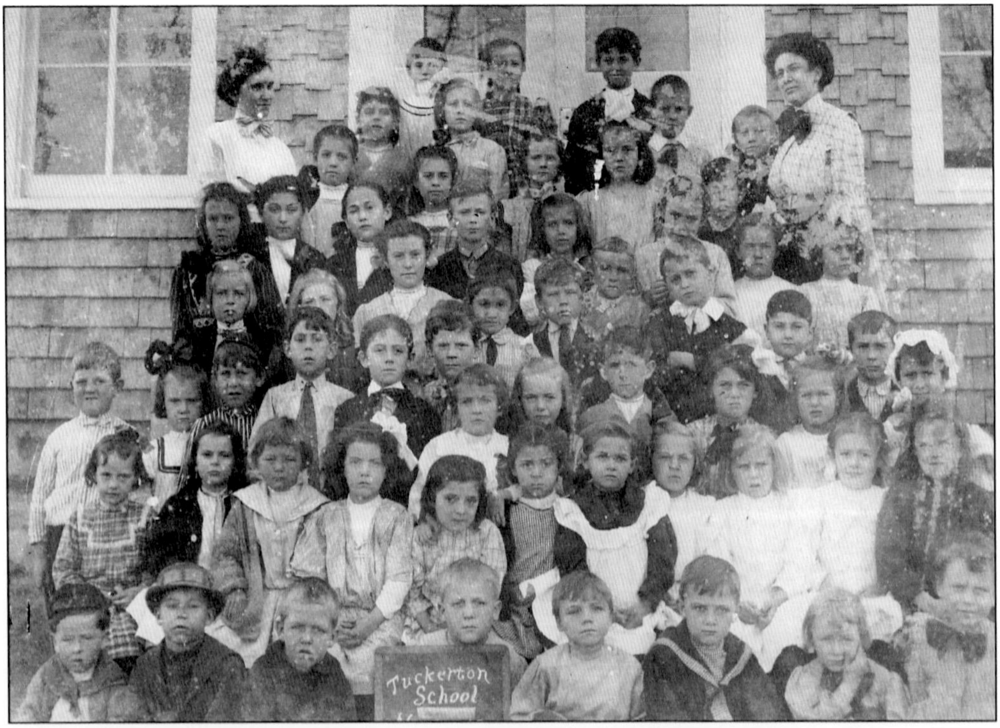

On November 12, 1900, these first, second, and third graders were attending the Tuckerton School at Clay and Marine Streets. Principal Gertrude Olmstead, who taught grades seven and eight, is at the upper right. The primary teacher, possibly Josie E. Kelley, is at the upper left. The pupils are quite nicely dressed which indicates the picture-taking was not a surprise. One little girl (third row, right end) and one little boy (first row, second from left) are sporting hats. Hair ribbons and a few bow ties can also be detected. (Courtesy THS.)

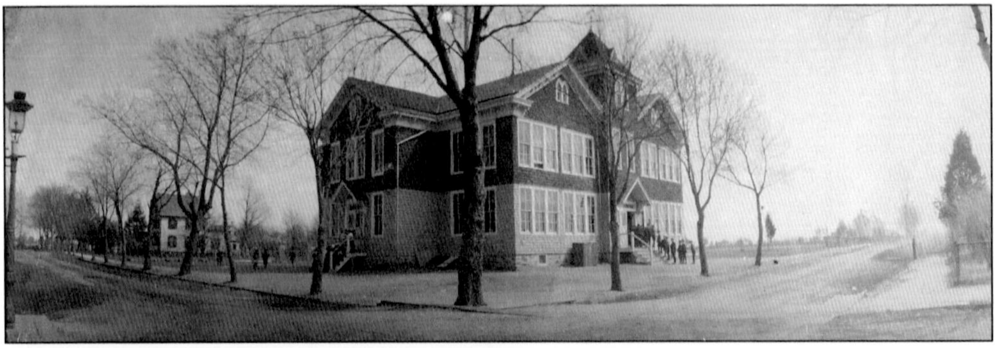

This Tuckerton school, which would eventually house all of the pupils of both Tuckerton and Little Egg Harbor, was built in 1873. Additions were made in 1910 and 1912 to provide for children from the West Tuckerton School, as well as classes for high school subjects. One half of the upstairs of this school was the "high school." A narrow space along the classroom wall was the typing section. The house down Marine Street, visible on the left, belonged to author Leah Blackman. (Courtesy THS.)

Hayes Parker, a 1927 graduate of the Wharton School of Business, was a well-known Tuckerton businessman. In 1930 he bought one of the shipping houses along the creek on Green Street. He dealt in the shipping of oysters, clams, and shellfish and in the operation of a marina. Community service included twenty-five years as a councilman and twenty-seven years on the board of education. Like his father, Barton, he lived almost a century and continued to enjoy gunning, fishing, and the bay throughout his life. (Courtesy *Tuckerton Beacon*.)

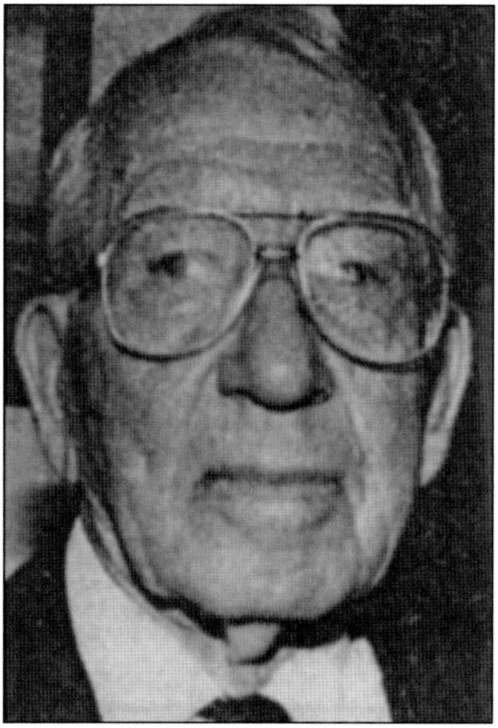

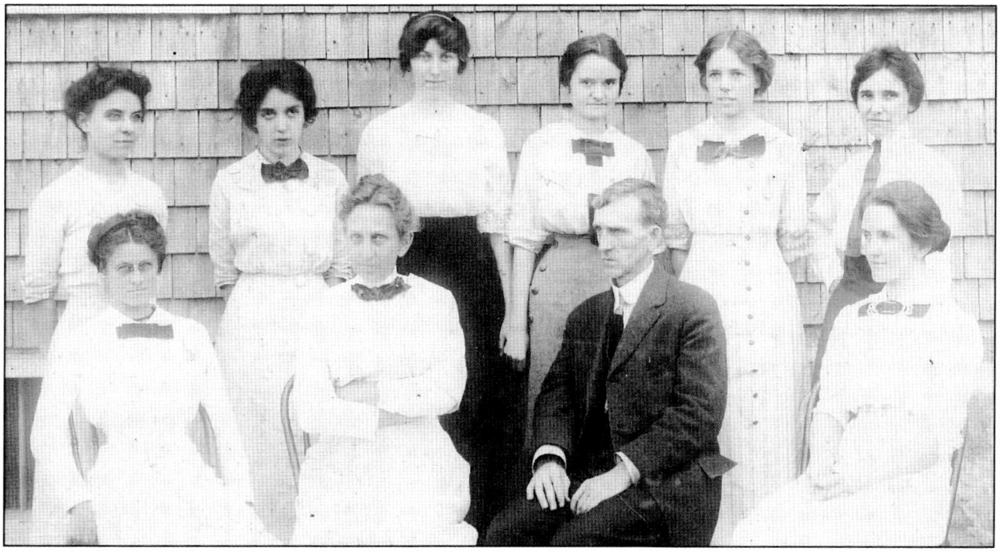

Principal A.J. Packard headed the staff of the Tuckerton School for three years. His staff in 1913/14 consisted of three high school teachers, including Gwendoline Bond (Peppler), standing at farthest left. Six teachers were assigned to grades one through eight. Mrs. Margaret K. Fox (seated second from the left beside Packard) taught grades seven and eight. Others were Florence Festerson and Margaret Stevens (high school), Maude Ireland (grades five and six), Nellie Falkinburg (grades four and five), Lina C. Marshall (grade three), Helen M. Allen (grade two), and Ethel D. Steelman (grade one). The West Tuckerton one-room school was closed in 1911. Pupils were transported to the school at Clay and Marine Streets, which was enlarged to eight rooms in 1910 and eleven rooms in 1912. (Courtesy OCHS.)

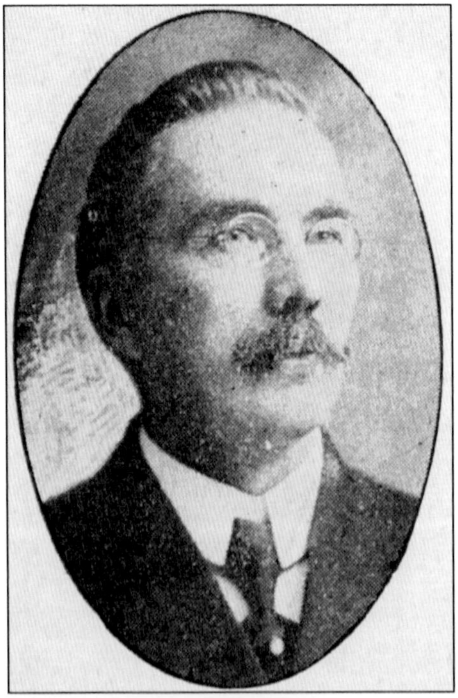

Frank R. Austin, born in Tuckerton on March 2, 1857, and educated in the local schools, became a prominent businessman and public official. He was the first mayor of the Borough of Tuckerton in 1901; a cashier and president of the Tuckerton Bank; and a member of the board of education, the board of health, Tuckerton Lodge #4, F & AM, and the Pohatcong Tribe of the Order of Red Men. (Courtesy THS.)

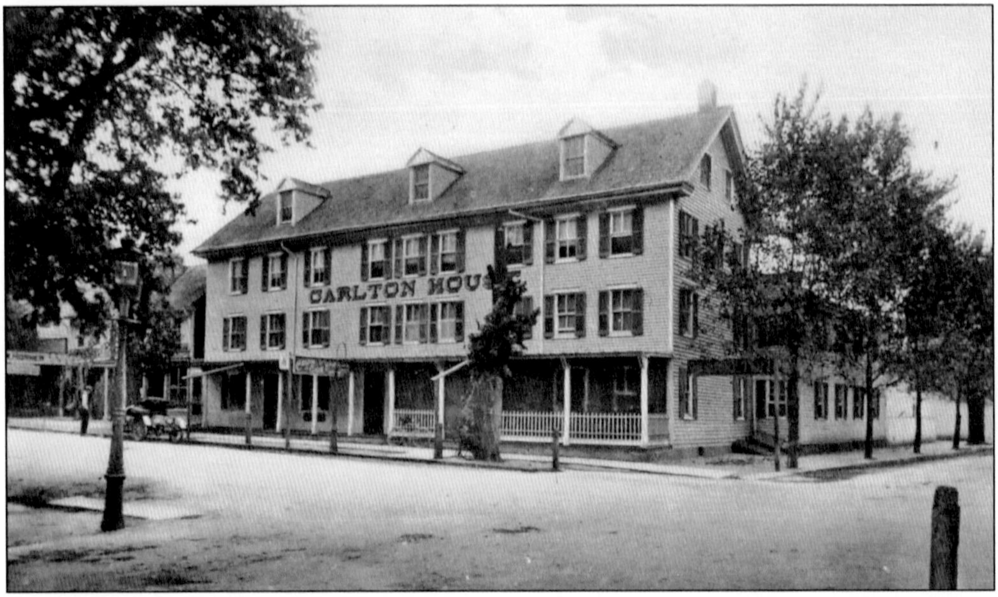

The Carleton House (later Carlton), the most prominent hotel in Tuckerton in 1879, was built as the Union House about 1800 by Ebenezer Tucker. It served as s post office and stagecoach stop and provided lodging for visitors to the shore. Henry and Louis Kumpf, proprietors in the late 1800s, provided splendid meals, large comfortable rooms, and genial hospitality. The Carlton was the only licensed house in Tuckerton with a well-stocked bar of choicest wines, liquors, and cigars as well as a popular pool room. It stood on the northeast corner of Main and Green Streets until it was razed in 1964. (Courtesy Michael Mangum.)

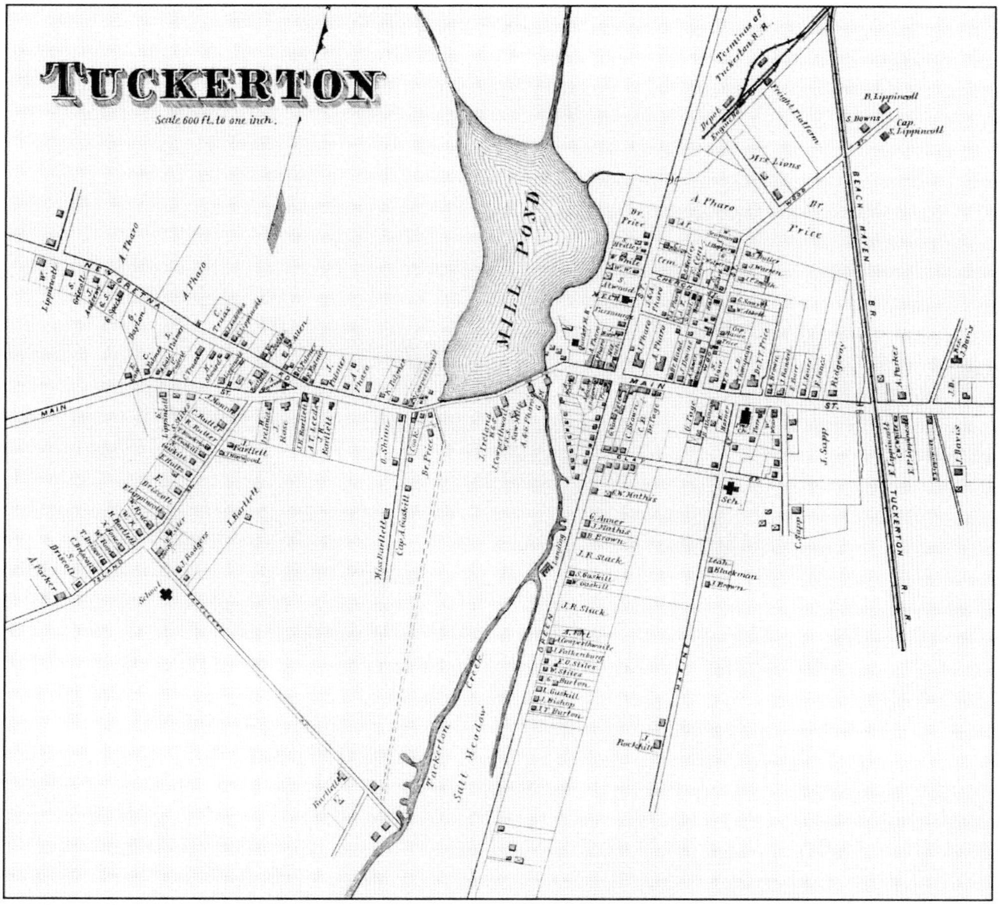

Settlers of Little Egg Harbor Township, which lies north and south of Tuckerton Borough today, knew a good thing when they saw it. It had fertile uplands and gigantic salt meadows as nurseries for fish and innumerable wild fowl. Tuckerton was a seventeenth-century bastion of civilization in a near-wilderness north of the Mullica River. The early residents had a distinct advantage in that the northeast bank of the creek was solid ground, so homes and businesses could be built along it for almost its entire length. Prior to 1798, when the name Tuckerton was introduced, the community was called Andrews' Mill, Shourds' Mill, Middle-of-the Shore, Clamtown, Fishtown, or Quakertown. Main Street shown on this map from the *Woolman and Rose Atlas* of 1878, is now part of Route 9. Green Street, which roughly parallels the creek, ran towards the bay and still does. A spur of the Tuckerton Railroad led to a dock at Edge Cove across Little Egg Harbor Bay from Beach Haven. Tuckerton was the second U.S. port of entry. Ocean County welcomed Little Egg Harbor Township in 1891 as part of a political deal. A note of interest: sketches for the *Atlas*, including the one of the Stafford Forge cranberry operation (see p. 26), were made by William F. Rose. The Rose family, of which he probably was a part, lived in Little Egg Harbor Township at one time. (Courtesy OCHS.)

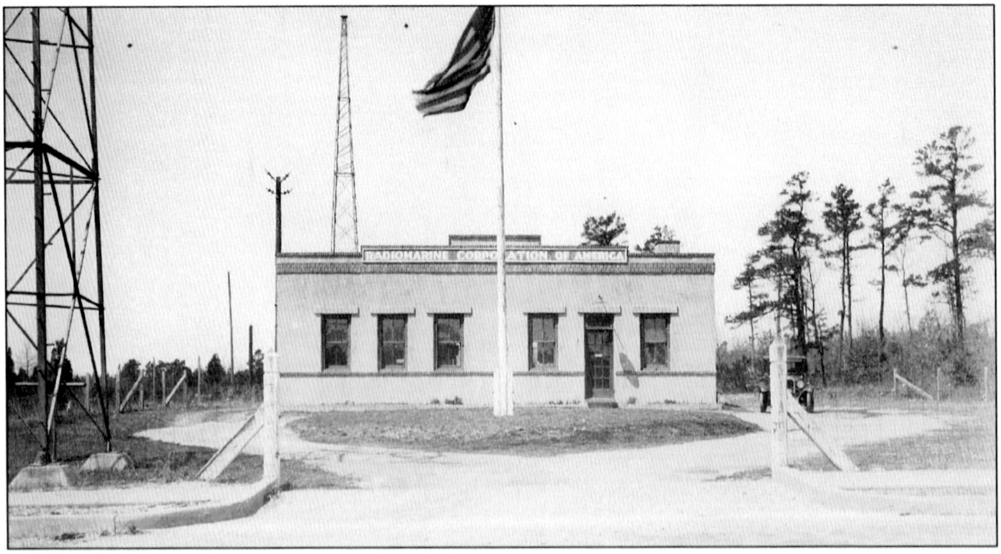

The Radiomarine Corporation of America Station, a subsidiary of RCA, was located on Route 9 north of the town. It was brought to Tuckerton in 1925 from Cape May so all of the transmitters could be housed in one building. In the 1920s the chief task of the company was relaying messages for passengers who wanted to buy and sell stocks. During World War II the station was closed because of radio silence regulations. It was reopened after the war and moved to West Creek in 1978. Later the station was operated as a private enterprise. (Courtesy THS.)

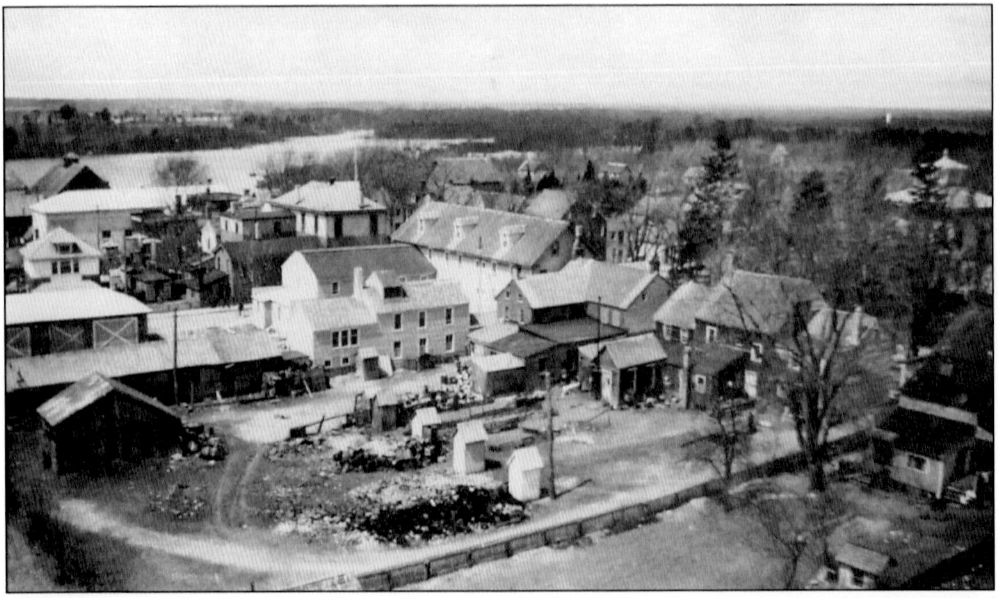

This view of Tuckerton is from the water tower, which stood in the center of the block bounded by Main, Clay, Green, and Marine Streets. The large building with three dormer windows is the Carlton Hotel. To its right are the store and home of the Horner family. Four outhouses can be seen behind these Main Street buildings. The large home on the right with the cupola is the home of J.J. Pharo. The Pohatcong Building is visible to the left of the Carlton Hotel. At the upper left the building with the small cupola is the old mill. (Courtesy THS.)

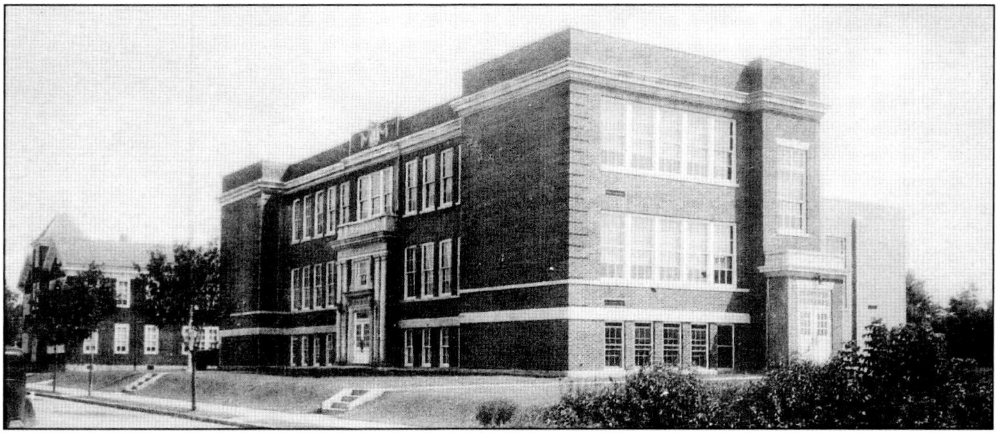

Tuckerton High School was built in 1927. Actually, high school classes were offered during the early 1900s in the grade school, the building at the left. It had two large classrooms upstairs on the Clay Street side. An area in the back of one was designated for typing and bookkeeping. All other high school subjects were taught in the remaining space. When Warren Rosenberger, who became superintendent of schools from 1930 to 1942, came in 1927, he taught European history, French I and II, civics, general science, and spelling. (Courtesy THS.)

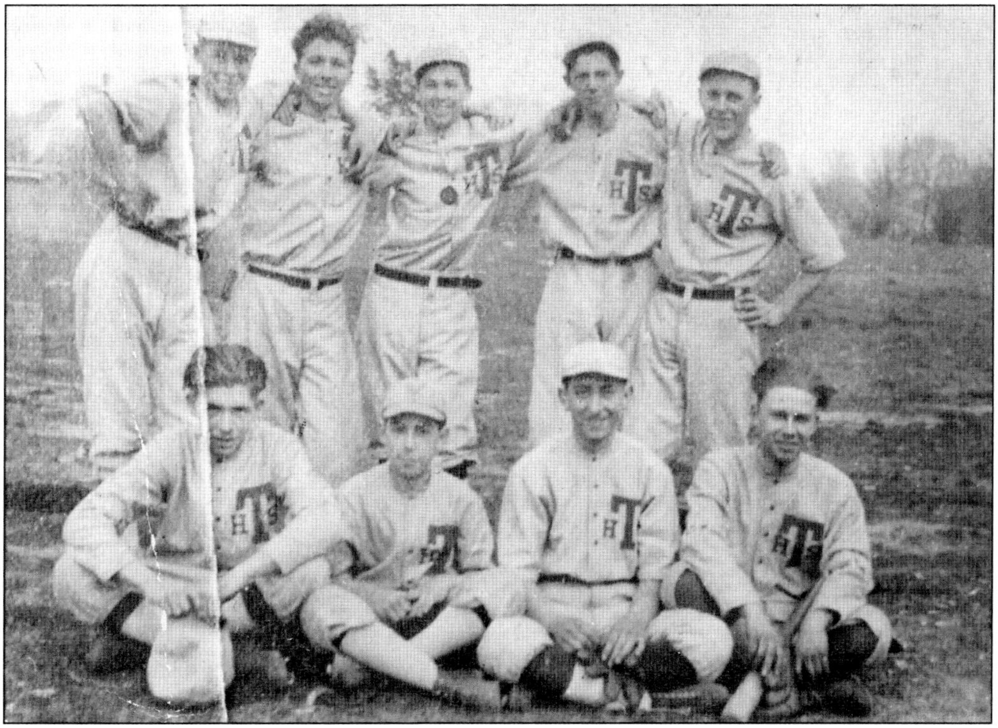

Baseball was popular at the shore long before other team sports. Shown above is the Tuckerton High School baseball team of 1914. From left to right are: (sitting) Paul Parker, Jack Webb, Walter Parsons, and Winfield Horner; (standing) Joe Mathis, Hayes Parker, Walter Loveland, Chester Parker, and James Bishop. In the first game they walloped Toms River, 14–8. Among other teams played were Beach Haven, Point Pleasant, Hammonton, and the Morris Guards. (Courtesy THS.)

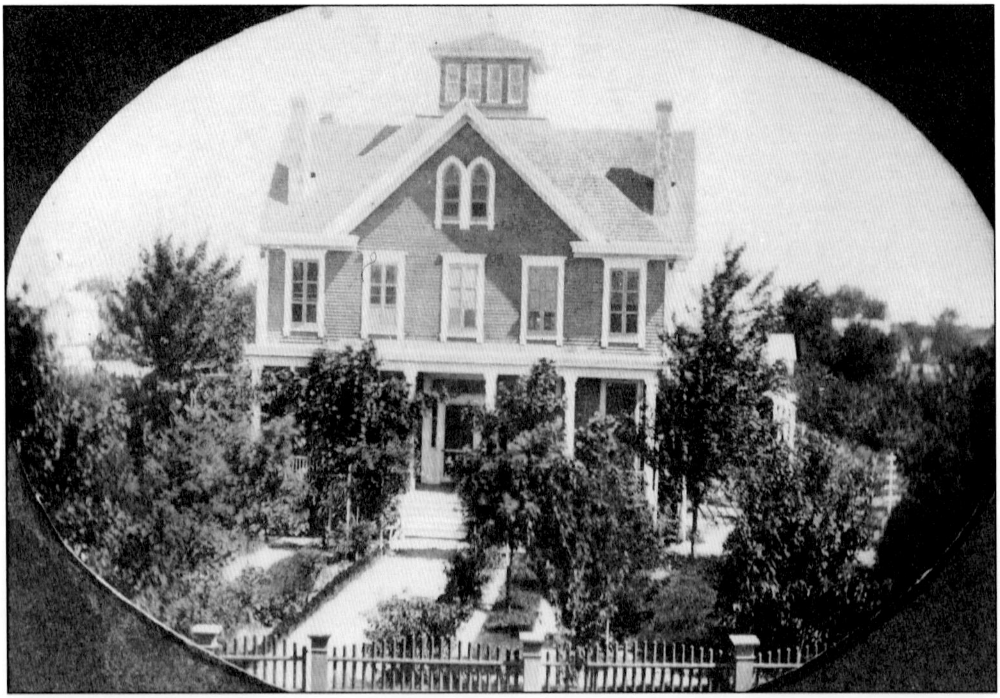

Archelaus Ridgeway Pharo built a large number of schooners and engaged in the coastal trade. He was influential in the creation and construction of the Tuckerton Railroad, which he later managed. Active in politics, Pharo held the office of freeholder and was a delegate to the Republican convention that nominated Abraham Lincoln. He was a member of the Society of Friends and served as clerk of the Little Egg Harbor Meeting. In the census of 1870 at age fifty-five, his occupation was "gentleman," and his real and personal estates were valued at $120,000. He died in 1886. (Courtesy THS.)

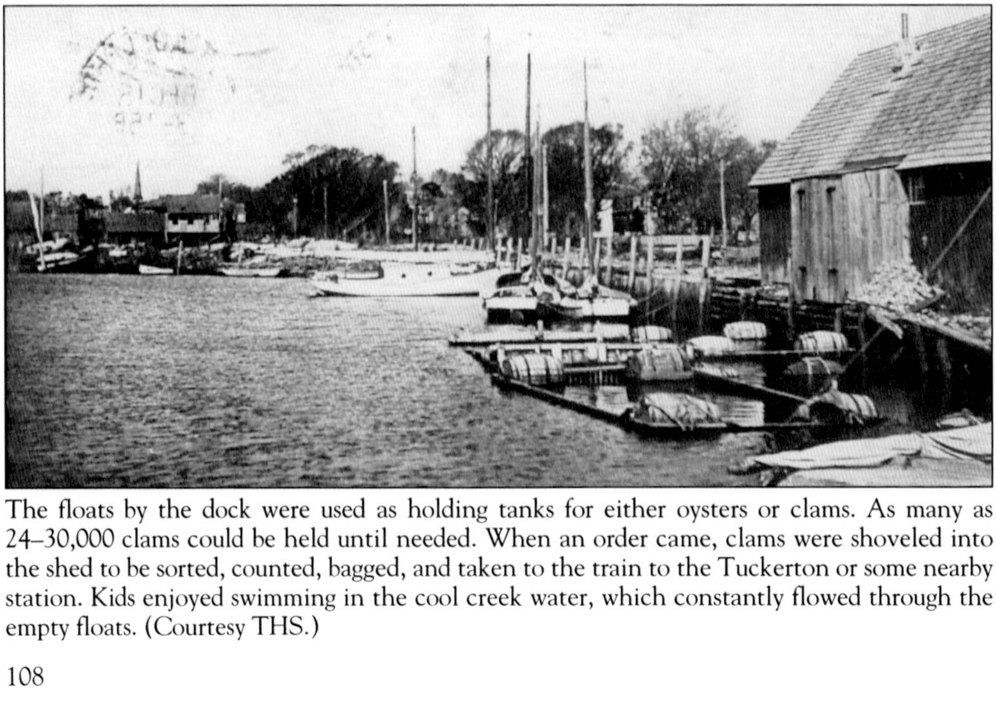

The floats by the dock were used as holding tanks for either oysters or clams. As many as 24–30,000 clams could be held until needed. When an order came, clams were shoveled into the shed to be sorted, counted, bagged, and taken to the train to the Tuckerton or some nearby station. Kids enjoyed swimming in the cool creek water, which constantly flowed through the empty floats. (Courtesy THS.)

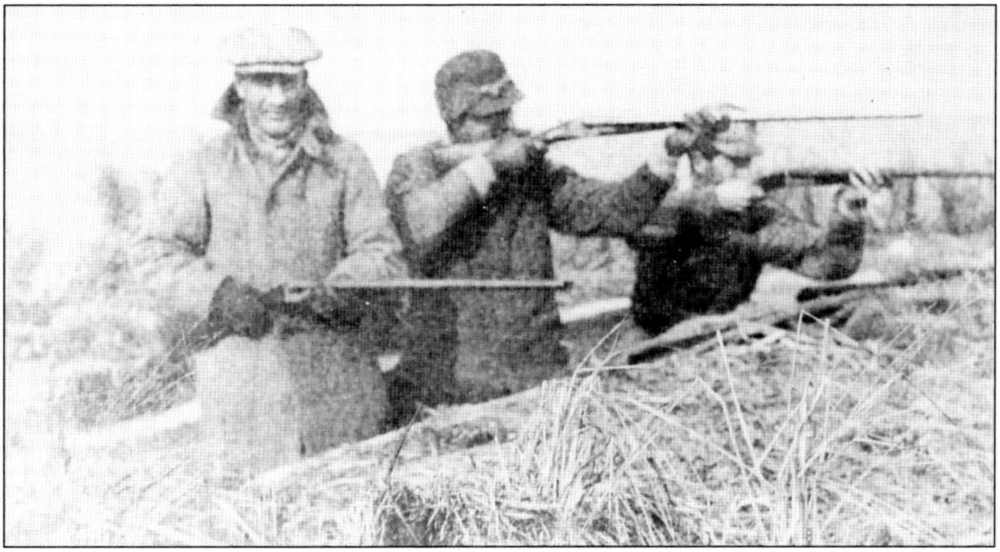

Just as residents of this downshore area have been doing for three hundred years, Claude Smith and his party brave the fog, mosquitoes, green head flies, wind, rain, and cold to enjoy the pleasures of hunting. Those gunning for geese, duck, or brant had to place their decoys within three rods of the marsh, island, bar, blank, blind (shown here), or ice. They could not hunt between sunset and sunrise. (Courtesy THS.)

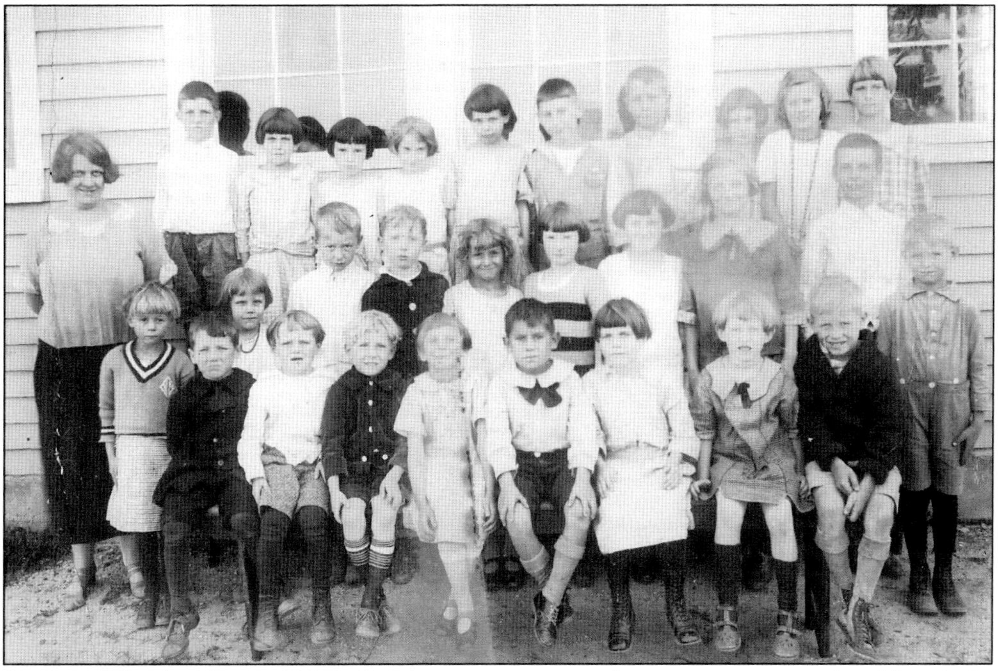

Between Manahawkin and New Gretna were many small communities, populated largely by one family whose name was given to that area. The Giffords and the Gales were both numerous about 2 miles southwest of Tuckerton. These pupils attended the Giffordtown School, which was opened before 1872 and was closed in 1950. Pupils bear such names as Mathis, Speck, Buelow, Jillson, Mott, and Cramer. (Courtesy THS.)

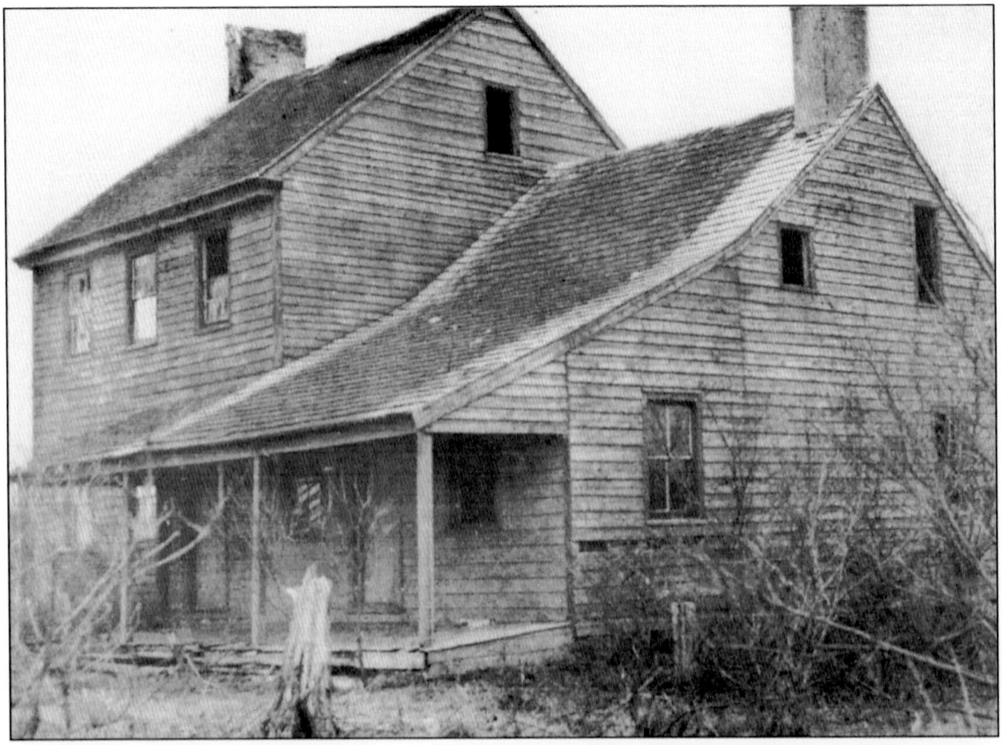

Bass River Township separated from Little Egg Harbor Township in 1864. Great John Mathis, the first white settler in this Bass River area, built a home on the present-day Dan's or Oak Island and later on the Bass River at the present site of Viking Yacht Company. He was called "Great" due to his stature as a wealthy landowner, ship builder, farmer, and financier who helped to fund the American Revolution. His Bass River home, shown here *c.* 1930, was rebuilt after being burned by the British. The house was demolished in the late 1960s. (Courtesy Franklin Gray.)

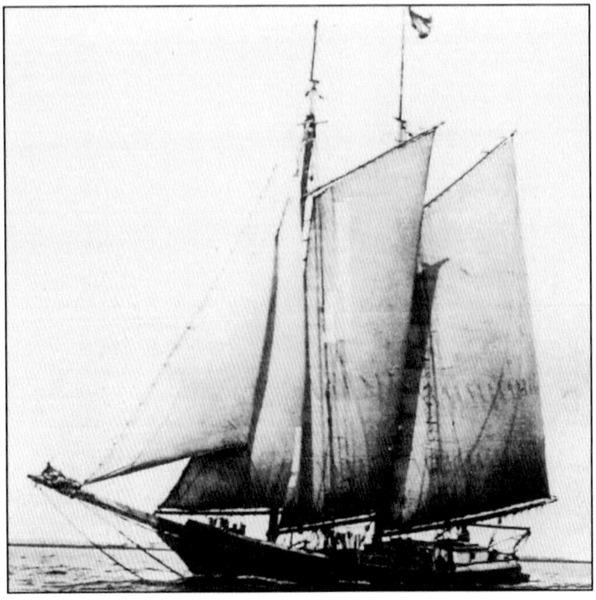

The principal industry in Bass River in the nineteenth century was ship building. The first shipyard was on the Great John Mathis property on the west bank of the river. Micajah Mathis Sr. built the brig *Argo* here about 1800. Capt. John Van Sant had a shipyard farther up the Bass River from 1791 until 1815. In a listing of merchant vessels in 1888, twelve operating schooners and one steam vessel were listed as having been built in Bass River. The schooner *Lizzie Belle* (pictured here), sailing out of Tuckerton, was built here in 1884. (Courtesy Mabel Mathis.)

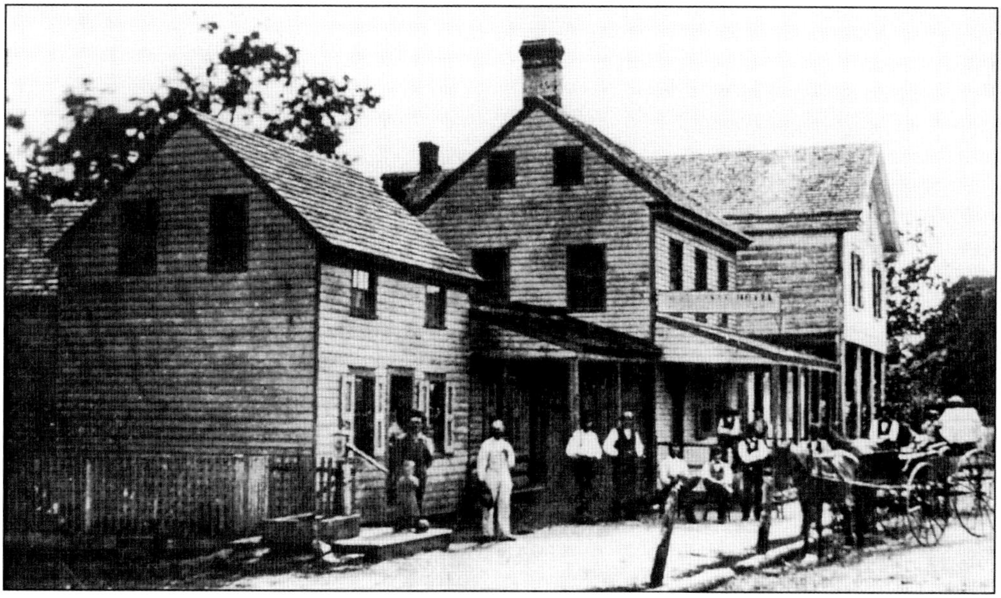

The Bass River Hotel was built in 1851 by Thomas French on the southwest corner of the Old New York Highway and Maple Avenue. Franklin Adams (wearing a white suit in the above picture) bought the hotel in 1856 and managed it and the adjoining post office until his death in 1885. The building of the hotel marked the beginning of New Gretna as the town center with the present Route 9 replacing Stage Road as the main transportation route. (Courtesy Franklin Gray.)

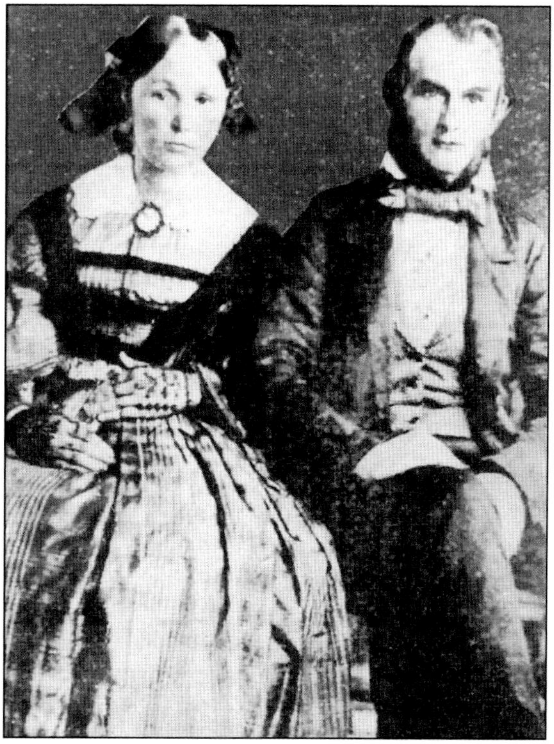

Franklin Adams and his wife, Mary Ann Mathis Adams, the youngest daughter of "Island Dan" Mathis, were well known for their hospitality during the many years of operating the Red Tavern and Bass River Hotel. (Courtesy Franklin Gray.)

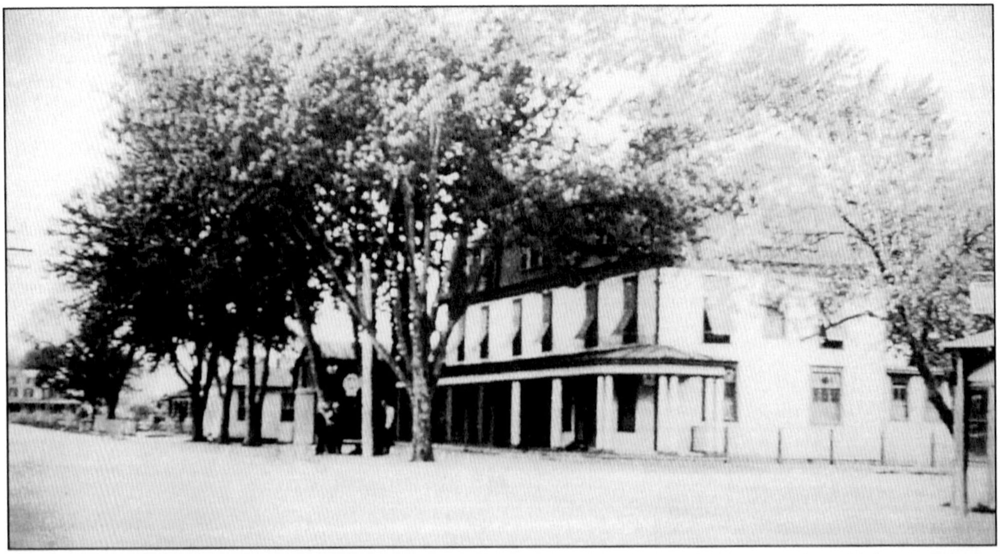

This early view, c. 1910, of the intersection of Old New York Road (Route 9) and North Maple Avenue shows the corner of Ashton Lamson's restaurant and the New Gretna Hotel. In its early days the hotel served as a stagecoach stop and inn. It became a popular boarding house for hunters and fishermen into the 1950s and a successful restaurant through the late 1980s. The building is presently vacant. (Courtesy Ruth Cramer Soles.)

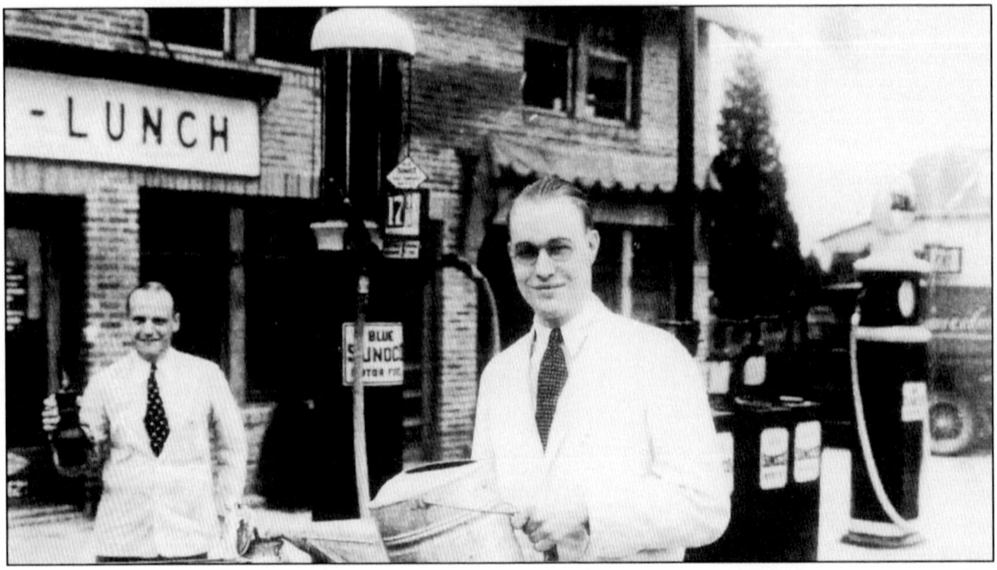

Small gas station-luncheonettes, the forerunners of today's convenience stores, were popular in Bass River Township in the 1930s and 1940s. The Cramer Brothers' facility on the northeast corner of New York Road and Maple Avenue replaced Ashton Lamson's restaurant, which burned down in 1929. Norman Mathis (right) and his boss, Frank Cramer, provide service with a smile in this c. 1950 photo. Today the building houses the Rustic Inn. (Courtesy Winfield Allen.)

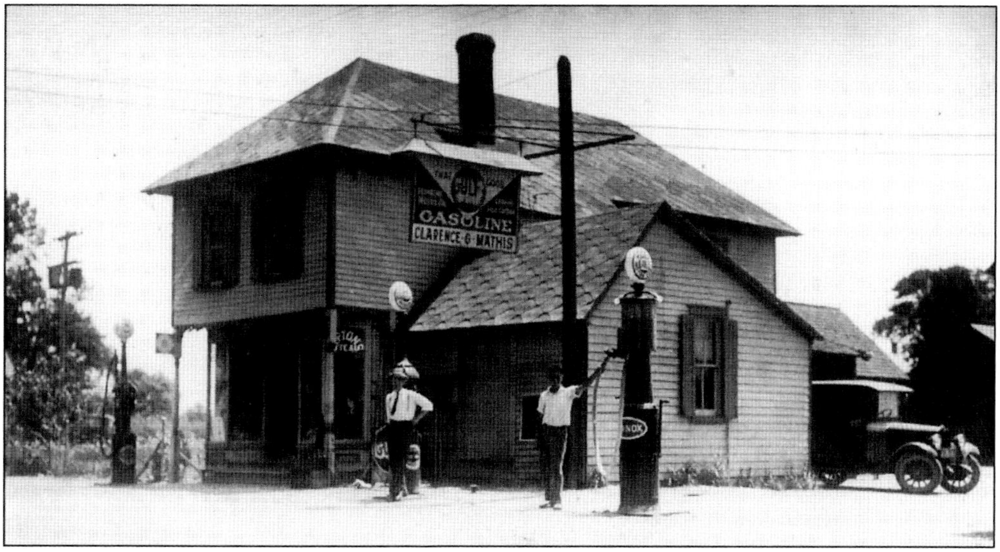

Residents of Bass River Township depended on small local general, grocery, hardware, millinery, and other stores for their everyday needs. Frequently small shops appeared in a front room of existing homes. The Mathis family maintained a store in New Gretna from the 1880s through 1954. "On account" purchases were recorded in a ledger. Norman G. Mathis (above right), the proprietor's son, worked in the store and frequently accompanied Delwin Downs (left), who made home deliveries for many years. (Courtesy Norman and Ann Mathis.)

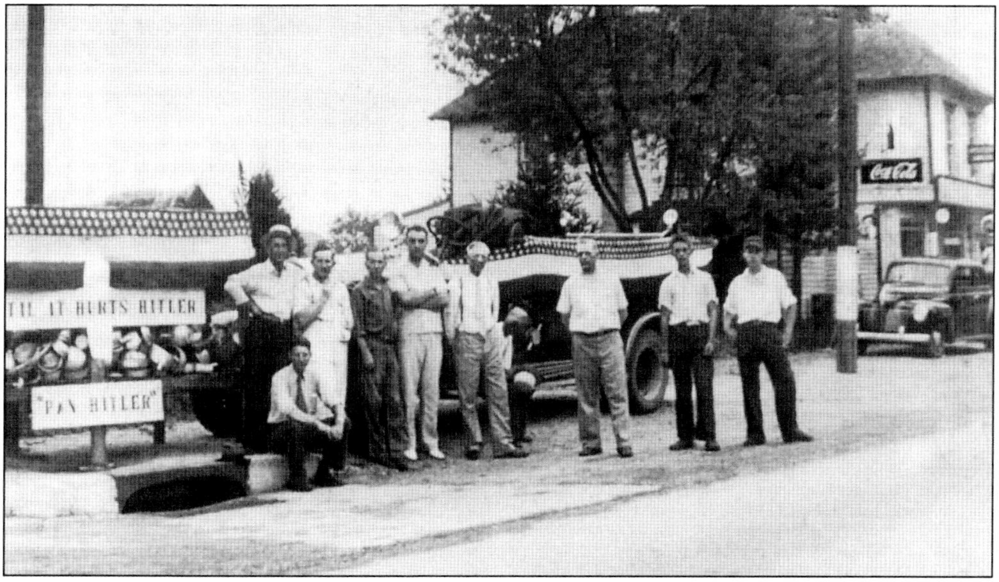

The New Gretna Volunteer Fire Company has been an important part of the civic and social life of the community, as evidenced by this World War II vintage photo showing members collecting aluminum for the war effort on the southwest corner of New York Road and Maple Avenue. Clarence Mathis' store can be seen on the right with his 1939 Chrysler parked in front. (Courtesy Norman and Ann Mathis.)

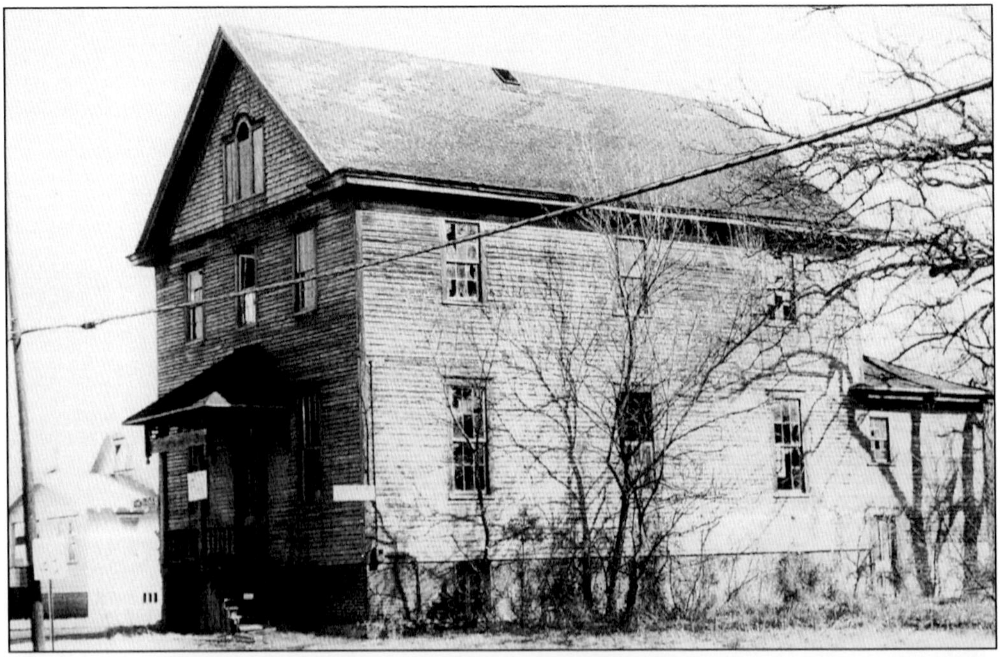

The Knights of Pythias Hall, built in the latter part of the nineteenth century, served as the meeting place for the Knights of Pythias and the Daughters of Liberty. It hosted traveling medicine shows, movies from Tuckerton, local government meetings, minstrel shows, school plays, and even classrooms, when the local school was being expanded. After falling into disrepair in the 1940s and 1950s, it was remodeled into a bakery in the 1970s. It was demolished in 1996. (Courtesy Col. Fred Cramer.)

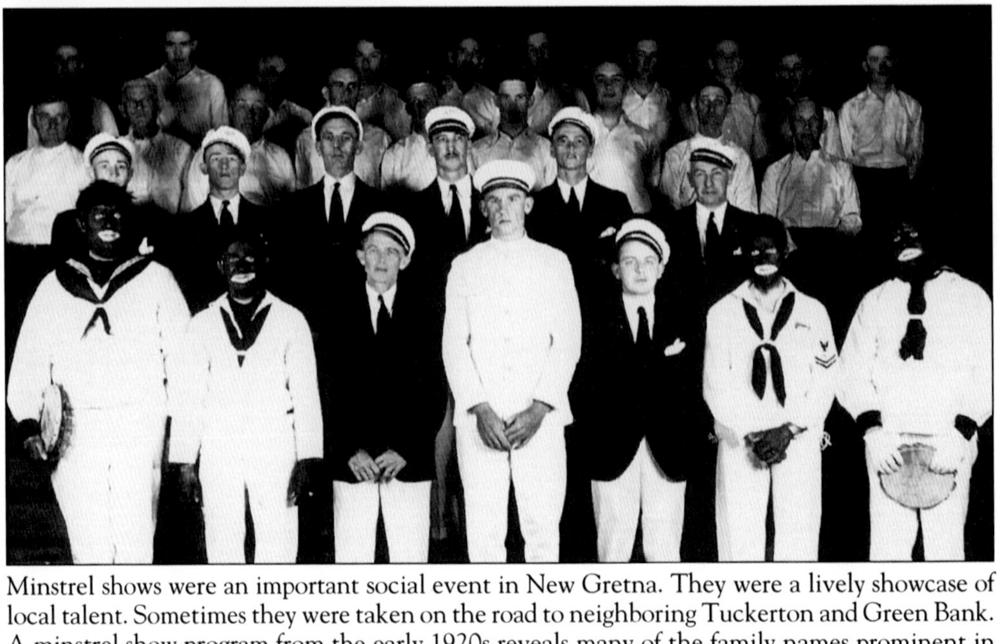

Minstrel shows were an important social event in New Gretna. They were a lively showcase of local talent. Sometimes they were taken on the road to neighboring Tuckerton and Green Bank. A minstrel show program from the early 1920s reveals many of the family names prominent in the area's history and still prevalent today: Cramer, Loveland, Mathis, and Sears. (Courtesy Helen S. Carty.)

NEW GRETNA MINSTRELS

Introducing **HOWARD MATHIS, Interlocutor**

END MEN

John S. Mathis	Russell Mathis

BALLADISTS

Clarence G. Mathis	Eugene Sears
Howard Mathis, Jr.	Bessie Mathis
Earl Cramer	Kirk Loveland
William Miles	Eugene Mathis

PIANIST

Miss Minnie Mathis

PART ONE

PROGRAM OF MUSICAL NUMBERS

Opening Chorus	Entire Company
Overture	Entire Company
To-morrow	Russell Mathis
Wake Up, Little Girl, You Are Dreaming	Eugene Sears
I'm Hungry for Beautiful Girls	J. S. Mathis
When the Bells in the Lighthouse Ring	C. G. Mathis
In the Little Red School-house	Mrs. Bess Mathis
When You're Gone I Won't Forget You	Earl Cramer
When Honey Sings an Old Time Song	Kirk Loveland
In My Home Town	H. Z. Mathis
Closing Chorus, "Some Sunny Day"	Entire Company

CURTAIN

INTERMISSION

Songs and Recitations	Mrs. H. R. Lindsley
Selection "Nuf Sed"	Billy Miles

PART TWO

Opening Chorus	Entire Company
Stand Up and Sing for Your Father (by request)	J. S. Mathis
When Evening Shadows Fall	Eugene Sears
Old Black Joe	C. G. Mathis
Yiddish Love	Russell Mathis
The Road to Home, Sweet Home	Kirk Loveland
Annie Laurie	Mrs. Bess Mathis

A 1920 minstrel show program featured local talent. The name "Mathis" appears nineteen times—a tribute to the early Great John Mathis family. Recreation took many forms in the downshore area, including cycling, baseball, sailing, debating, picnicking, and church socials. (Courtesy Jean and Murray Harris.)

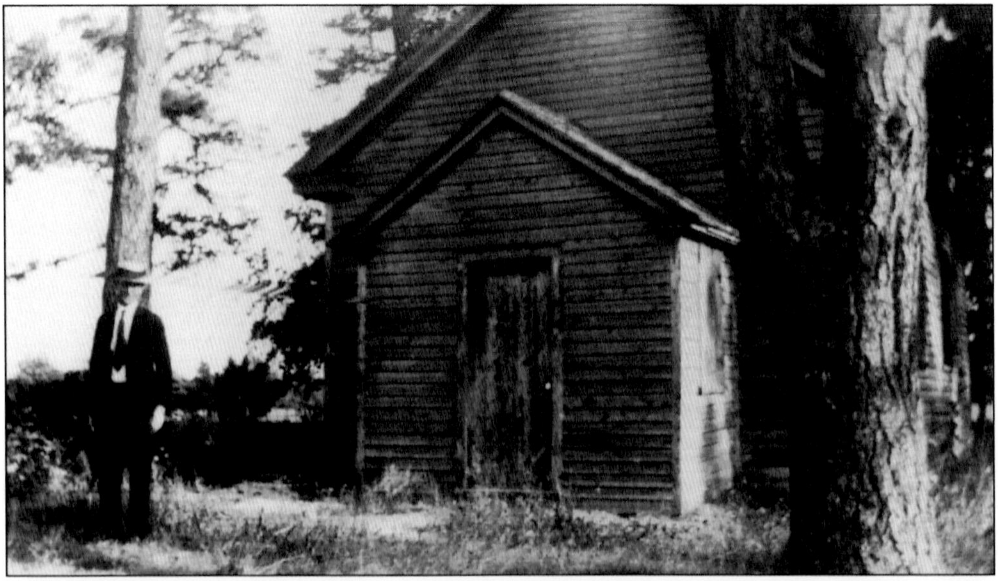

Charles H. Adare, Civil War veteran who died in an accident at Pleasant Mills in 1882, stands outside the Mathistown schoolhouse where four of his children attended school in the 1880s. His daughter Rachel Adare Carr remembered all of the children using the same cup to get drinking water out of a bucket. The school was closed in 1900 when the New Gretna School was constructed on North Maple Avenue. Today it is a remodeled home at its original site on New York Road. (Courtesy Thomas and Judy Cramer.)

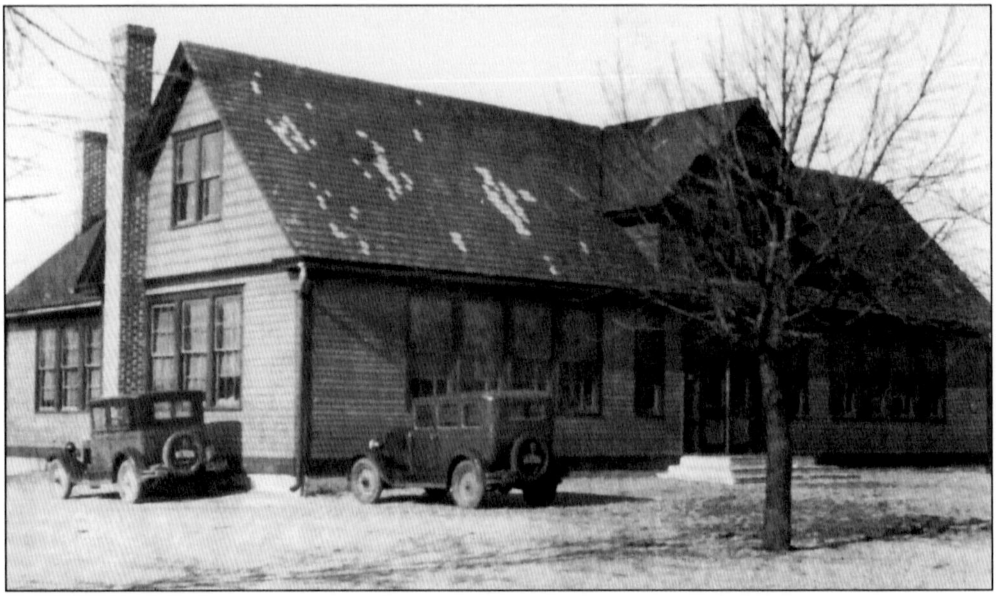

In 1883 there were five one-room schoolhouses in Bass River Township located in the Union Hill (Leektown), Squab Hill, Mathistown, Frogtown, and Harrisville sections. In 1898 the Squab Hill school was moved and joined to a new one-room structure, creating a two-room school at the present North Maple Avenue site. The one-room schools were then closed as the new building served all of the township's pupils. The two-room building was remodeled through the years and is now part of the present school facility. (Courtesy Steve Eichinger.)

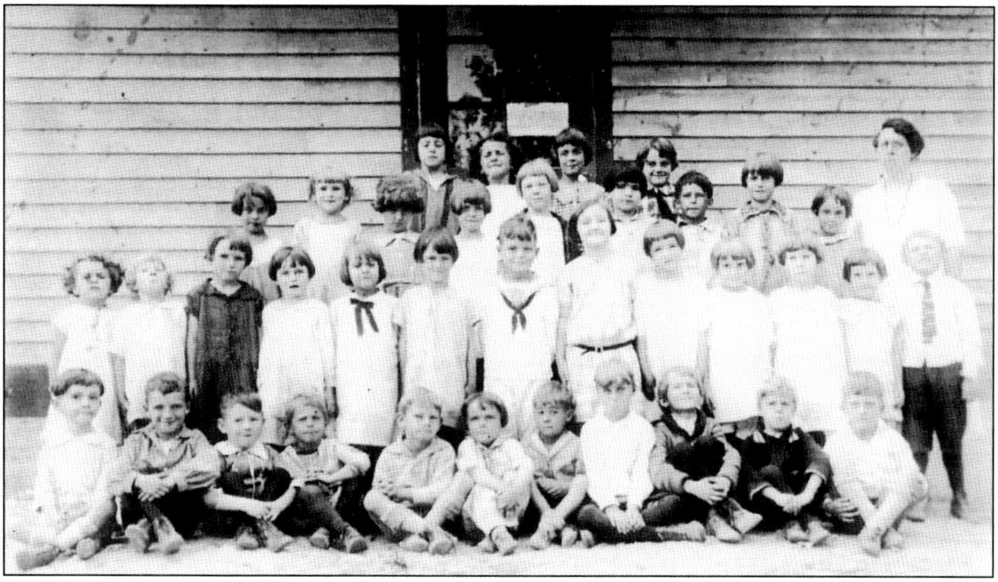

Margaret Adams began her forty-and-a-half-year teaching career in 1895 at the age of sixteen in the Mathistown schoolhouse. She became teaching-principal of the New Gretna School in 1907. Miss Margaret is shown here c. 1926 with her class of children from the Adams, Allen, Bozarth, Cramer, Downs, Lambert, Leepa, Leek, Loveland, Mathis, Prince, Robbins, Sears, and Wiseman families. Many of these families still live in the area today. (Courtesy Myrtle Falkinburg.)

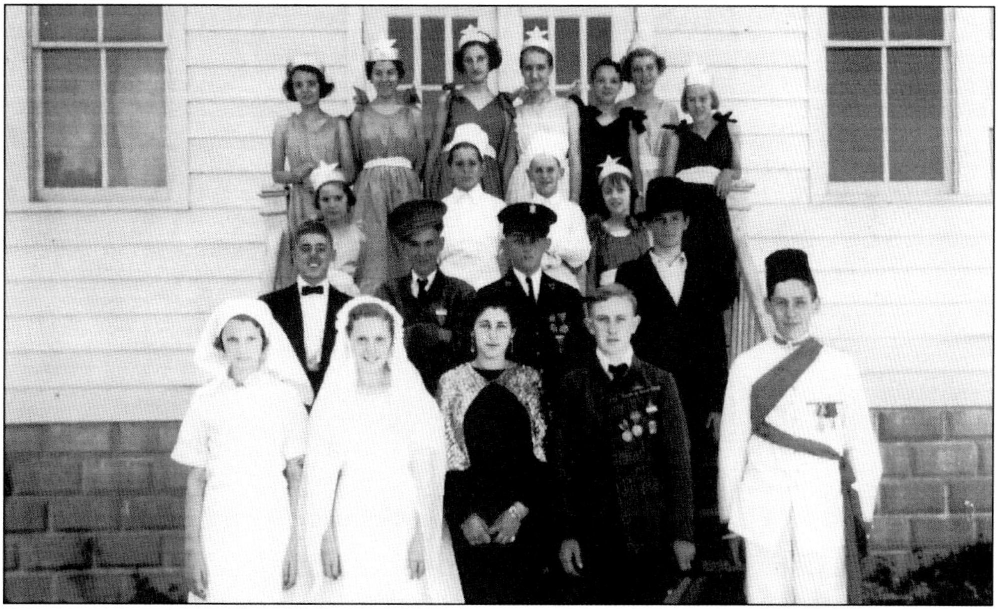

New Gretna school students had "graduation plays" in the 1930s and 1940s. The cast from the 1936 play posed on the steps of the Civic Hall, which was built by the New Gretna Civic Association, a group of local women. It was used for church and community bazaars and dinners, community meetings, school plays, card and jigsaw puzzle parties, movies, and dances. Later it housed a roller skating rink and a sewing factory and is now the home of the New Gretna Volunteer Fire Company. (Courtesy Naomi Maurer.)

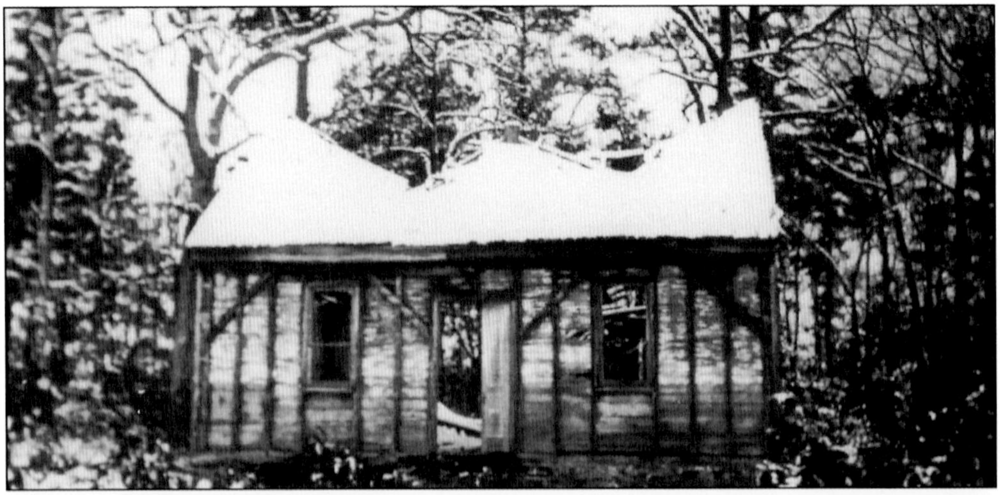

Early in the nineteenth century the Society of Friends split into two orthodox and conservative branches. The orthodox Hicksites built this meetinghouse at Bridgeport, Wading River, in 1825 between the present Adams-Leek-McKeen Cemetery and Leektown Road, near the McKeen Hotel. As membership dwindled, Lucy Evans, the group's leader, sat silently by herself as both minister and congregation until her death in 1834. Her tombstone can be found today beside the quiet wooded area that once was the Quaker Meeting House. (Courtesy Burlington County Historical Society.)

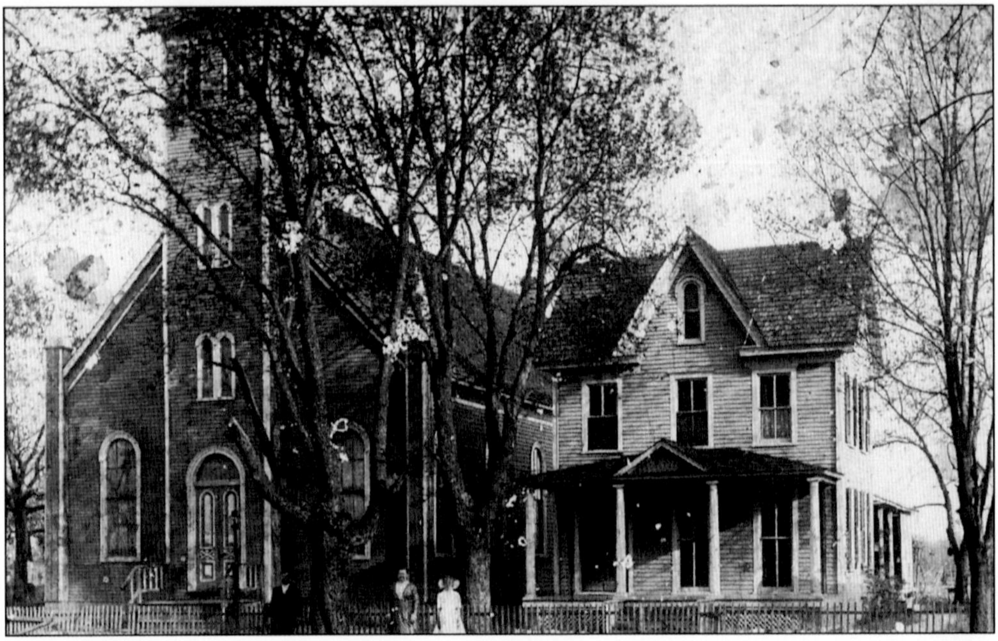

The Methodists in the Bass River area first held meetings in private homes until a meetinghouse was erected at the site of the present Hillside Cemetery in the Frogtown section of the township in 1800. In 1852 the present church was built on New York Road on land donated by Enoch Adams and Micajah Mathis. The parsonage was built in 1884. The old meetinghouse was moved to the south side of the cemetery road and was used as a one-room schoolhouse until 1898. It was demolished in 1915. (Courtesy St. Paul's United Methodist Church.)

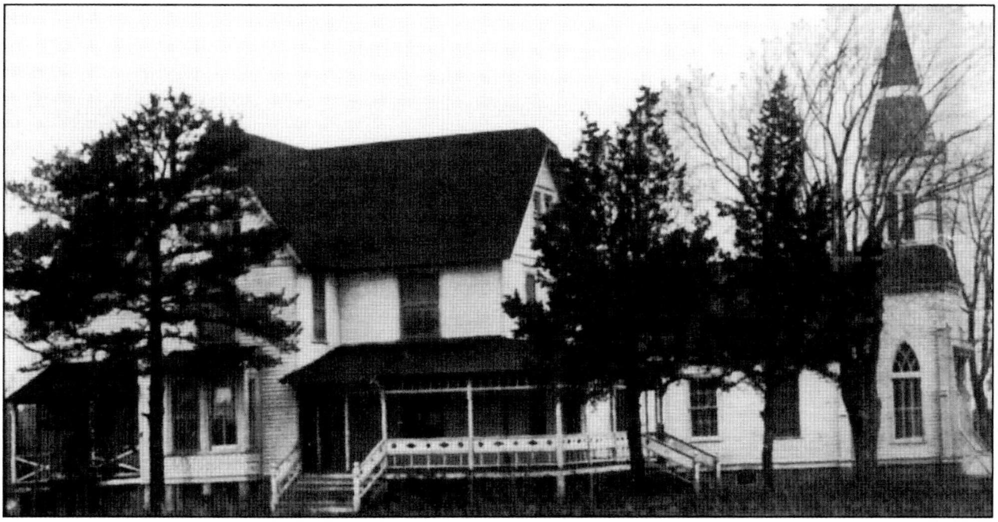

Presbyterian services were first held in Bass River by the Reverend John Brainard in the house of Captain Charles Loveland and later at the house of John Leek. Services continued in private homes and schools until 1851, when the present church was completed on land donated by Joseph Cramer. The manse was constructed in 1912 for the Reverend S.G. Webb and his new bride. Charles Loveland and John A. Cramer were the carpenters. The beautiful memorial stained-glass windows were installed in the church in 1928. (Courtesy June LeMunyon.)

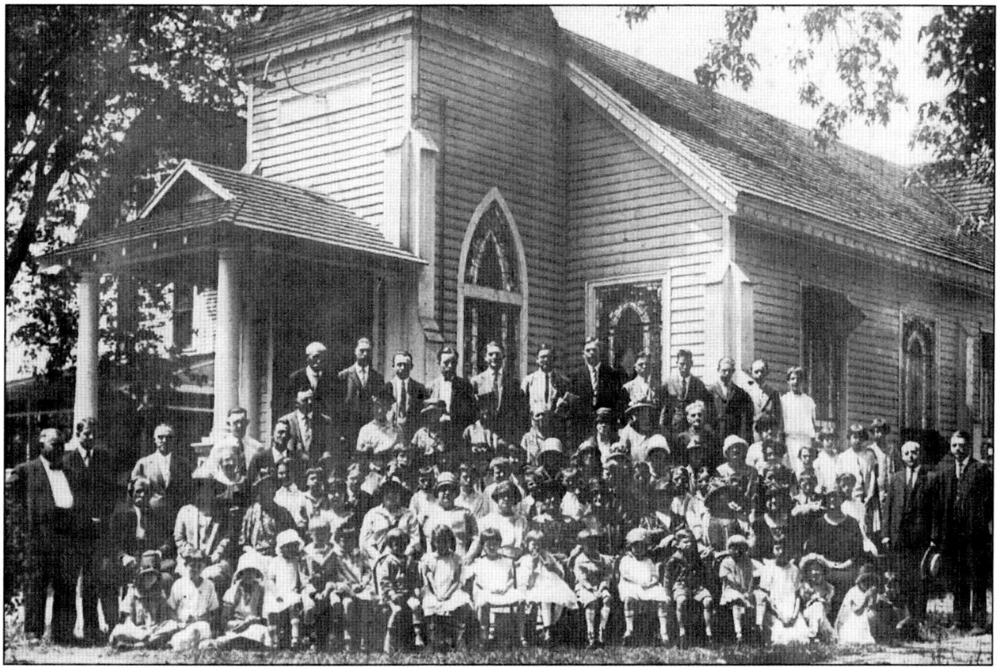

The New Gretna First Presbyterian Church was a vital and active force in the community in the latter part of the nineteenth and first half of the twentieth century, as evidenced by the large congregation posing outside the church in the mid-1920s. The beautiful stained-glass windows were donated by prominent families in the community: Adams, Cramer, French, Loveland, and Mathis. (Courtesy Donald Cramer.)

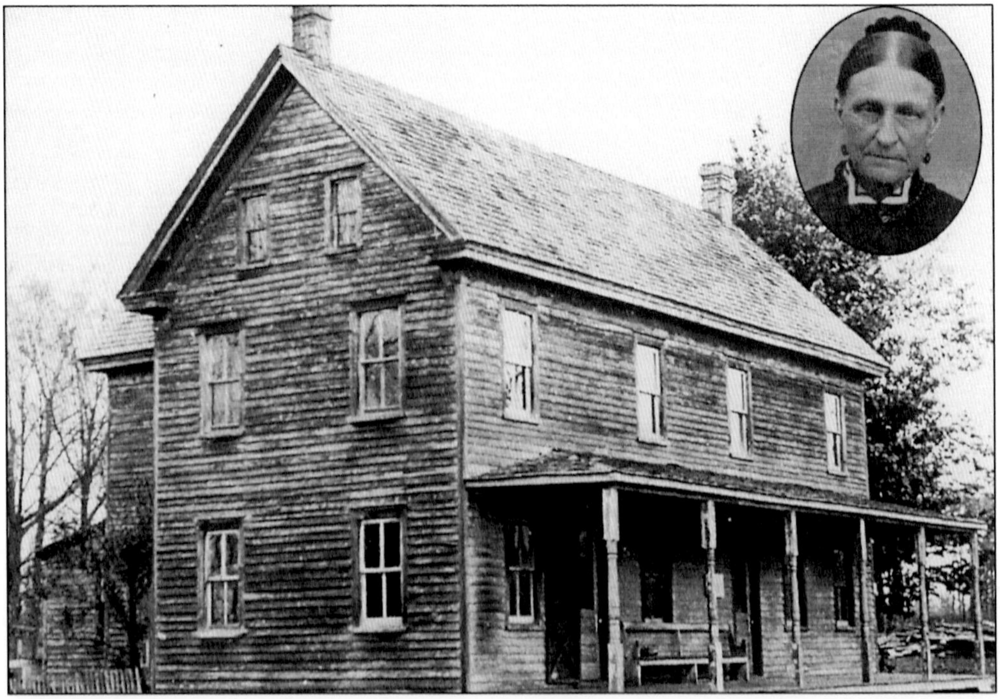

Robert McKeen bought the large house on the Wading River from John Leek III, and he converted it into an inn, where it served as a hotel, stagecoach stop, store, and post office for almost a century. Robert's daughter Catherine ran the inn from 1845 until her death in 1890. She also served as postmistress from 1858 and tended the Wading River Bridge for many years. Many of the Leeks and McKeens are buried in the Adams-Leek-McKeen (Old Bridgeport) Cemetery in back of the inn. (Courtesy Steve Eichinger.)

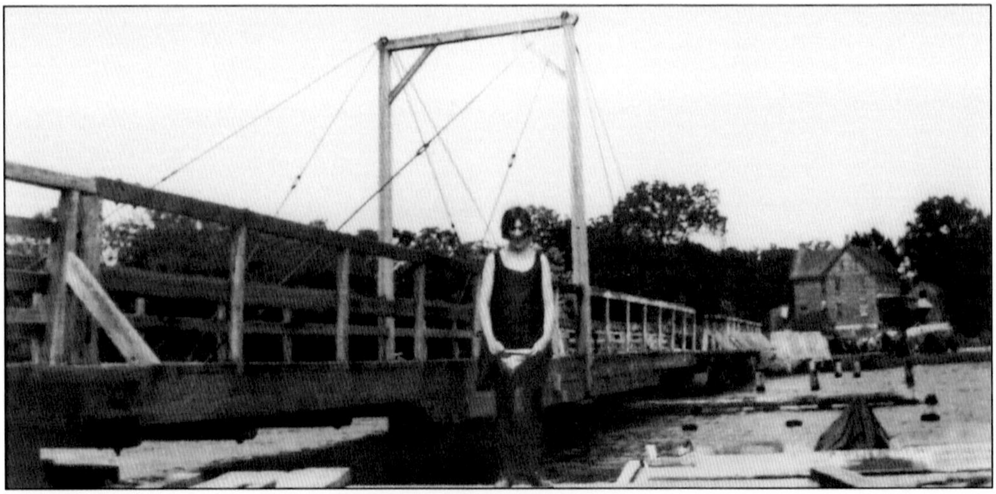

The first bridge constructed over a navigable portion of the area rivers was a wooden swing bridge constructed in 1814 over the Wading River at Leek's wharf in Bridgeport. It was replaced by a lift bridge in the 1930s, which was, in turn, replaced by a concrete and steel bridge in the late 1980s. The bridge has been a favorite spot for fishing and swimming. The old McKeen Hotel can be seen in the background of this c. 1915 photo, showing Frances Gale enjoying a swim. (Courtesy Steve Eichinger.)

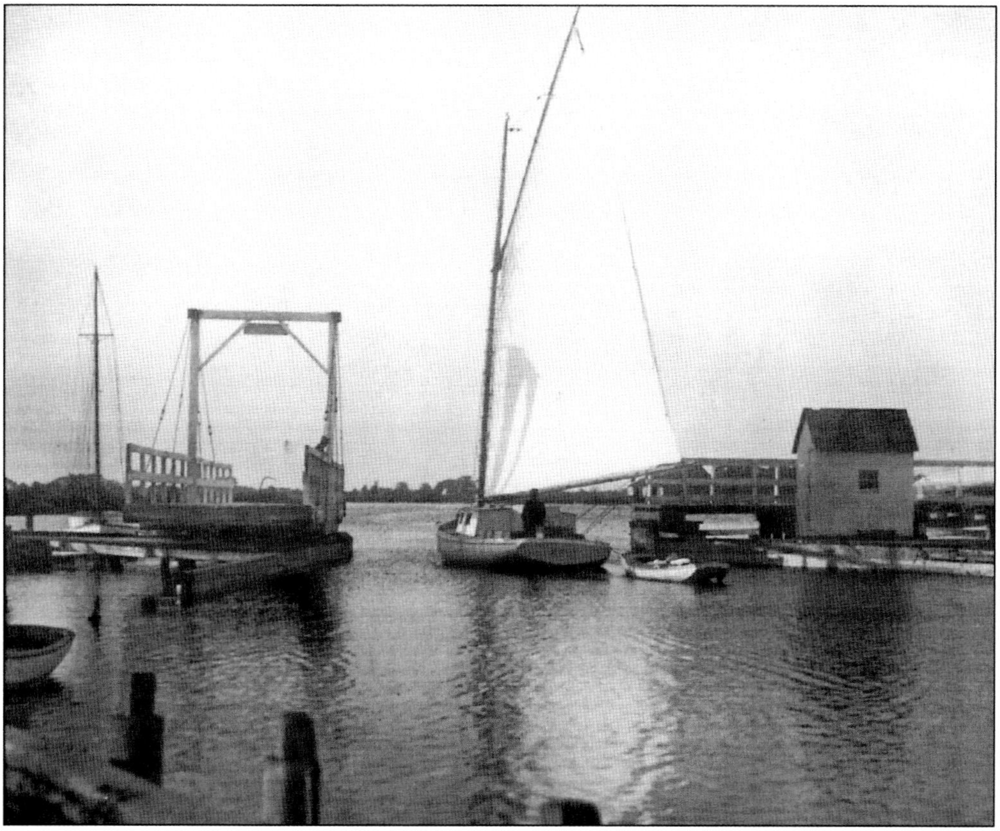

The Bass River bridge, a wooden swing bridge built in 1824, provided a more direct route from Tuckerton to the town center of New Gretna. In the latter part of the 1800s and early 1900s, schooners, often laden with store goods for local use, passed through the bridge on their way to load charcoal for the New York City and Philadelphia market. A large number of clamming and oystering garveys and fishing boats also kept the bridge tender busy. (Courtesy THS.)

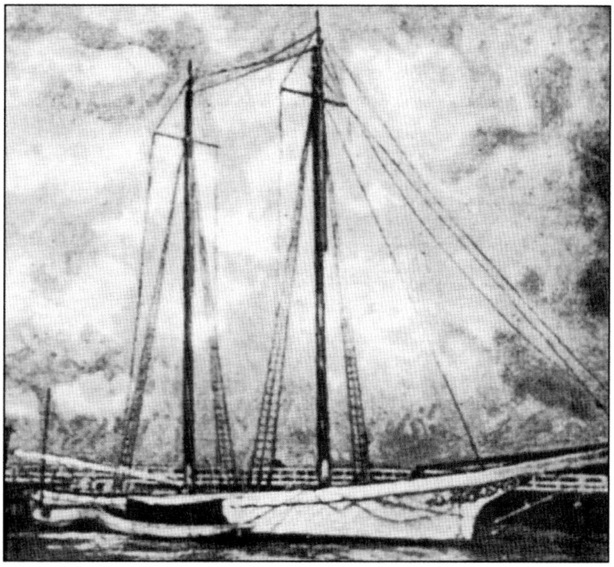

The presence of an America's Cup defender, the yacht *Columbia*, was symbolic of the importance of ship building to the local economy. It gave employment to lumbermen, haulers, carpenters, iron workers, blacksmiths, caulkers, sail makers, and crew members. The *Columbia* was captained by Thomas A. Mathis, born in New Gretna in 1869. He became a state senator, the New Jersey secretary of state, and a major force in Republican politics for over forty years. (Courtesy Walter and Margaret Roberts.)

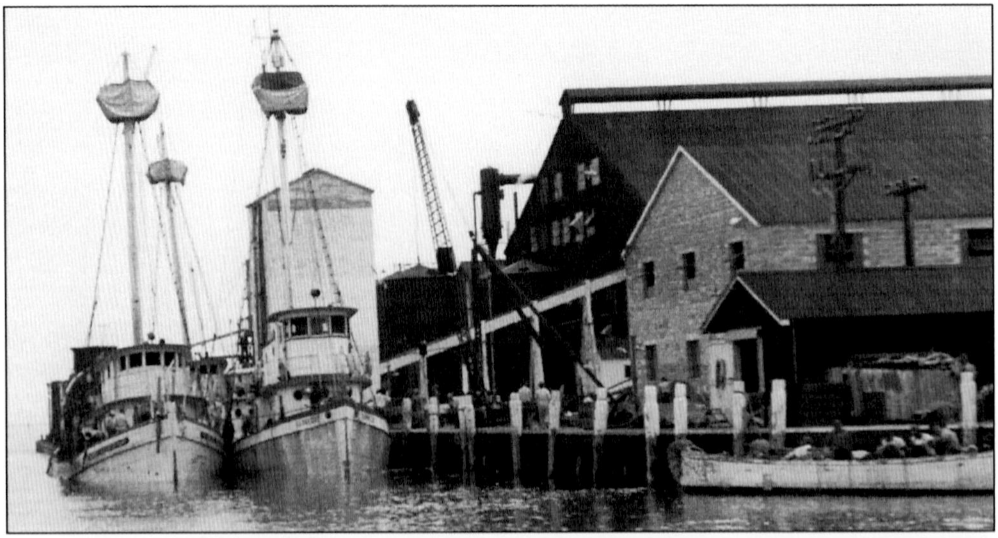

The Tuckerton-Little Egg Harbor area had been a major menhaden center since the mid-1800s with a fish factory operating on Story Island in Little Egg Harbor Bay and later on Crab Island in Great Bay, pictured above in 1954. Menhaden were processed into fertilizer, fish oil, fish solubles used in the cosmetics industry, fish meal used as poultry and livestock feed, and fish flour. The factory closed in 1969 when the great schools of menhaden disappeared. It is now owned by the State of New Jersey. (Courtesy Burrell Adams.)

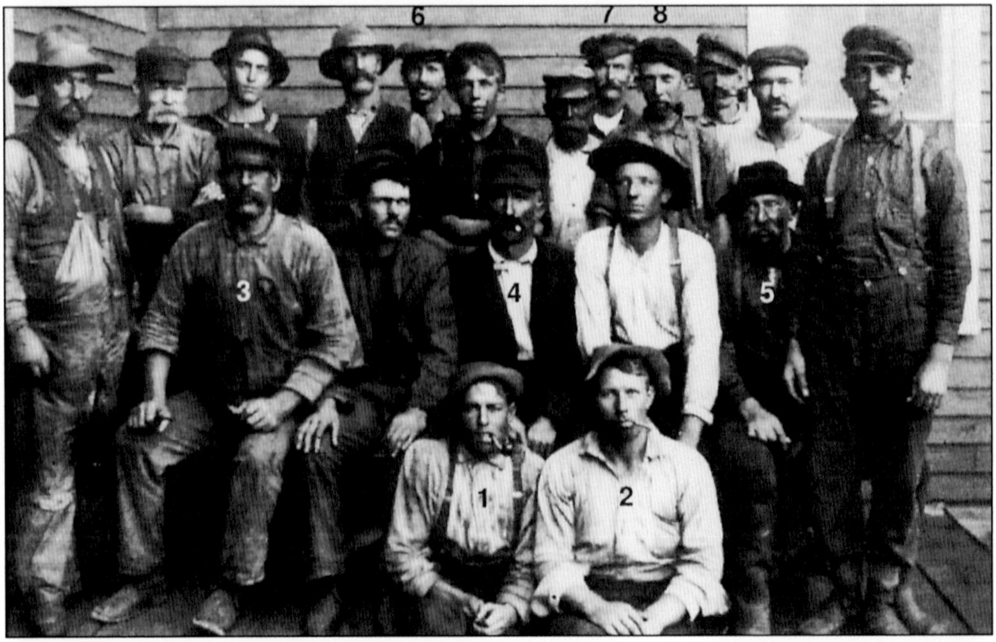

Fishing steamers out of Tuckerton and Bass River employed many local men. Most provided menhaden for the Story Island fish factory in Little Egg Harbor Bay and the Crab Island fish factory in Great Bay. The steamer *Adroit's* nineteen-member crew, c. 1900, included the following men from Bass River: Ira Jerue (1), Mark Leeds (2), Levi Chew (3), Joseph Hickman (4, captain), Asbury Mathis (5), Malcolm Billsborough (6, pilot), Joseph Loveland (7), and Marvin Mathis (8). (Courtesy Horace Somes Jr.)

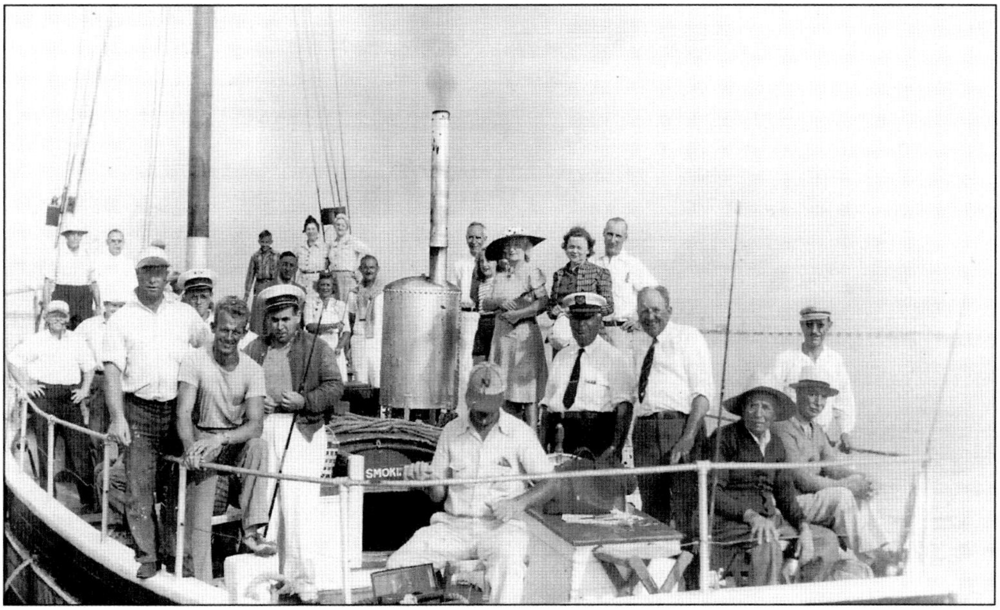

The *Onley* is a good example of local watermen's adaptation to changing times. Originally a catboat transporting cargo, she was retrofitted with a diesel engine. Captain Starns sailed her out of Atlantic City as a pleasure craft during the summer months. She was used to transport green oysters from New York and New England during the fall and winter seasons to Cramer's Oyster House at Amasas Landing on the Bass River. They were then transplanted into the clean waters of the Bass and Mullica Rivers for later harvesting. (Courtesy George Hedervary.)

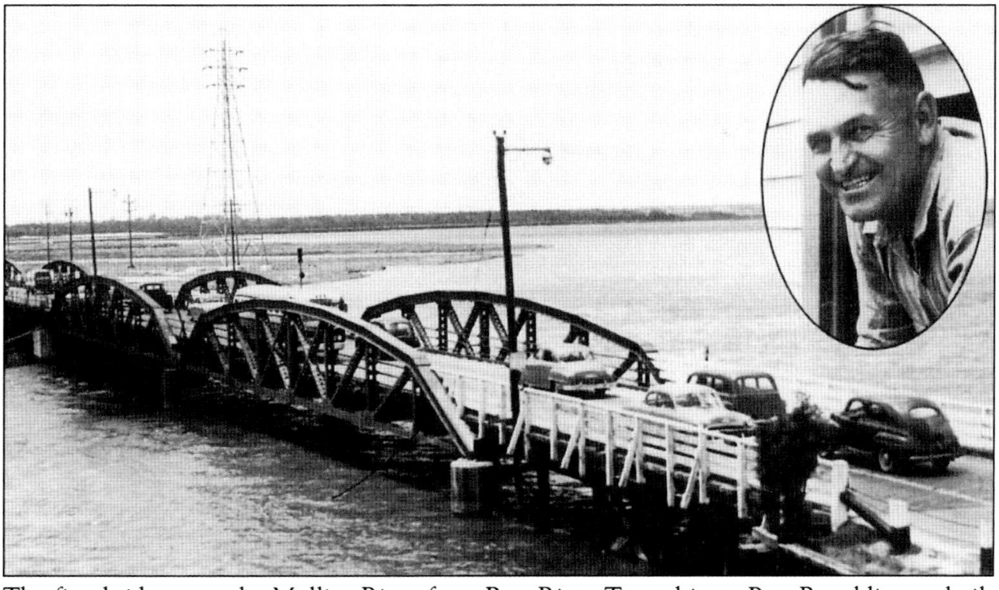

The first bridge over the Mullica River from Bass River Township to Port Republic was built in 1856. This iron bridge was constructed in 1915 through 1917 and was tended for thirty-two years by Horatio "Tater" Cramer (inset). It was dismantled in the late 1960s after completion of the present Garden State Parkway bridge and moved to Chincoteague, Virginia, where it is still in use today. (Courtesy William Augustine Collection, Rutgers University, and Esther Slota (inset).)

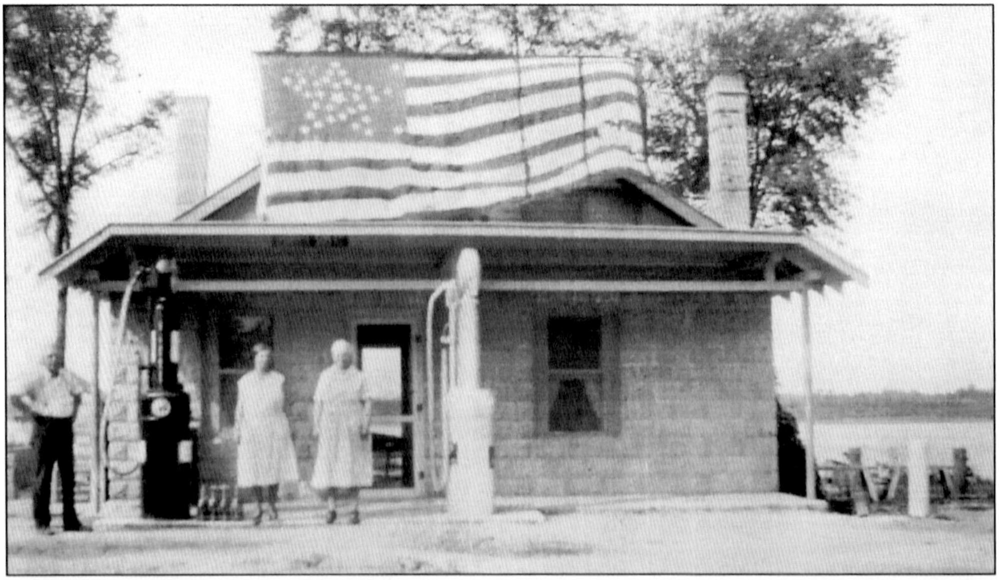

Samuel and Martha Adams Merchant operated a small gas station on the banks of the Wading River just down the street from the McKeen Hotel in the Bridgeport (Wading River) area of Bass River. The flag on the roof of this Independence Day photo, *c.* 1920, is said to have been made by Catherine McKeen in 1876 for the country's centennial celebration. Martina Adams, age sixteen, a great-grandniece of Catherine McKeen, stands between the Merchants. The gas station is now the home of Martina's son, Lee Eichinger. (Courtesy Lee Eichinger.)

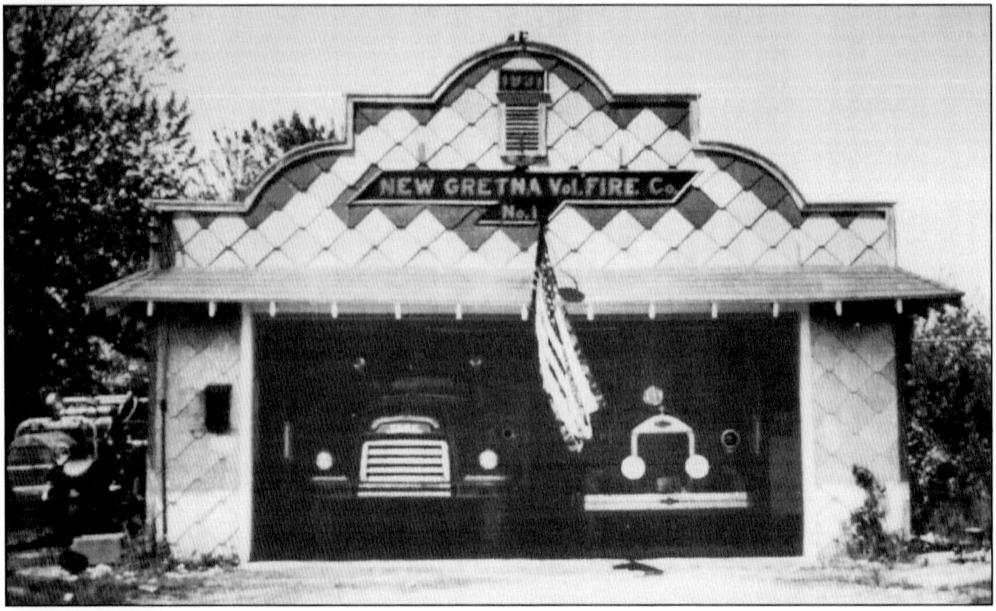

The New Gretna Volunteer Fire Company was founded in 1929, shortly after Ashton Lamson's restaurant on the northeast corner of New York Road and Maple Avenue burned. The firehouse shown above, *c.* 1954, was sold to the township fathers and remodeled in the late 1970s to become the township's first municipal building. Previously, township offices were held in various locations, including the old Bass River Hotel, the Knights of Pythias Hall, and the local school. (Courtesy New Gretna Volunteer Fire Company.)

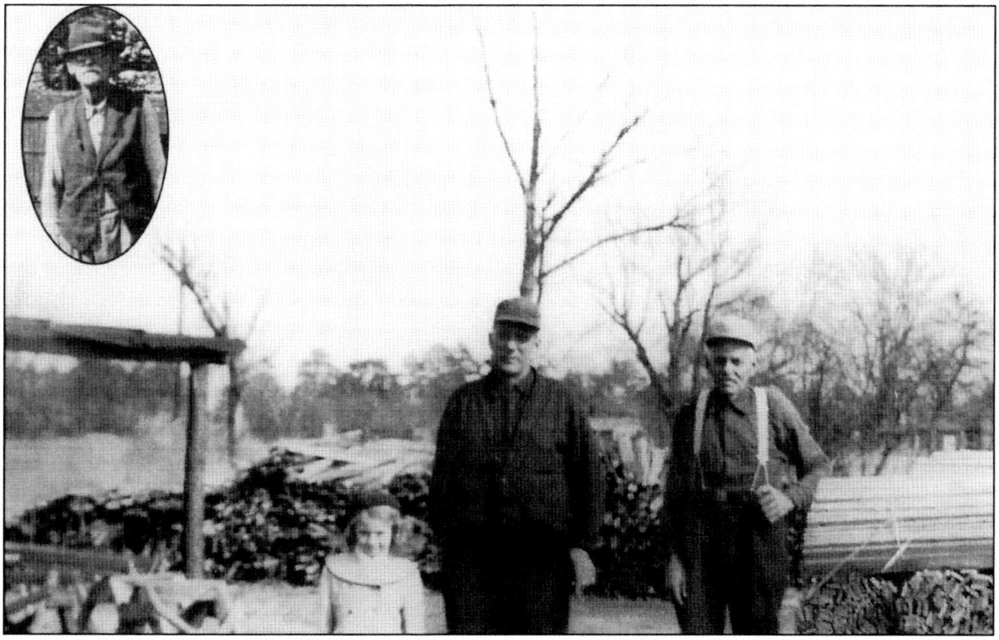

Bass River sawmills provided white Jersey cedar lumber for boat and home building. The first sawmill, owned by Ebenezer Tucker, was at the head of the west branch of the Bass River in the mid-1700s. It was burned by the British in 1778. James Howard Bozarth (right) operated a mill at Leektown with his son Horace (left), shown here with granddaughter Patricia Wilson in 1948. Howard's father, Charles Bozarth (inset), a Civil War veteran, worked in many area mills including the Batsto sawmill. (Courtesy Patricia Wilson Groff.)

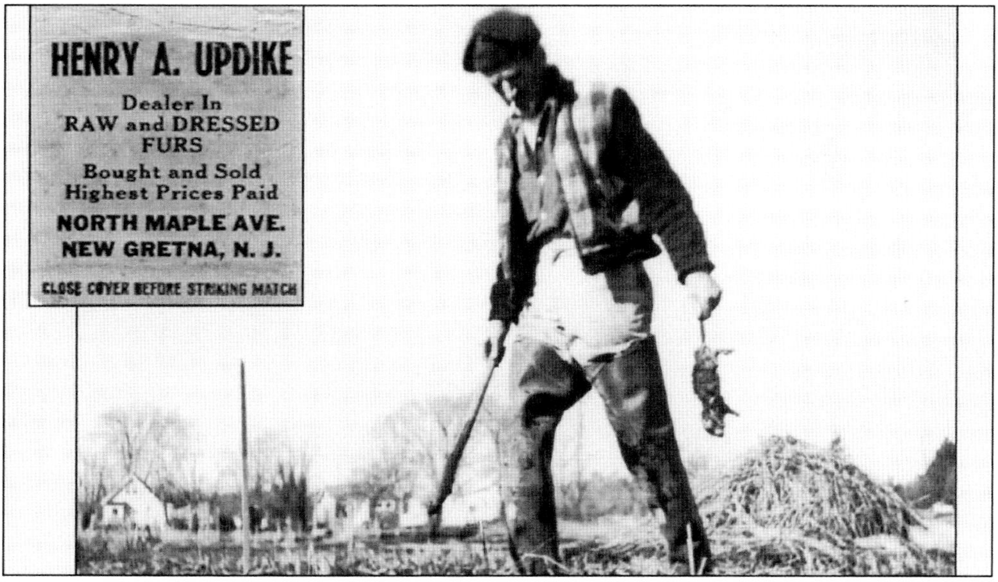

Trapping of mink, otter, and muskrat was a profitable trade in Bass River Township because of the extensive watershed areas formed by the Mullica, Wading, and Bass Rivers. Local trappers and fur dealers prospered. Joe Cramer, shown trapping muskrat on his North Maple Avenue property, sold the "rats" to Henry Updike, a local fur dealer. A muskrat mound can be seen in the background. (Courtesy Stansbury Cramer and Harry DeVerter (inset).)

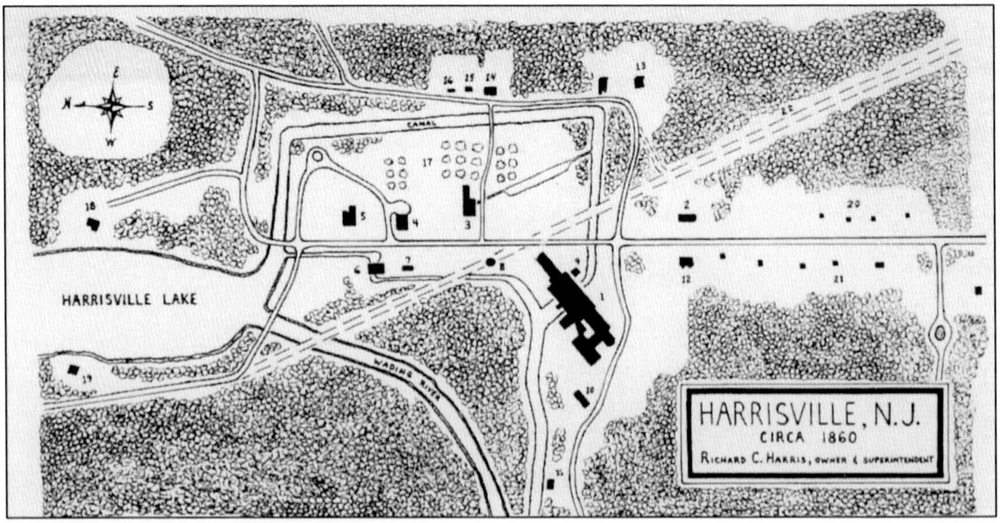

Harrisville became a thriving community in the nineteenth century with a store, church, school, sawmill, gristmill, tenant houses, owners' mansions, a farm, and a main street lighted by gas lamps surrounding the large papermill. Sold to Joseph Wharton at a sheriff's sale in 1896, it became a part of the Wharton tract with neighboring Martha and Calico. Wharton's plan to pipe the pure underground water to Philadelphia was thwarted when the New Jersey legislature passed a law banning the export of water across state lines. The area is now a part of the Wharton State Forest. (Courtesy Angelo N. Dellomo Jr.)

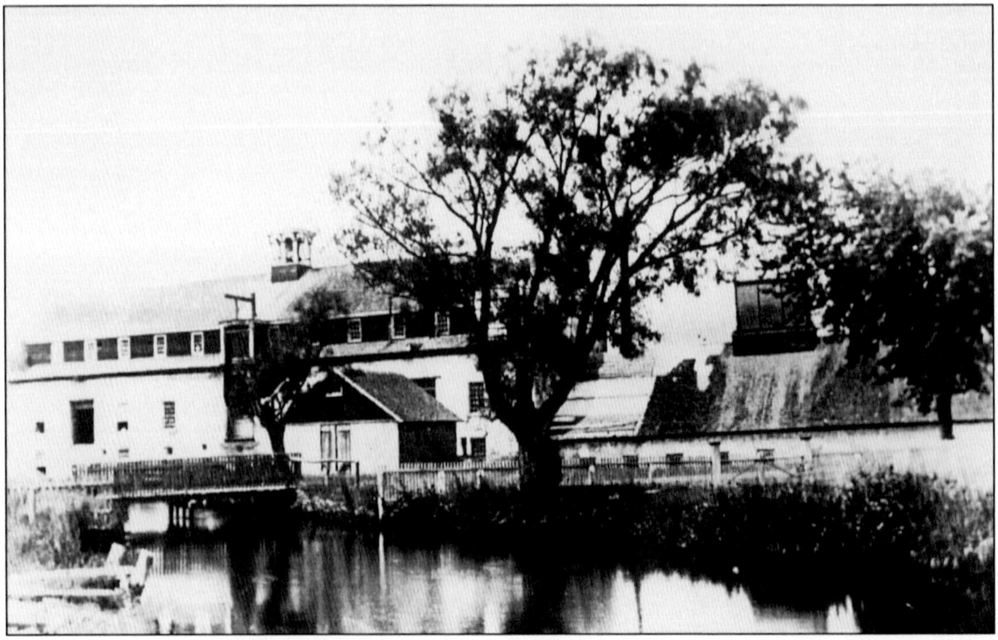

Isaac Potts, a Philadelphia iron master who built Martha Furnace in 1793, constructed the Wading River Forge and Slitting Mill in 1795 on the site that became Harrisville. After passing through various owners, the property was purchased by William McCarthy, who built a successful papermill in 1834. In 1851 McCarthyville became Harrisville when it was purchased by Richard and William Harris. It was the largest papermill in New Jersey in the 1850s, producing nearly a ton of paper a day. (Courtesy Steve Eichinger.)

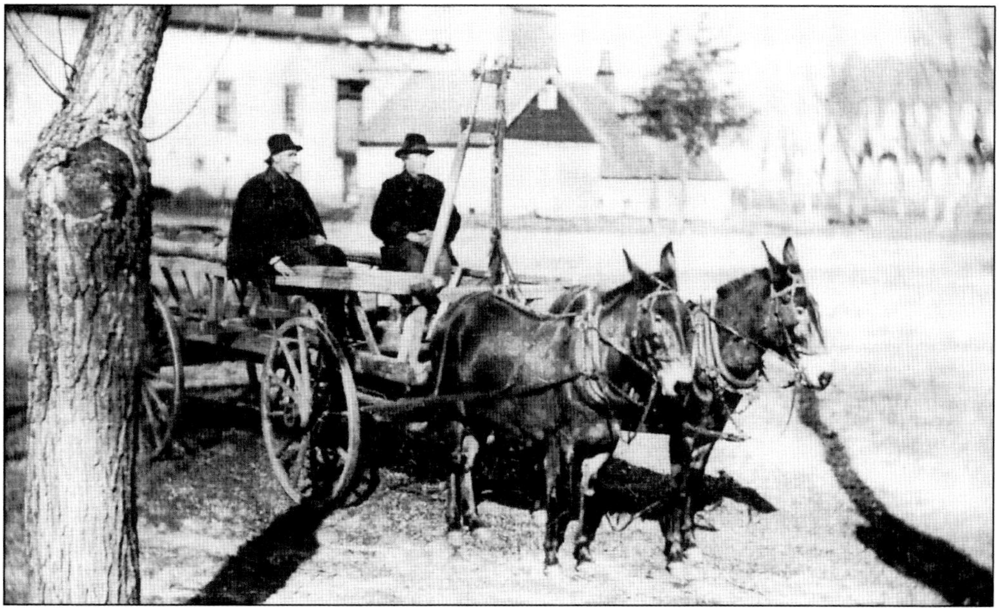

Harrisville, the center of an industrial area with five bog iron furnaces, including neighboring Martha, provided jobs not only for the workers living in the tenant houses, but also for residents of nearby towns, including Bass River. The papermill manufactured a heavy grade brown paper from old rope cuttings, bagging imported from Philadelphia, and salt hay from local marshes. Samuel McKeen (left) and Austin Downs delivered salt hay to the main plant seen in the background. (Courtesy Steve Eichinger.)

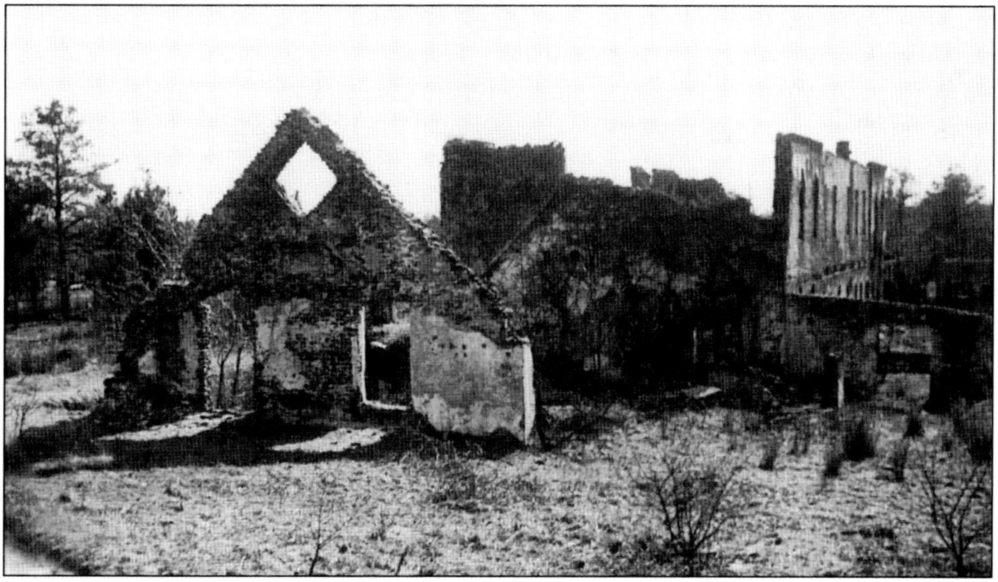

The paper business declined through the 1880s. The factory was sold at the sheriff's sale in 1891. Fires destroyed a large part of the town in 1893 and the remainder of the town and the papermill in 1910. Massive sandstone and brick ruins existed for decades and were a popular destination for day trips and picnics. Today only a small portion of a wall exists behind a chain link fence on the west side of Route 542. (Courtesy William Augustine Collection, Rutgers University.)

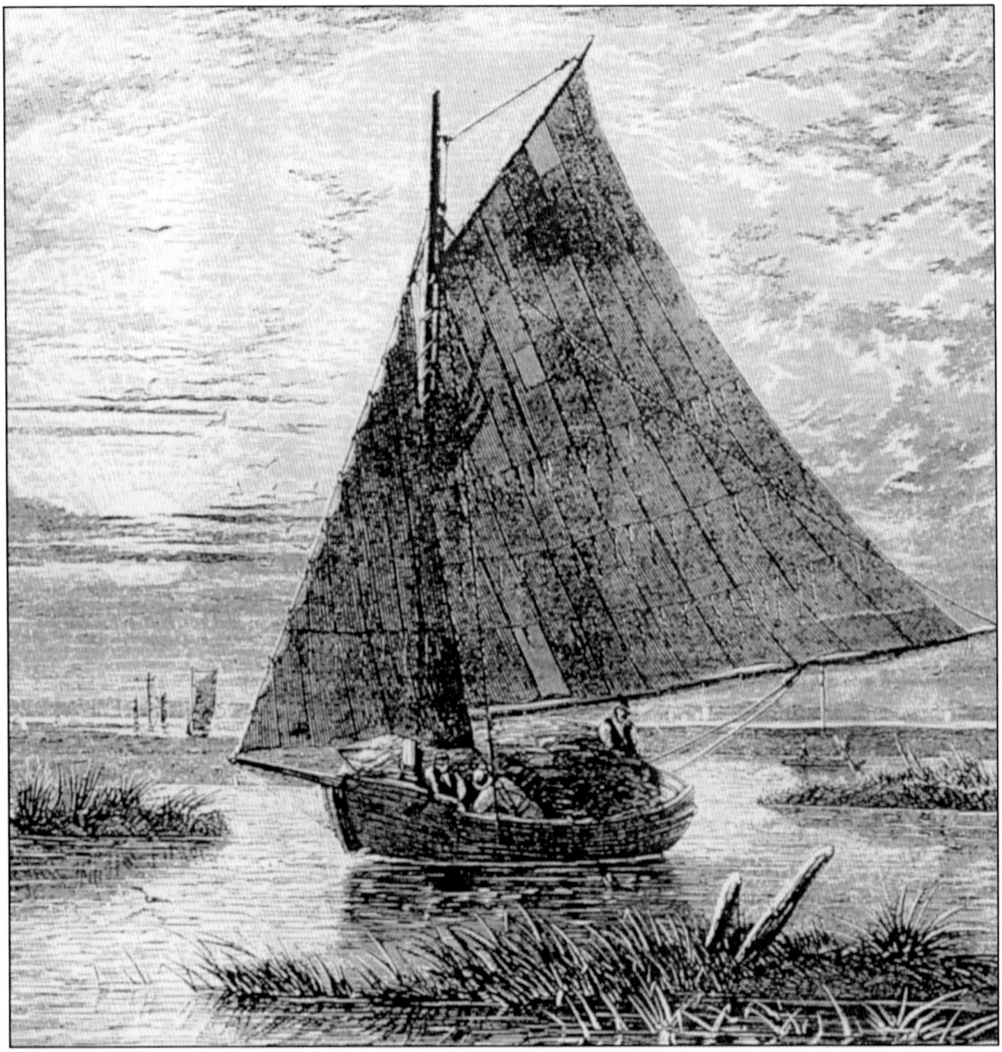

This sketch of the salt meadows and bay was drawn by Granville Perkins for the *American Agriculturist* in September 1869. The old boat with patched sails was loaded with punk, a kind of submerged peat which was employed by farmers in the shore area. These saltwater meadows were described in the article accompanying the sketch as more level than a western prairie, and were it not that salt water limits the selection of plants that can be grown, they would be most valuable for cultivation because they are so rich in organic matter. In the nineteenth century there were long stretches of salt meadows broken only by bays and creeks along the Jersey coast. Many farmers used these meadows for grazing cattle and sheep. Some animals were even taken by boat to the barrier island and left to graze during the warmer months.

It seems most appropriate to use a boat scene as this photographic tribute to a way of life draws to a close. Boats brought whalers to our shores, brought immigrants into Tuckerton, and were essential to making a living in this area. They extended the reach of the railroads and their passengers, carried hunters to their blinds or served as their blinds, carried trading goods up and down the East Coast, served as the means of travel along with the stagecoach prior to the arrival of the first train, and encouraged sport fishing and racing. The design and creation of a boat is a work of art, and its movement on the water will always be a subject for painters and photographers. (Courtesy BBD & BM.)